CISSP in 21 Days

Second Edition

Boost your confidence and get the competitive edge you need to crack the exam in just 21 days!

M. L. Srinivasan

BIRMINGHAM - MUMBAI

CISSP in 21 Days

Second Edition

First published: December 2008

Second edition: June 2016

Production reference: 1240616

Published by Packt Publishing Ltd.
Livery Place
35 Livery Street
Birmingham
B3 2PB, UK.
ISBN 978-1-78588-449-8

www.packtpub.com

Credits

Author

M. L. Srinivasan

Reviewer

John T. Schreiner

Commissioning Editor

Veena Pagare

Acquisition Editor

Divya Poojari

Content Development Editor

Arun Nadar

Technical Editor

Rupali R. Shrawane

Copy Editor

Yesha Gangani

Project Coordinator

Ritika Manoj

Proofreader

Safis Editing

Indexer

Rekha Nair

Production Coordinator

Melwyn Dsa

About the Author

M. L. Srinivasan is the founder and CEO of ChennaiNet, an India-based technology company focused on information technology and information security-related product development, services, and training. He's a Certified Information System Security Professional (CISSP) and Certified Information Security Management System Lead Auditor.

Popularly known as MLS, the author is an information technology and information security professional and has about 25 years' experience in various IT domains, such as software programming, hardware troubleshooting, networking technologies, systems administration, security administration, information security-related consulting, auditing and training.

He has been an avid trainer throughout his career and has developed many short-term and long-term training programs. He has been invited to speak at many international conferences and seminars on information security. Currently he is associated with NIIT Technologies (USA), and CA Technologies (USA) as a senior instructor covering various product-based training on CA identity manager, CA SiteMinder (Single Sign-On), CA ControlMinder (AccessControl), CA Federation Manager, and CA DataMinder products.

He was a specialist IT and IS auditor with Det Norske Veritas (DNV), India region. He has performed many quality and information security audits for hundreds of medium and large organizations in the past.

About the Reviewer

John Schreiner is a Major in the United States Marine Corps and a networking and security instructor. He serves as a Company Commander, responsible for training Marines on the East Coast on the latest commercial technologies (Cisco, Microsoft, Riverbed, Harris, and so on.). John brings experience teaching CISSP, Security+, and CCNA: Security.

 John holds a CISSP, CCNA: Security, CCNP, CCDP, WCNA, and various other certifications. He also blogs at http://www.unadulteratednerdery.com/. In addition to this title, John was the technical reviewer for *Cisco Unified Communications Manager 8: Expert Administration Cookbook, Tanner Ezell, Packt Publishing*.

> *I'd like to thank my amazing wife, Jacki, whose steadfast support and embrace of my nerdy endeavors are a constant reminder that she's the best thing that has ever happened to me.*

www.PacktPub.com

For support files and downloads related to your book, please visit www.PacktPub.com.

Did you know that Packt offers eBook versions of every book published, with PDF and ePub files available? You can upgrade to the eBook version at www.PacktPub.com and as a print book customer, you are entitled to a discount on the eBook copy. Get in touch with us at service@packtpub.com for more details.

At www.PacktPub.com, you can also read a collection of free technical articles, sign up for a range of free newsletters and receive exclusive discounts and offers on Packt books and eBooks.

https://www2.packtpub.com/books/subscription/packtlib

Do you need instant solutions to your IT questions? PacktLib is Packt's online digital book library. Here, you can search, access, and read Packt's entire library of books.

Why subscribe?

- Fully searchable across every book published by Packt
- Copy and paste, print, and bookmark content
- On demand and accessible via a web browser

Free access for Packt account holders

If you have an account with Packt at www.PacktPub.com, you can use this to access PacktLib today and view 9 entirely free books. Simply use your login credentials for immediate access.

To my Father who is the guiding force for everything I do

Table of Contents

Preface

Certified Information System Security Professional (CISSP) is a coveted certification for an information security professional to achieve. Certified individuals are considered experienced and knowledgeable information security professionals. This is due to the fact that the certification's requirements are that the candidate not only has to pass the exam, but have 4 to 5 years of relevant practical experience in one or two domains of information security.

The exam is conducted by the International Information System Security Certification Consortium (ISC)²®, a nonprofit consortium that is the globally recognized Gold Standard for certifying information security professionals throughout their careers. (ISC)²® was founded in 1989 by industry leaders and has certified over 1,00,000 information security professionals across the globe.

While preparing for CISSP™, a candidate has to study many books and references. There are many books that cover the CISSP™ CBK™ domains in depth and provide a starting point for a thorough preparation for the exam. References to such books are covered in the references chapter at the end of this book. However, since there are many concepts spread across the eight security domains, it is an important starting point as a guide to explore deeper concepts, as well as refresh many concepts that need to be revised before the exam. This book addresses the requirements of the initial preparation for the exam, as well as revisiting the key concepts in these eight domains. To facilitate such a need core concept, the eight CISSP information security domains are explained in a short, simple, and lucid form.

What this book covers

Chapter 1, *Day 1 – Security and Risk Management - Security, Compliance, and Policies*, covers the foundational concepts in information security, such as Confidentiality, Integrity, and Availability (CIA) from the first domain of CISSP Common Body of Knowledge (CBK)®.

Chapter 2, *Day2 – Security and Risk Management - Risk Management, Business Continuity, and Security Education*, covers risk management practices that include the identification of risks through risk analysis and assessment, and mitigation techniques such as reduction, moving, transferring, and avoiding risks. An overview of business continuity requirements, developing and documenting project scopes and plans, and conducting business impact analyses is provided. Further more policies and practices pertaining to personnel security are covered.

Chapter 3, *Day 3 – Asset Security - Information and Asset Classification*, covers the classification of information and supporting assets; the collection of information, its handling and protection throughout its lifecycle, and ownership of information and its privacy; and data retention requirements and methods.

Chapter 4, *Day 4 – Asset Security - Data Security Controls and Handling*, covers data security controls that include Data Loss Prevention strategies, such as data at rest, data in transit, data in use, and data handling requirements for sensitive information.

Chapter 5, *Day 5 – Exam Cram and Practice Questions*, covers important concepts and information from the first two domains of the CISSP CBK, namely Security and Risk Management and Asset Security. They are provided in an exam-cram format for fast review and serve to reinforce of the two domains covered in the previous four chapters.

Chapter 6, *Day 6 – Security Engineering - Security Design, Practices, Models, and Vulnerability Mitigation*, covers concepts for using secure design principles while implementing and managing engineering processes. Information security models and system security evaluation models with controls and countermeasures, and security capabilities in information systems, are also covered. Also, vulnerability assessment and mitigation strategies in information systems, web-based systems, mobile systems, and embedded and cyber-physical systems are covered in detail.

Chapter 7, *Day 7 – Security Engineering - Cryptography*, covers the application of cryptography in information security requirements. Various concepts such as the cryptographic life cycle, types of cryptography, public key infrastructure, and so on are covered with illustrations. The methods of cryptanalytic attack are covered in detail with suitable examples.

Chapter 8, *Day 8 – Communication and Network Security - Network Security*, covers foundational concepts in network architecture and network security. IP and non-IP protocols, and their applications and vulnerabilities, are covered in detail, along with wireless networks and their security requirements. Application of cryptography in communication security, with illustrations and concepts related to securing network components.

Chapter 9, *Day 9 – Communication and Network Security - Communication Security*, covers communication channels such as voice, multimedia, remote access, data communications, virtualized networks, and so on, and their security requirements. Preventing or mitigating network attacks is also covered, with illustrations.

Chapter 10, *Day 10 – Exam Cram and Practice Questions,* covers important concepts and information from the third and fourth domains of the CISSP CBK, namely security engineering and communication and network security. They are provided in an exam cram format for fast review and serve to reinforce the two domains covered in the previous four chapters.

Chapter 11, *Day 11 – Identity and Access Management - Identity Management,* covers provisioning and managing the identities and the access used in the interaction between humans and information systems. Core concepts of identification, authentication, authorization, and accountability, are covered in detail. Concepts related to identity as a service or cloud-based third-party identity services are covered, as well as security requirements in such services, with illustrations.

Chapter 12, *Day 12 – Identity and Access Management - Access Management, Provisioning, and Attacks,* focuses on access control concepts, methods, attacks, and countermeasures in detail.

Chapter 13, *Day 13 – Security Assessment and Testing - Designing and Performing Security Assessment and Tests,* covers tools, methods, and techniques for identifying and mitigating risks due to architectural issues using systematic security assessment and testing of information assets and associated infrastructure. Security control requirements and their effectiveness assessment are also covered.

Chapter 14, *Day 14 – Security Assessment and Testing - Controlling, Analyzing, Auditing, and Reporting,* covers management and operational controls pertaining to security process data. Analyzing and reporting test outputs, either automated or through manual methods, and conducting or facilitating internal and third-party audits, are covered in detail.

Chapter 15, *Day 15 – Exam Cram and Practice Questions,* covers important concepts and information from the fifth and sixth domains of the CISSP CBK, namely Identity and Access Management and security assessment and testing. They are provided in an exam cram format for fast review and serve to reinforce the two domains covered in the previous four chapters.

Chapter 16, *Day 16 – Security Operations - Foundational Concepts,* covers physical security strategies that include secure facility and website design, data center security, hazards, and media storage. Concepts on logging and monitoring activities, investigations, security in the provision of resources, operations security, and resource protection techniques are covered in detail.

Chapter 17, *Day 17 – Security Operations - Incident Management and Disaster Recovery,* covers incident management, disaster recovery, and business continuity-related concepts that pertains to security operations.

Chapter 18, *Day 18 – Software Development Security - Security in Software Development Life Cycle,* covers the application of security concepts and the best practices for the production and development of software environments. Security in the software development life cycle is also covered in detail.

Chapter 19, *Day 19 – Software Development Security - Assessing Effectiveness of Software Security,* covers assurance requirements in software and ways to assess the effectiveness of software security. It also covers the different methods and techniques to assess the security impact of acquired software.

Chapter 20, *Day 20 – Exam Cram and Practice Questions,* covers important concepts and information from the seventh and eighth domains of the CISSP CBK®, namely security operations and software development security. They are provided in an exam cram format for fast review and serve to reinforce the two domains covered in the previous four chapters.

Chapter 21, *Day 21 – Exam Cram and Mock Test,* consists of an exam cram from all the eight domains in CISSP CBK®.

What you need for this book

There are no software/hardware requirements for this quick reference and revision guide. You only need to build your confidence with the systematic study and revision of the concepts in the information security domain to crack the CISSP examination.

Who this book is for

This book is for all aspirants who are planning to take the CISSP examination and obtain the coveted CISSP certification that is considered the "Gold Standard" in Information Security personal certification.

It assumes that the candidate already has sufficient knowledge in all the eight domains of the CISSP CBK by way of work experience and knowledge gained from other study books. This book provides concise explanations of the core concepts that are covered in the exam.

Conventions

In this book, you will find a number of text styles that distinguish between different kinds of information. Here are some examples of these styles and an explanation of their meaning.

Code words in text, database table names, folder names, filenames, file extensions, pathnames, dummy URLs, user input, and Twitter handles are shown as follows: "In a three-way handshake, first the client (workstation) sends a request to the server (for example, `www.some_website.com`)."

New terms and **important words** are shown in bold.

 Warnings or important notes appear in a box like this.

 Tips and tricks appear like this.

Reader feedback

Feedback from our readers is always welcome. Let us know what you think about this book-what you liked or disliked. Reader feedback is important for us as it helps us develop titles that you will really get the most out of.

To send us general feedback, simply e-mail `feedback@packtpub.com`, and mention the book's title in the subject of your message.

If there is a topic that you have expertise in and you are interested in either writing or contributing to a book, see our author guide at www.packtpub.com/authors .

Customer support

Now that you are the proud owner of a Packt book, we have a number of things to help you to get the most from your purchase.

Downloading the color images of this book

We also provide you with a PDF file that has color images of the screenshots/diagrams used in this book. The color images will help you better understand the changes in the output. You can download this file from `http://www.packtpub.com/sites/default/files/downloads/CISSPin21DaysSecondEdition_ColorImages.pdf`.

Errata

Although we have taken every care to ensure the accuracy of our content, mistakes do happen. If you find a mistake in one of our books-maybe a mistake in the text or the code-we would be grateful if you could report this to us. By doing so, you can save other readers from frustration and help us improve subsequent versions of this book. If you find any errata, please report them by visiting `http://www.packtpub.com/submit-errata`, selecting your book, clicking on the **Errata Submission Form** link, and entering the details of your errata. Once your errata are verified, your submission will be accepted and the errata will be uploaded to our website or added to any list of existing errata under the Errata section of that title.

To view the previously submitted errata, go to `https://www.packtpub.com/books/content/support` and enter the name of the book in the search field. The required information will appear under the **Errata** section.

Piracy

Piracy of copyrighted material on the Internet is an ongoing problem across all media. At Packt, we take the protection of our copyright and licenses very seriously. If you come across any illegal copies of our works in any form on the Internet, please provide us with the location address or website name immediately so that we can pursue a remedy.

Please contact us at `copyright@packtpub.com` with a link to the suspected pirated material.

We appreciate your help in protecting our authors and our ability to bring you valuable content.

Questions

If you have a problem with any aspect of this book, you can contact us at `questions@packtpub.com`, and we will do our best to address the problem.

1
Day 1 – Security and Risk Management - Security, Compliance, and Policies

Information security and risk management are analogous to each other. The security and risk management domain forms the baseline for all information security concepts and practices. This is the first domain in CISSP CBK. Concepts on the key areas explained in this domain are across the next seven domains of CISSP, and will serve as the conceptual foundation for more complicated topics. Hence, a strong foundational knowledge in this domain will help the students in understanding the concepts in the rest of the domains.

A candidate appearing for the CISSP exam is expected to have foundational concepts and knowledge in the following key areas of the *security and risk management* domain:

- Asset protection
- Confidentiality, Integrity, and Availability (CIA)
- Security governance principles
- Compliance
- Legal and regulatory issues that pertain to information security in the global context
- Professional ethics
- Personnel security policies
- Risk management principles
- Threat modeling
- Business continuity planning

- Security risk considerations in acquisition strategy and practice
- Security education training and awareness

This chapter gives an overview of Security, Compliance, and Policies using a high-level illustration. This is followed with an overview of asset and asset protection. Furthermore, the concepts of **Confidentiality, Integrity, and Availability (CIA)** are explained with suitable examples. Security governance principles, compliance frameworks, and legal and regulatory issues that can impact on compliance are covered from a global perspective. Management practices that relate to security policies, standards, procedures and guidelines, as well as personnel security policies, are covered toward the end.

Overview of security, compliance, and policies

Asset protection forms the baseline for security. Unintended disclosure and unauthorized modification or destruction of an asset can affect security.

Observe the following illustration:

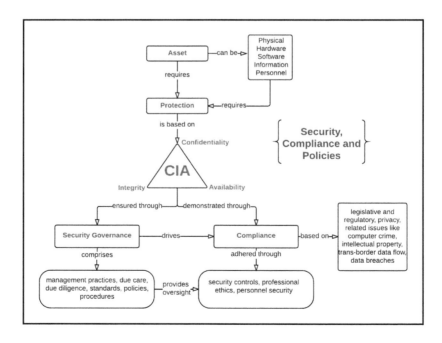

- Asset requires protection
- Protection is based on the requirements of Confidentiality, Integrity and Availability (CIA) for the
- Security is ensured through Security Governance that comprises management practices and management oversight
- Security is demonstrated through compliance that could be legal or regulatory
- Compliance consists of adherence to applicable legal and regulatory requirements; applicable policies, standards, procedures and guidelines; and personnel security policies
- Compliance can be affected by security issues

Asset

Assets can be tangible, that is, perceptible by touch. An example of a tangible asset could be a desktop computer or a laptop. Assets can be intangible, that is, not have physical presence. An example of an intangible asset could be a corporate image or an intellectual property, such as patents.

Assets are used by the organization for business processes. Every asset, whether tangible or intangible, has a certain intrinsic value to the business. The value can be monetary, or of importance, or both. For example, a simple firewall that costs less than $10000 may be protecting important business applications worth millions of dollars.

If an asset is compromised, for example, stolen or modified, and the data or a secret information is disclosed, it will have an impact that could lead to monetary loss, customer dissatisfaction, or legal and regulatory non-compliance.

An asset can be hardware, software, data, process, product, or infrastructure that is of value to an organization, and hence, needs protection. The level of protection is based on the value of the asset to the business.

To assess protection requirements, assets are grouped based on the type of assets, such as tangible or intangible, physical or virtual, and computing or noncomputing. For example, a computer can be a physical asset as well as a computing asset, such as hardware.

 Note that equipment, such as plumbing tools, can also be called hardware in some countries. However, in the information security domain, hardware generally implies computing and computer-related equipment.

Assets are generally grouped as follows:

- **Physical assets**: They are tangible in nature and examples include buildings, furniture, **Heating, Ventilating and Air Conditioning (HVAC)** equipment, and so on.
- **Hardware assets**: They are related to computer and network systems. Examples include, servers, desktop computers, laptop, router, network cables and so on.
- **Software assets**: They are intangible assets that an organization owns a license to use. In general, organizations may not have **Intellectual Property Rights (IPR)** over such assets. Examples include, **Operating Systems (OS)**, **Data Base Management Systems (DBMS)**, office applications, web server software, and so on.
- **Information assets**: They are intangible in nature. They are owned by the organization. Examples include, business processes, policies and procedures, customer information, personnel information, agreements, and formulas developed in-house or purchased outright.
- **Personnel assets**: People associated with the organization, such as employees, contractors, and third-party consultants, are grouped under this type.

 Note that, in certain accounting practices, software can also be classified under **Property, Plant and Equipment (PPE)**. However, in the information security domain, software is classified as an intangible asset. Besides, software or information may be stored in hardware or physical assets, such as on hard disk or DVD.

Asset protection

In the information security domain, asset protection involves security management practices that are subjected to business and compliance requirements. Such practices for asset protection are called security controls.

Types of security controls include:

- Physical entry controls to an office building that allow only authorized personnel
- Monitoring controls, such as CCTV, for surveillance of critical assets
- Controls, such as locks, for hardware assets for protection from theft
- Tamper proofing controls, such as hashing and encryption, for software and data asset
- Copyrights or patent for information assets to protect legal rights
- Identity management systems to protect personnel assets from identity theft

This is not a comprehensive list of security controls. This book provides hundreds of such requirements and controls in subsequent chapters. However, a requirement or a control is not determined ad-hoc. Instead, asset protection requirements are identified through a structured method of risk analysis, evaluation, and assessment. Similarly, controls are identified through risk mitigation strategies. Risk assessment and risk mitigation strategies are covered in the next chapter.

Hence, asset protection requirements are based on risk. In order to understand risk, to perform risk assessment and select controls for asset protection, the concepts of CIA have to be understood first.

Confidentiality, Integrity, and Availability (CIA)

Information is a business asset and adds value to an organization. Information exists in many forms. It may be printed or written on paper, stored in electronic media, transmitted by electronic means, or spoken in conversations.

Information and its associated infrastructure are accessed and used in business by employees, third-party users or by automated processes. For example, an HR Manager accessing employee profile database through a database application. Each component in this activity, that is, HR manager, employee profile database, and the database application is called **entities**. Other examples would be a time-based job scheduler, such as cron in UNIX, such as operating systems, or a task scheduler in Windows, such as operating systems updating information through a script in a database. Here, scheduler application, the script or application it runs, and the data being accessed are entities.

Information assets and associated entities have certain levels of CIA requirements. A level could be a numeric value or representational value, such as high, low, or medium. The CIA triad is frequently referred to as **tenets** of information security. Tenet means *something accepted as an important truth*. The CIA values of an asset are established through risk analysis, which is a part of risk management. Concepts of risk management are covered in the next chapter.

Information security is characterized by preserving CIA values of an asset. Preserving is to ensure that the CIA values are maintained all the time and at all the locations. Hence, for an effective information security management, defining and maintaining CIA values is a primary requirement.

Confidentiality

Information needs to be disclosed to authorized entities for business processes, for example, an authorized employee accessing information about the prototype under development on the server. **Confidentiality** is to ensure that the information is not disclosed to unauthorized entities, for example, confidentiality is often achieved by encryption.

Integrity

Information has to be consistent and not altered or modified without established approval policies or procedures. **Integrity** is to maintain the consistency of the information internally as well as externally. This is to prevent unauthorized modification by authorized entities, for example, an update to the database record is made without approval.

Integrity is also to prevent authorized modification by unauthorized entities, for example, when malicious code is inserted in a web application by an unethical hacker. In this scenario, a hacker (an unauthorized entity) may modify an application through an established procedure (authorized update).

Availability

Availability is to ensure that information and associated services are available to authorized entities as and when required. For example, in an attack on the network through **Denial-of-Service (DoS)**. Sometimes, an authorized update to an application may stop certain essential services and will constitute a breach in availability requirements, for example, inadvertently tripping over a server power cable may constitute as an availability breach.

Security governance

Information security for a long time was considered as a purely technical domain. Hence, the focus was to define and manage security predominantly through the Information Technology department in many organizations. It was more like protecting only the Information systems, such as computers and networks.

Information exists in many forms and the levels of assurance required vary, based on their criticality, business requirements and from legal, regulatory compliance requirements. Hence, the focus has to be on protecting the *information* itself, which is essential and much broader in scope compared to focusing only on Information Technology.

Information is a business asset and valuable to organizations. Information has a lifecycle. It could be handled, processed, transported, stored, archived, or destroyed. At any stage during the lifecycle, the information can be compromised. A compromise can affect the CIA requirements of the information.

Information protection is a *business responsibility*. It involves governance challenges, such as risk management, reporting, and accountability. Hence, it requires the involvement of senior management and the board to provide a strategic oversight for implementing and ensuring continual effectiveness.

Strategy, goals, mission, and objectives

Aligning and integrating information security with enterprise governance and IT governance frameworks is the primary **strategy** for the senior management and the board. It includes the definition of the current state of security and establishing goals and objectives to align with the corporate mission.

For such a strategy, **goals** and **objectives** will include understanding protection requirements, which are based on the value of information, expected outcomes of the information security program, benefits that are quantifiable, and methods to integrate information security practices with organizational practices.

A corporate mission is based on the definition of the business, its core purpose, values and beliefs, standards, and behaviors. An information security **mission** defines security requirements, their purpose, focus on risk management, commitment to continual maintenance, and the improvement of the information security program. Hence, aligning information security mission with the corporate's mission is one of the primary strategies of security governance.

Organizational processes

To support the information security strategy and to meet the goals and objectives, **organizational processes** need to be aligned to the mission. Such processes include defining the roles and responsibilities of the personnel involved with effective implementation and day-to-day management; establishing monitoring mechanisms that include reporting, review and approval processes, and ensuring that management support is available to such organizational processes.

Security roles and responsibilities

Information security is everyone's responsibility in any organization. Specific **security roles and responsibilities** are to be considered from the security governance perspective. Hence, the information security responsibilities of the board of directors/trustees, executives, steering committee, and chief information security officer are important at management level.

Control frameworks

To support the information security strategy and the mission, **control frameworks** are established by the organization. Such frameworks contain controls under three broad categories, namely, management, administrative, and technical.

Management controls

Management controls are characterized by stating the views of the management and their position in particular topics, such as information security.

For example, the **Information security policy** is a management control, wherein the management states its intent, support, and direction for security.

Administrative controls

While a policy is a high-level document that provides the intent of the management, **administrative controls** are to implement such policies.

For example, **procedures, guidelines, and standards** are administrative controls that support the policies. These are covered later in this chapter.

Technical controls

Information is stored and processed predominantly in IT systems. Hence, **technical controls** are established to support management and administrative controls in the information systems.

Firewall, intrusion detection systems, antivirus, and so on, are some examples of technical controls.

Due diligence and due care

It is important that intent and management support to information security programs is visible across the organization to investors and customers. Hence, an organization should demonstrate due diligence and due care pertaining to information security processes and activities.

Understanding risk and estimating the same, in view of the organizations' mission, prevailing threats, vulnerabilities, and attacks, and legal, regulatory compliance, form a part of the due diligence process by the management.

Implementing security governance by way of organizational processes, defining roles and responsibilities, establishing risk management processes, and monitoring effectiveness of the information security controls are **due care** activities by the management.

Compliance

Information security breaches in the past two decades have necessitated new security-related legal and regulatory frameworks or updates to existing legal and regulatory frameworks to include security-related compliance provisions across various countries. Requirements to comply with legal and legislative frameworks have increased exponentially due to global nature of the Internet, cross-border information exchange, electronic commerce, and services. Compliance frameworks are abundant with terms and jargon that a security professional should be aware of. Following are some of the legal and regulatory frameworks, terms, and jargons that are relevant to the Information Security domain.

Legislative and regulatory compliance

Common law is a law that is developed based on the decisions of courts and tribunals rather than through statutory laws (legislative statutes). The legal system that uses common law is called **common law legal systems**. Countries, such as the United Kingdom, the United States of America (most of the states in the USA), Canada, Australia, South Africa, India, Malaysia, Singapore, and Hong Kong follow common law.

There are three categories under common law that are generally established:

1. **Regulatory law**, also called as **Administrative law**, primarily deals with the regulations of administrative agencies of the government.
2. **Criminal law** deals with the violations of government laws. Criminal laws are filed by government agencies against an individual or an organization. The punishment under criminal laws includes imprisonment as well as financial penalties.
3. **Civil law** deals with the lawsuits filed by private parties, such as corporations or individuals. Punishments under this law are financial or punitive damages or both.

Statutory law, **legislative statute**, or **statute law** is a legal system that is set down by the legislature or executive branch of the government. Statutory law under certain instances is also termed as **codified law**.

Religious are legal systems based on religious principles. Examples include Hindu, Islam, and Christian laws.

Civil Law laws are legal systems based on religious principles. Examples include Hindu, Islam, and Christian laws.

Civil Law is a legal system based on codes and legislative statutes as opposed to common law. France, Germany, and many other countries in the world follow civil law. Hence, there is a civil law category in the common law system and a civil law system itself.

Privacy requirements in compliance

Privacy is protection of **Personally Identifiable Information** (PII)about individuals or **Sensitive Personal Information** (SPI) that can be used to identify a person in context with a group. Protection under privacy is from disclosure or selective disclosure based on the individual's preferences.

National Institute of Standards and Technology (**NIST**) has published a guide to protecting the confidentiality of the personally identifiable information-wide NIST special publication 800-122. As per the guide, PII is defined as *any information about an individual maintained by an agency, including (1) any information that can be used to distinguish or trace an individual's identity, such as name, social security number, date and place of birth, mother's maiden name, or biometric records; and (2) any other information that is linked or linkable to an individual, such as medical, educational, financial, and employment information.*

Privacy laws deal with protecting and preserving the rights of an individual's privacy.

A few examples of privacy laws in the United States include the following:

- Health Insurance Portability and Accountability Act (HIPAA)
- Financial Services Modernization Act (GLB), 15 U.S. Code: 6801-6810
- Final Rule on Privacy of Consumer Financial Information, 16 Code of Federal Regulations, Part 313

In the UK, they include the following:

- Data Protection Act 1998 (United Kingdom)
- Data Protection Directive (European Union)

Licensing and intellectual property

Intellectual Property (**IP**) refers to creative works using intellect, that is, mind, music, literary works, art, inventions, symbols, designs, and so on fall under intellectual property. The creator of such intellectual work has certain exclusive rights over the property. These exclusive rights are called **Intellectual Property Rights** (**IPR**).

Intellectual property law is a legal domain that deals with Intellectual Property Rights (IPR).

Following are some of the IPR-related terminologies:

- **Copyright**: This is an intellectual property that grants exclusive rights to the creator of the original work, such as deriving financial benefits out of such work, ownership credits, and so on. Others do not have 'right to copy' such work. Copyright is country-specific.

- **Patent**: This is a set of exclusive rights granted to the inventor of new, useful, inventive, and industry applicable inventions. This right excludes others from making, using, selling, or importing the invention. Patents are granted for a specific period of time. A patent is a public document.
- **Trademark**: This is a unique symbol or mark that is used by individuals or organizations to uniquely represent a product or a service. Trademark is also used to distinguish from products and services of other entities.
- **Trade secret**: This is a formula, design, process, practice, or pattern that is not revealed to others. This is to protect the information being copied and gain competitive advantage.

Legal and regulatory issues

Information compromise or security breach that could lead to civil or criminal liability on the part of an organization will be grouped under legal and regulatory issues. For example, if a hacker intrudes into a system, obtains **Personally Identifiable Information (PII)**, and publishes the same in an Internet portal, then the liability for failure to protect such information falls on the organization.

The following list of issues may have legal or regulatory ramifications.

Computer crimes

A computer crime is a fraudulent activity that is perpetrated against computer or IT systems. The motivation could be for financial gain, competitive gain, popularity, fame, or adventure.

In computer crime, the term *computer* refers to the role it plays in different scenarios. Whether the crime is committed against a computer, whether the crime is committed using the computer, whether the computer is incidental in the crime, or a combination of all the three.

The following paragraphs provide some of the common computer crimes. Remember, CIA compromise or breach will be the end result of a crime.

Fraud

Manipulation of computer records, such as data diddling, salami slicing, or any other techniques, or a deliberate circumvention of computer security systems, such as cracking or unethical hacking for monitory gain, is termed as **fraud**.

 Data diddling is a malicious activity to change the data during input or processing stage of a software program to obtain financial gain.
Salami slicing, also known as **penny shaving**, is a fraudulent activity to regularly siphon extremely small quantity of money so as to prevent from being observed or caught.

Hacking refers to the discovery of vulnerabilities, holes, or weaknesses in computer software and associated IT systems either to exploit the same for improvising the security or to prevent intentional fraud. **Hackers** are persons who do hacking. However, hacking is classified with different names to distinguish the objective:

- **Black-hat hackers** are people with malicious intent, who compromise the computer systems to commit crime. Such a hacker is called a **cracker** and the malicious hacking activity is termed as **cracking**.
- **White-hat hackers** or **ethical hackers** are people who try to compromise the computer systems to discover holes and improve the security.
- **Grey-hat hackers** are ambiguous wherein their actual intention is not known.

Theft

Identity theft is to steal someone's identity. The intention is to pretend to be someone else to commit fraud. Stealing passwords, login credentials, and credit card information are examples of identity theft.

Intellectual property theft is stealing software code or designs for financial gain.

Malware/malicious code

A **malware** is **mali**cious soft**ware** that is designed to compromise, damage, or affect the general functioning of computers, gain unauthorized access, collect private, and sensitive information and/or corrupt the data.

Writing or spreading malware is a computer crime. Viruses, worms, Trojan horses, spyware, such as Key logger, and so on are examples of malware and are explained as follows:

- A **computer virus** is a malicious program or a malicious code that attaches to files and can spread from one file to another file or from one computer to another computer. Technically, a virus can spread or infect the computer if the user opens the infected file.
- **Worms** are similar to viruses, but are self-replicating and propagating. Generally, worms do not require the human intervention of opening an infected file.
- A **Trojan horse** is a malware that hides its identity within a legitimate program. Users are tricked into opening the file containing the malware by way of social engineering.

- Social engineering is a type of nonintrusive attack in which humans are tricked into circumventing security controls. Some of the attacks, such as phishing and **Cross Site Request Forgery** (**CSRF**), use social engineering techniques. More details about CSRF are covered in Chapter 6, *Day 6 – Security Engineering – Security Design, Practices, Models and Vulnerability Mitigation*.

- **Spyware** is a malicious code that tracks the user actions. Examples of user actions include web browsing patterns, files opened, applications accessed, and so on. A spyware is best explained as a snooping software.
- **Key loggers** are a type of spyware that capture keystrokes and transmit them to an attacker's server. Sensitive information, such as username and passwords, are captured using key loggers. Key loggers can be a hardware or software.

Cyber crime

Criminal activities that are perpetrated using communication networks, such as the Internet, telephone, wireless, satellite, and mobile networks, are called as **cyber crimes**:

- **Cyber terrorism** is a type of cybercrime perpetrated against computers and computer networks and they generally are premeditated in nature. The objective of the attacks could be to cause harm based on social, ideological, religious, political, or similar objectives.

- **Cyber stalking** is a type of cybercrime in which the offender harasses or intimidates the victim using the Internet and other electronic means. It is a criminal offence under various state anti stalking, harassment laws.
- **Information warfare** is a type of cybercrime to destabilize the opponent, such as corporations and institutions, to gain a competitive advantage. For example, false propaganda, web page defacement, and so on.
- **Denial-Of-Service (DoS)** attack or **Distributed Denial-Of-Service (DDoS)** attacks are cybercrimes where websites or corporate systems of the corporations or computer systems of any user, made inaccessible by way of multiple services, request to overload the web and application servers. Eventually, the servers stops responding to genuine requests. (Ro)botnets are increasingly used for such crimes. A botnet is an army of computers listening to a control center system for executing orders. Generally, computers in a bot network are compromised systems through security vulnerability exploitation.

 More details about botnets are covered in `Chapter 6`, *Day 6 – Security Engineering – Security Design, Practices, Models and Vulnerability Mitigation*.

Making and digitally distributing child pornography is a cyber crime.

Digitally distributing and storing copyrighted materials of others without the copyright owner's explicit permission is a cyber crime.

Using e-mail communication to disrupt or send unsolicited commercial e-mails or induce the user to perform certain actions to steal information or money fall under cyber crime.

Following are examples of such crimes:

- Sending **Unsolicited Commercial Email** (UCE) is called **spamming**. It is a cyber crime that clogs the networks and intrudes into the privacy of the user.
- **Phishing** is a type of cyber crime wherein a user is lured to an attacker constructed illegitimate website that looks similar to actual website the user intended to visit. For example, online banking websites, e-mail login pages, and so on. A successful phishing attack would result in the capture of user credentials by the attacker.
- **Pharming** is a type of cyber attack wherein a user is redirected to a malicious website constructed by the attacker. Generally, this type of redirection happens without user acceptance or knowledge.

- **SMiShing** is a type of cyber attack using mobile networks. In this attack, **Short Messaging Service (SMS)** is used to lure the user to the attacker-constructed malicious websites. This is similar to phishing.
- **Harassment** in the form of cyberstalking, cyberbullying, hate crime, online predating, and trolling are crimes that target specific individuals.

Importing and exporting controls

Many countries have import and export restrictions pertaining to the encryption of data. For example, encryption items specifically designed, developed, configured, adapted, or modified for military applications, command, control, and intelligence applications are generally controlled based on munitions lists.

Transborder data flow

The transfer of computerized data across national borders, states or political boundaries are termed as transborder data flow. Data can be personal, business, technical, and organizational. Legal issues that arise out of such data is related to ownership and the usage.

Data breaches

By definition, a data breach is a security incident in which sensitive, protected, or confidential data is copied, transmitted, viewed, stolen, or used by an individual unauthorized to do so. It can also be owing to unintentional information disclosure, data leak, or data spill.

Data breach can happen owing to hacking (unethical means), organized crimes, negligence in the disposal of media, and so on.

Data breach is a security incident, and hence, many jurisdictions have passed data breach notification laws.

In the United States, data breach-related laws are categorized as security breach laws. National Conference of State Legislatures in the United States defines the provisions of such laws as:

Security breach laws typically have provisions regarding who must comply with the law (e.g. businesses, data/ information brokers, government entities, and so on); definitions of "personal information" (e.g. name combined with SSN, drivers license or state ID, account numbers, and so on.); what constitutes a breach (e.g. unauthorized acquisition of data); requirements for notice (e.g. timing or method of notice, who must be notified); and exemptions (e.g. for encrypted information).

Professional ethics

The information security profession is based on trust, as the professional may be handling sensitive or confidential information. Ethically sound and consistently applied code of professional ethics need to be adhered to by the professional.

Codes of ethics

These are based on the safety of the commonwealth, duty to principals, such as employers, contractors, people whom a professional works for, and to each other. It requires that professionals adhere, and be seen to adhere, to the highest ethical standards of behavior.

(ISC)^2 code of professional ethics

International Information System Security Certification Consortium (ISC)^2 has a published code of professional ethics for its members provided as follows:

- Protect society, the commonwealth, and the infrastructure
- Act honorably, honestly, justly, responsibly, and legally
- Provide diligent and competent service to principals
- Advance and protect the profession

Security policies, standards, procedures, and guidelines

Policies, standards, procedures, and guidelines form a quartet of organizational mechanisms in protecting information:

- **Security policies** are high-level statements that provide management intent and direction for information security. They describe the *what* of the description.

- **Security standards** provide prescriptive statements, control objectives, and controls for enforcing security policies. In a way, they provide the *how* of the description. They can be internally developed by the organization and/or published by standard bodies, such as **National Institute of Standards and Technology (NIST), International Organization for Standardization (ISO)**, or country-specific standard bodies.
- **Security procedures** are step-by-step instructions to implement the policies and standards.
- **Security guidelines** provide the best practice methods to support security controls selection and implementation. They can be used in whole or part while implementing security standards.

  For example, NIST Special Publication 800-14, *Generally Accepted Principles and Practices for Securing Information Technology Systems* provides procedures and guidelines for *System security life cycle*.

International Organization for Standardization (ISO) along with **International Electro-Technical Commission (IEC)** has published code of practice guidelines and a standard for **Information Security Management System (ISMS)**. They are as follows:

- **ISO/IEC 27002**: Code of practice for information security. This standard provides a list of best practices an organization could adopt for security management.
- **ISO/IEC 27001**: This standard specifies the **management framework** required for Information Security and is a certifiable standard. Organizations can seek certification against this standard for their **Information Security Management System (ISMS)**.

Personnel security policies

Personnel security policies concern people associated with the organization, such as employees, contractors, and consultants. These policies encompass the following:

- Screening processes to validate security requirements
- Understanding their security responsibilities
- Understanding their suitability to security roles
- Reducing the risk of theft, fraud, or the misuse of facilities

Employment candidate screening

Background verification checks are primarily used in employment candidate screening processes. They may include the following:

1. Character references to evaluate the personal traits of the applicant. Best practice guidelines indicate character references from at least two entities, such as from business and personnel.
2. Completeness and accuracy of the applicant's curriculum vitae and the verification of claimed academic and professional qualifications are critical checks in the screening process.
3. Identity checks by verifying identification documents.
4. Checking criminal records as well as credit checks.

Employment agreement and policies

Besides general job roles, based on the business requirements, information security responsibilities that include information handling requirements should form part of the employment agreement and policies.

Employees should also be aware of organization's information security policies, and when they are given access to sensitive or confidential information, they need to additionally sign confidentiality and nondisclosure agreements.

Employment termination processes

Employee termination processes have to be in accordance with the established security policies and practices. The primary objective of the process is to ensure that employees, contractors, and third-party users exit or change employment as per established procedures without compromising security. The procedures may include termination of responsibilities, return of assets, removal of access rights, and so on.

Vendor, consultant, and contractor controls

Third-party users, such as vendors, consultants, and contractors, need access to the information and associated systems based on the job function. Information protection starts from screening process, confidentiality, and nondisclosure agreements.

Compliance and privacy

Adherence to policies, procedures, and so on, performing job functions as per the legal, regulatory requirements, and adherence to privacy protection mechanisms, are applicable across the board in an organization.

Summary

This chapter has covered foundational concepts in Information Security. In a nutshell, assets such as physical, hardware, software, information and personnel require protection. Protection of assets is based on CIA requirements. CIA values are determined using risk assessment methods (covered in the next chapter). Information security is ensured through security governance and demonstrated through compliance.

Continued in the next chapter are topics, such as understanding and applying risk management concepts, threat modeling, and establishing business continuity requirements in this first domain.

Sample questions

Q1. Which one of the following statements about security standards reflect the most appropriate definition?

1. Security standards are step-by-step instructions to implement a security policy
2. Security standards contains prescriptive statements, control objectives, and controls for implementing security
3. Security standards document best practices
4. Security standards are technology specific blue print diagrams

Q2. Security breach laws typically have provisions regarding who must comply with the law and additional applicable provisions. Which one of the following may not be an applicable provision?

1. Definitions of personnel information
2. Exemptions
3. What constitutes a breach
4. Requirements for certification

Q3. Which statements, among the following are published by (ISC)^2 in the Code of professional ethics (this is a drag and drop type of question. Here you can draw a line from the list of answers from the left to the empty box on the right-hand side)?

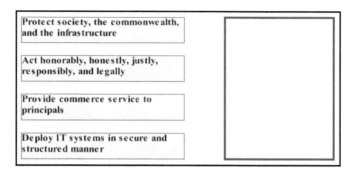

Q4. A security practitioner is evaluating a privacy breach scenario for an ecommerce order placement and process setup. Choose a location where a possible privacy security breach could happen due to insecure implementation (this is a hot spot type of question. Place a tick mark in the appropriate circle).

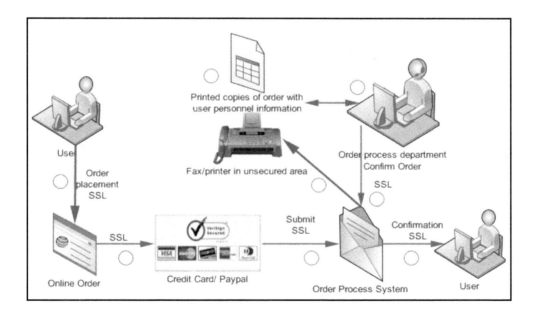

2
Day 2 – Security and Risk Management - Risk Management, Business Continuity, and Security Education

This chapter gives an overview of risk management, business continuity, and security education using a high-level illustration. Understanding and applying risk management concepts, threat modeling, and establishing business continuity requirements are some of the main topics covered in this chapter. A brief overview of integrating security risk considerations into information systems' acquisition, strategy, and practice are covered. Establishing and managing information security education, training, and awareness programs and recommendation of best practices are provided towards the end of the chapter.

Overview of risk management, business continuity, and security education

Asset protection forms the baseline for security. Unintended disclosure, unauthorized modification, or destruction of an asset can affect security.

Observe the following illustration:

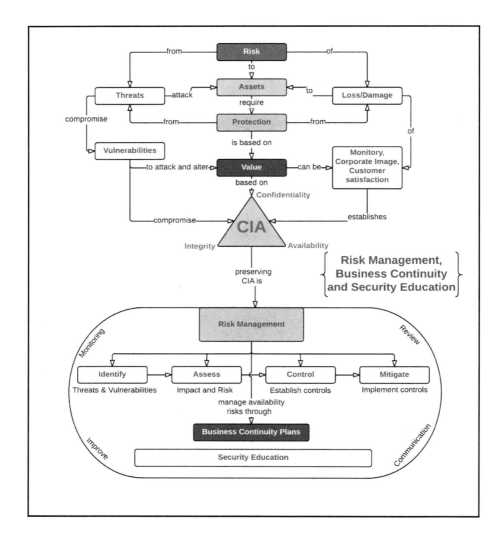

Fig 1

- Risk is to assets from threat sources.
- The asset requires protection from attacks.
- Protection is based on the value of the assets. The value can be based on monetary value, anticipated loss due to customer dissatisfaction, damage to corporate image, or all of the above.

- Risk management is to identify, assess, control, and mitigate risks.
- Risk management consists of monitoring, reviewing, communicating, and improving mechanisms.
- Risks that compromise the availability of assets and resources are treated through **Business Continuity Plans (BCP)**.
- Security education is an integral part of risk management.

These concepts are covered in detail in the rest of this chapter.

Risk management

Risk is defined as an exposure to loss, injury, or damage due to threats, vulnerabilities, and attacks. Risk management is to manage the risks.

Identifying threats and vulnerabilities, attacks, estimating potential impact, and establishing and implementing suitable controls to treat the risk are functional steps in risk management. Monitoring, reviewing, communicating the results, and improving the security posture are continual improvement processes in the risk management cycle.

 Security posture is an overall plan of the organization pertaining to security. It includes security governance, policies, procedures, and compliance.

Observe the following illustration, which is a typical web application network infrastructure consisting of the N-tier architecture:

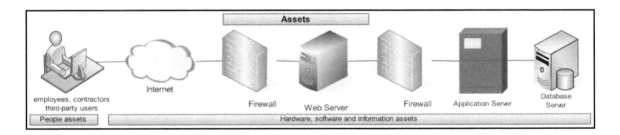

Fig 2

In the preceding architecture, various assets are involved in the business process of accessing, updating, or modifying the information. For example, an employee (people asset) accesses a web application (information asset) in a web server (hardware and software assets). The web application accesses the application server, which in turn accesses and processes the data in the database server. In this chain of connections and processes, each asset will have certain levels of CIA requirements. For example, the applications in the application server and the data they access will have higher confidentiality and integrity requirements than the web server. Also, observe that there are some existing controls, such as the firewall, authentication systems, and access control mechanisms.

 From the information security perspective, a corporation has to evaluate the risk of security compromise to the system, data, or physical assets and estimate potential loss through threat, vulnerability, and attack analysis.

Threats, vulnerabilities, and attacks

Threat is an event that could compromise the information security by causing loss or damage to assets. The threat is predominantly external to an organization. Examples of threats are fire, flood, hacking, and so on.

Vulnerability is a hole or a weakness in the system. Threat can exploit vulnerabilities through its agents called **threat agents**. For example, having no antivirus software is a vulnerability, which a threat agent like a virus could exploit. Similarly, hacking is a threat that could exploit a weakness in the system through its agent, for instance, a hacker.

A threat event exploiting a vulnerability is called as an **attack**. The end result of an attack can lead to a **security violation**. An attack either compromises a security control or lack of it and can affect the CIA requirements of the asset.

 Having vulnerabilities and threats alone may not end in attacks. An attack can be a motivated action to commit financial fraud or adventure action, such as stopping a service or adversarial action for competitive gain, revenge, and so on. Proper assessment has to be done to ascertain the chance of an attack, the tenet of CIA it can affect, and the resulting damage if the attack succeeds. In a nutshell, attacks can either be motivated or inadvertent.

Threat risk modeling

Observe the following illustration, which now provides threat and vulnerability scenarios in the same network depicted earlier. It is apparent, that due to vulnerabilities in the system, threat agents may be able to attack and possibly succeed in penetrating the network and obtain confidential information, alter sensitive data, or stop a service. However, we still do not know yet that such an attack could materialize with prevailing controls in place. But we will be able to estimate the possible impact if such an attack materializes. In other words, we will be able to estimate potential loss.

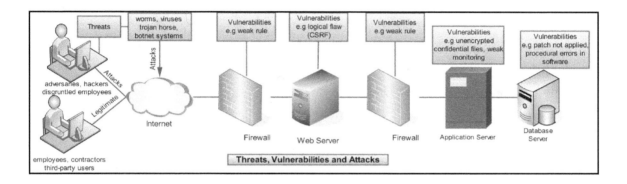

Fig 3

Hence, in a threat risk modeling process, the following steps are necessary to estimate potential loss:

1. Identify assets and their CIA requirements.
2. Identify threats to those assets.
3. Identify vulnerabilities in those assets.
4. Identify attack possibilities.
5. Identify existing controls.
6. Perform vulnerability assessment and penetration tests on the assets and the infrastructure.
7. Estimate risk (potential loss).

We have reviewed assets and CIA requirements of assets in the previous chapter. The rest of the steps are covered in the following topics.

Threat and vulnerability analysis

In a threat risk-modeling scenario, the infrastructure/application has to be broken down into various types of assets. Observe the following flow diagram:

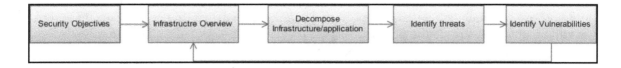

Fig 4

During threat and vulnerability analysis, the following questions are pertinent to determine the risks:

Q1. What are the security objectives (requirements)?

> Security objectives are based on policies, such as the information security policy, legal/regulatory requirements as mandated in privacy laws, Service Level Agreements (SLA) as required in infrastructure availability, or data integrity assurance requirements as required in financial transactions.

Q2. What is the overall infrastructure?

> What are the individual components in the infrastructure? What are the CIA values of the assets (people, infrastructure, application, data, and so on)? Will the CIA values change due to certain factors? If so, what are those factors?

> Infrastructure consists of physical security requirements, such as secure locations, and environmental requirements, such as clean power, heating, ventilation and air conditioning, and so on.

> Application security requirements are based on access control, data flows, trust boundaries, and so on.

Q3. What threats are applicable based on the type of assets (threat register)? What are the prevailing threats to these assets?

> Identify and document threats to the infrastructure, threats to the application, and threats to data.

Q4. What are the vulnerabilities (vulnerability register) that these threats can compromise? Which of these vulnerabilities are identified in these assets?

> Identify and document vulnerabilities in infrastructure, applications in data flow, and so on.

When a corporation compiles the answers to the preceding questions, it is in the process of threat and vulnerability analysis. The end result of such an exercise will be a documented matrix of assets, threats, and vulnerabilities.

Attack analysis

Based on the matrix of threats and vulnerabilities and based on the results of security testing, a few attack scenarios can be constructed. Such a scenario is called as an attack tree.

Observe the following single dimensional attack tree. This attack tree is based on *Fig 2* in the previous page:

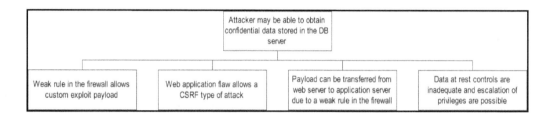

Fig 5

 Note that some of the technical jargon used in the illustration, such as custom payload, CSRF, and so on, is covered in `Chapter 6`, *Day 6 – Security Engineering – Security Design, Practices, Models, and Vulnerability Mitigation.*

Hence, an attack tree is constructed based on the following questions:

Q1. What are the various attacks that are possible based on the type of assets (attack vectors)?

> Attack possibilities can be created based on vulnerability assessment, penetration testing, application security testing, and also based on the existing documentation of attacks that are available from trusted sources.

Q2. What will happen when the attack succeeds?

> Identify the system or data that will be compromised, CIA values that will be affected and so on. It is also important to identify cascading effects of such a compromise. For example, if an attacker compromises a webserver, will the other servers that have trust relationships established with the webserver be compromised?

Q3. What will be the loss? Is the loss quantifiable?

> Identify loss in terms of money, time to recover, policy violation and its impact, loss of competitive advantage, customer loss, compliance violation and its impact, and so on.

> Threat, vulnerability, and attack analysis provide information to perform risk analysis. Few online dictionaries and databases are available that provide common weaknesses and attack possibilities to applications or to infrastructure and so on. References and URLs for such resources are provided in `Chapter 5`, *Day 5 – Exam Cram and Practice Questions.*

Risk analysis

Risk is an exposure to loss or damage due to threats, vulnerabilities, and attacks. Hence, risk analysis is used to estimate the probability of an attack, identify prevailing controls and their effectiveness in combating the attacks, and estimate the consequence of such an attack in terms of potential loss.

Risk has to be understood from the following perspectives:

- **Risk to what?**

  > Risks are generally to assets. Assets can be tangible or intangible.

- **Risk from what?**

  > Risks are from threat sources, such as earthquakes, floods, hacking, fires, viruses, disgruntled employees, and so on.

- **Risk of what?**

> When an asset is compromised by a threat, it may result in a security violation. Hence, there could be loss or damage. The damage can be monetary loss, image loss, customer loss, or legal issues. Hence, there is a risk of losing money, a risk of losing customers, or a risk of facing legal/regulatory consequences due to the security breach.

The damage caused due to a security violation is called as an **impact**. The magnitude of such an impact is the potential loss or, in other words, risk.

If the magnitude of an impact can be calculated in monetary terms (say, a dollar value), then the risk is defined in quantitative terms. If the magnitude cannot be determined in terms of monetary value, but can be measured in relative terms (such as high, medium, or low), then the risk is defined in qualitative terms.

In terms of information security, ISO/IEC 27000 defines risk as the **probability** of a threat exploiting the vulnerability and the **consequence** of loss or damage to the asset due to that event. This is called probability versus consequence analysis and is a type of risk analysis.

> Different types of risk assessments can be conducted based on the type of assets and applicability and based on regulatory requirements. Some of them are, Operationally Critical Threat, Asset, and Vulnerability Evaluation (OCTAVE), Asset based risk assessment method based on ISO/IEC 27005, NISTSP 800:30, DREAD, and so on. References to many such risk assessment methodologies and a brief overview of them are provided in Chapter 5, *Day 5 – Exam Cram and Practice Questions*.

The results of probability versus consequence risk analysis will provide four scenarios. Refer to the following illustration (*Fig 6*):

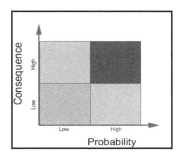

Fig 6

- The probability is low and the consequence is low, represented as the green zone at the bottom left corner
- The probability is low and the consequence is high, represented as the amber zone at the top left corner
- The probability is high and the consequence is low, represented as the amber zone at bottom right corner
- The probability is high and the consequence is high, represented as the red zone on top right corner

By systematically analyzing the probability of a threat exploiting vulnerability and the related consequences, one can deduce the risk.

The process of determining the risk level in terms of threats and a vulnerabilities and the probability versus consequence analysis is called **risk analysis**. In other words, risk analysis is a systematic process of identifying the risks and estimating the loss if the risk materializes.

In the risk analysis process, related parameters of threats, vulnerabilities, and attacks are taken into consideration to derive a value. The value can be a number (quantitative) or an expression (qualitative). This derived value is called the **risk value**. For example, an insurance agent may consider different parameters, such as age, health conditions, hereditary diseases, habits, and so on, before determining a premium for life insurance. Similarly, in information security, parameters are based on assets, their required CIA values, threats, vulnerabilities, and attacks.

Risk analysis process involves two distinctive activities. One is to measure the impact of the risk. The analysis process tries to estimate the loss in terms of monetary value if a risk materializes. However, assets are tangible or intangible in nature. It is not possible to always determine the value of assets in monetary terms. Hence, two types of analysis are used to determine loss expectancy. One is called quantitative risk analysis and the other is called qualitative risk analysis.

Both quantitative and qualitative risk analysis processes require that the value of the asset is determined. The terms of reference by which the significance of the risk is determined called are **risk criteria**.

Quantitative risk analysis

This type of risk analysis provides risk values in numeric terms. For example, monetary loss. In other words, *quantify the risk or derive a dollar value of a risk*. Mathematical models are available to estimate the monetary value of a risk. One such model is provided here.

When a threat event happens, the percentage of loss of an asset is based on its exposure level to that particular threat. Generally, an exposure level is represented in terms of a numerical value between 0 and 1.

For example, refer to the network diagram in *Fig 3*. The web server has a higher exposure level from external sources than the application server . It is possible to approximate this exposure level based on threats, vulnerabilities, and attacks. The primary firewall in *Fig 3* has a weak rule that allows a custom payload to be deployed on the web server. If the web server contains a confidential file that can be obtained due to the attack, then the exposure value of the web server and the file will be 1.

If an exposure value is represented in percentage, then the percentage will be called the **Exposure Factor (EF)** of that asset. In the preceding web server example, the exposure value will be 1, which will give an exposure factor of 100%. Exposure factor is calculated based on the other controls that are in place. For example, if the web server is protected with a host-based firewall or privilege-based access controls are implemented, then the exposure factor will be less.

When a monetary value or a dollar value is assigned for the expected loss due to a single threat event, it is called **Single Loss Expectancy (SLE)**, whereas, the monetary value of the asset is called the **Asset Value (AV)**.

SLE is the *AV* multiplied by the *EF*. In other words, *SLE = AV X EF*. In the previous example, assuming the asset value of the confidential file is $10, then *SLE = 10 X 100% = $10*.

The estimated frequency or probability of a threat event occurring in a year is called **Annualized Rate of Occurrence (ARO)**. For example, if the web server is compromised five times in a year, ARO = 5.

When SLE is multiplied by ARO, the resultant value is called **Annualized Loss Expectancy (ALE)**. In this example, *ARO = 10×5 = $50*.

ALE is a dollar figure that is a quantified financial loss per annum.

Qualitative risk analysis

Qualitative risk analysis provides risk values in relative terms, such as a rating scales. For example, high, medium, or low; or a grading scale of 1, 2, 3; or red, amber, green, and so on.

For example, if an asset value is categorized as high, medium, or low based on the business impact, then the risk will be based on such rating scales rather than monetary values.

Risk treatment

Using risk analysis methods, either quantitative or qualitative risk values are obtained. This activity of assigning values to risk is called **risk estimation**. Once the risks are identified, it is important to understand their significance in terms of the impact to the business. This process of estimating the impact is called **risk evaluation**. Overall, the process of risk analysis and risk evaluation is called **risk assessment**.

Based on the risk assessment, suitable strategies are devised to mitigate the risks. These strategies are called **controls** or **counter measures**, which are **safeguards** against the risk. There are four types of risk mitigation strategies followed in the information security domain:

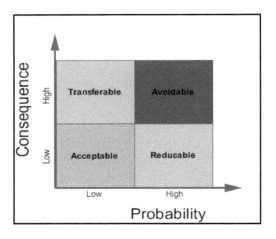

Fig. 7

- Risk acceptance is a strategy adopted when both probability and consequence are low. For example, if the cost of protecting the file is higher than the cost of controls, then the risk may be accepted. That is, the consequence is lower than the control cost.
- Risk reduction is a strategy adopted when the probability is high and the consequence is low. For example, not storing a confidential file in the web server or controls, such as encryption, will reduce the risk of disclosure of confidential files.

- Risk transfer is a strategy adopted when the probability is low and the consequence is high. For example, threat event, such as earthquakes or other natural calamities. When the probability is low and the consequence is high, implementing a control may be cost prohibitive, but accepting risk could be catastrophic. In situations like these, transferring risk through insurance would be most appropriate.
- Risk avoidance is a strategy adopted when both the probability and the consequence are high. Risks that will have a catastrophic impact on the business have to be avoided or, by using disaster recovery methods, moved to an acceptable level.

Suitable plans need to be drawn up and controls are identified to mitigate the risks. Such plans are called **risk treatment plans**.

Coordinated activities to manage the risk by way of risk assessment, risk treatment, risk acceptance, risk communication to stakeholder, risk monitoring, and risk review are collectively called **risk management**.

Due to the heterogeneous nature of information systems, even after applying the controls, it may not be possible to assure either 100% security or 0% risk to assets. There is an amount of risk that will remain after implementing safeguards. This risk is called **residual risk**. For example, assume the SLE for the company website is 50,000. The EF is currently 1. Firewall A will reduce the EF to .10 and cost 10,000. Firewall B will reduce the EF to .0 and cost 50,000. Going with Firewall A will cost 40,000 less, but will still leave you with 5,000 of residual risk. Given that it would cost 40,000 to remove 5,000 of the risk, it is prudent to allow residual risk instead of implementing additional controls. In this scenario, risk acceptance is the best strategy.

Business continuity management

Generally, risk mitigation strategies for confidentiality and integrity-related risks are implemented through various operational and technical means. They are covered in domains, such as cryptography, telecommunication network security, access control, and so on. Risk mitigation strategies to address risks in terms of the availability of assets is addressed through the business continuity management processes.

In the business continuity domain, the focus is on specific threat events that could have a devastating impact on the functioning of the organization as a whole and the IT infrastructure in specific. Examples of such events are fires, floods, earthquakes, tornados, terrorist attacks, and so on.

Generally, an organization may not have controls to prevent such events. Such events are termed as **disruptive events**. In other words, an event that could impact regular operations for a prolonged period of time is a disruptive event. Hurricane Katrina, the attacks on the World Trade Center in 2001, or the collapse of large organizations, such as Enron, are examples of disruptive threat events.

Business continuity management involves the following:

- Risk analysis and review to identify disruptive threat events
- Business Impact Analysis (BIA) to estimate potential
- Strategies for safeguarding business interests
- Business Continuity Plans (BCP) that are instituted to respond to potential threats
- Tests and exercises to verify the continuity processes
- Regular and systematic reviews through program management

Business continuity management consists of policies as stipulated by the senior management, processes that involve business continuity-related activities, people with required skill sets, and infrastructure resources to support critical business functions.

The Business Continuity Planning (BCP) process

Addressing the risks by way of plans and procedures for the continuation of business operations during and after a disruptive event is called **Business Continuity Planning (BCP)**. The aim is to prevent interruptions to business operations.

This domain is concerned with the continuation of critical business processes and business support systems in the event of an incident, emergency, or disaster. For example, critical business processes may include accounting, payroll, Customer Relationship Management (CRM), and so on.

BCP involves the following:

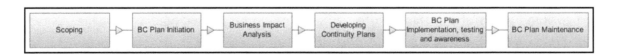

Fig. 8

1. Scoping in terms of assets, operations, and business processes.
2. Initiating the planning process.

3. Performing Business Impact Analysis (BIA).
4. Developing the BCP.
5. Implementing, testing, and creating awareness.
6. Maintenance of plans.

While designing the BCP, availability should be considered the primary factor. The objective of BCP is to avoid any serious damage to the business also to enable the recovery of information systems within an acceptable timeframe. This time frame is derived from Business Impact Analysis.

 Business Impact Analysis (BIA) is a type of risk assessment exercise that tries to assess qualitative and quantitative impacts on the business due to a disruptive event. Qualitative impacts are generally operational impacts, such as the inability to deliver, while quantitative impacts are related to financial losses.

BCP best practices

BCP should be as follows:

- **Appropriate**: The scoping process should cover the essential resources
- **Adequate**: Based on BIA, the adequacy of available resources pertaining to continuity and recovery should be established
- **Complete**: The plan should include all of the resources required based on the analysis

BCP resources should include the availability of processes and the availability of people to implement the processes.

The BCP process should include testing the plans and day-to-day functions/activities to be performed to make the plan effective and ready at all times.

BCP measures should include preventative measures to control known issues and facilitating measures to act in a timely manner on the issues that are not under the control of the organization.

BCP should identify mission-critical systems, business impact due to the nonavailability of critical systems (loss of revenue, loss of profits, inability to comply with laws, damage to reputation, and so on), preventive controls, and recovery controls.

BCP objectives should include recovery time by way of Recovery Time Objectives (RTO) and recovery points by way of Recovery Point Objectives (RPO).

Recovery Time Objective (RTO): A timeframe within which the systems should be recovered (indicated in terms of hours/days). For example, if RTO is less than 8 hours, then a virtual environment with active/passive data center will an be significantly faster.

Recovery Point Objective (RPO): The maximum period of time (or amount) of transaction data that the business can afford to lose during a successful recovery. For example, if RPO is 10 mins, then the backup plan should be to conduct backups every 10 mins.

Business continuity procedures should include the procedure for testing plans and the procedure for updating plans.

The BCP should include the following:

- Notification
- Call trees
- Response teams
- Updating mechanism for contacts
- Step-by-step procedure for recovery
- Appropriate testing
- Restoring normalcy to the primary website or stable state
- Required records and the format of the records
- Awareness of people

Security risk considerations in acquisitions, strategy, and practice

Information systems include various components, such as operating systems and application software, which may be off-the-shelf products or custom developed applications, database management systems, infrastructure, and so on. During development and/or implementation, security risks should be considered based on security requirements. Some such requirements are listed here:

- Security requirements analysis and specifications
- Security risks in the processing of data

- Need for cryptographic controls
- Risks in system operations
- Risks in development and support processes
- Technical vulnerability management
- Risks in outsourced software development

 Note that detailed information and best practices are provided in various chapters throughout this book.

Information security education, training, and awareness

The information security domain consists of many concepts and definitions. Besides, information security initiatives in an organization will have many policies, procedures, as well as technology components. In order to have an effective security posture within the organization, it is important that people or personnel are aware of security requirements, organization-specific security policies and procedures, and most importantly, particular personnel-specific roles and responsibilities pertaining to security.

Security awareness and training is one of the core components of the risk management program in any organization. The objective is to ensure that the personnel are aware of the security requirements and are trained to handle day-to-day security events.

National Institute of Standards and Technology (NIST) publication 800-14 – *Generally Accepted Principles and Practices for Securing Information Technology Systems*, recommends seven steps for a security awareness and training program. The standard groups the best practices into three broad areas, which are identification, management, and the evaluation of training and awareness programs.

- In the identification phase, an organization would establish scope, goals and objectives, training staff identification, and the audience.
- In managing the program, an organization would motivate the management and employees, manage administration, and maintain the training and awareness programs.
- Periodically, an organization will evaluate the program for its effectiveness.

The international standard ISO/IEC27002 *Information technology – Security techniques-code of practice for information security management* is an acknowledged International Standard that provides some of the best practices in various domains of information security. The standard defines the following good practices a security professional should be aware of pertaining to *Security Awareness and Training*:

- Based on their job function, the standard emphasizes that all employees and, where relevant, contractors and third-party users should be provided with appropriate awareness training as well as regular updates in organizational policies and procedures.
- The induction program should consist of awareness training that covers the organization's security policies and the security expectations. The personnel should undergo such training before any access to information or services are granted to them.
- The training program should contain the security requirements of the organization, legal responsibilities, business controls and, most importantly, correct usage instructions that relate to information processing facilities.
- Procedures related to log-on, appropriate usage of systems, networks, software packages, and the explanation of disciplinary processes in case of policy or procedure violations should be part of the training.
- The training should also focus on known threats and enhance the awareness of security incidents and problems and the way to respond to them based on the personnel's role.

Summary

This chapter has covered foundational concepts in risk management. In a nutshell, risks are from threat sources to assets. When a threat event exploits a vulnerability, it results in a security violation, which could compromise the established CIA requirements of assets. Risks to assets may cause loss or damage, which is estimated through risk analysis methods. Security risks are managed through risk assessment, control implementation, risk monitoring, and review procedures.

In the next two chapters, we will cover asset protection and security that forms the basis for selection and implementation of technical and administrative controls.

Sample questions

Q1. Which one of the following is correct?

1. Qualitative risk analysis is to qualify the risk and quantitative risk analysis is to measure the same
2. Qualitative risk analysis is to qualify the risk and quantitative risk analysis is to monitor the same
3. Qualitative risk analysis provides scaled values while quantitative risk analysis provides monetary values
4. Qualitative risk analysis is to quantify the risk and quantitative risk analysis is to measure the same

Q2. The risk that remains after implementing a safeguard is known as what?

1. Relative risk
2. Quantitative risk
3. Residual risk
4. Qualitative risk

Q3. Which objectives, among the following, are established in the Business Continuity Planning (BCP) domain (this is a drag and drop type of question. Here you can draw a line from the list of answers from left to the empty box on right)?

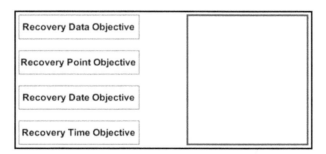

3
Day 3 – Asset Security - Information and Asset Classification

Information security is the preservation of confidentiality and integrity and the availability of assets. Assets have intrinsic value to the business and are classified into various types. The type of asset and its value are used to determine the required level of security assurance.

This chapter provides an overview of asset security. The concepts and techniques that pertain to information assets are covered in detail throughout this chapter. Data security concepts and controls are also covered in detail using suitable illustration and examples.

This chapter covers the following:

- Overview of asset security
- Overview of information and asset classification
- Asset ownership
- Classification types in government
- Classification types in corporations
- Overview of data privacy
- Overview of data retention strategies

Overview of asset security – information and asset classification

Asset protection forms the baseline for security. Unintended disclosure, unauthorized modification, or destruction of an asset can affect security. In other words, confidentiality, integrity, and/or availability requirements will be affected.

As covered in Chapter 1, *Day 1 – Security and Risk Management – Security, Compliance, and Policies*, assets are grouped based on their type, such as physical, hardware, information, and so on. Similarly, assets are further classified based on their value and sensitivity. Value can be monetary or based on other qualitative factors, such as loss in terms of people, property, or image. Sensitivity is based on confidentiality factors and the effect of disclosure to national security. For corporations, sensitivity is based on the extent of the loss of corporate image.

Observe the following illustration:

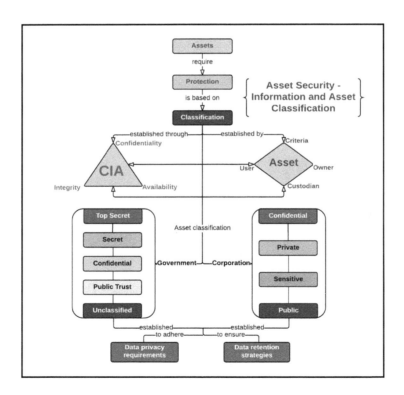

Asset classification and control

Information is a business asset and is of value to an organization. Information can exist in various forms, such as printed on paper, spoken in conversations, stored in electronic media, transmitted through e-mails and messages, and so on. Hence, irrespective of the location of the asset, its protection is vital and is based on the classification. In turn, classification is based on confidentiality, integrity, and availability requirements.

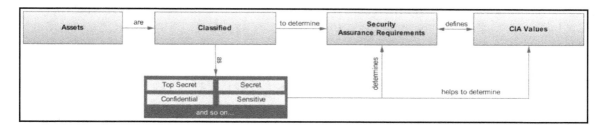

Asset classification is based on asset value. Various parameters are used in the industry to derive asset value. In general, asset value is based on the impact to the corporation in the event of disclosure, alteration, or destruction. Impacts could be loss of business, loss of corporate image, customer dissatisfaction, and so on. Hence, parameters to derive asset value may include, monetary value, intellectual property value, competitive advantage, privacy requirements, legal and regulatory requirements, and so on. Security controls for asset protection are based on its value and its sensitivity. Hence, the asset type and its value determine the level of security assurance required. Information assurance requirements establish the required CIA values.

In a nutshell, asset classification is used to identify the type of information based on its value, sensitivity, and the degree of assurance required. Classification helps to devise suitable security controls.

The following parameters are applicable to information assets:

- **Classification criteria**: Information assets are generally classified based on the following:
    - Value
    - Age
    - Useful life
    - Personnel association based on privacy requirements, such as the damage caused by loss or damage

- **Owner**: The owner of the information asset is responsible for its protection. The owner plays the role of determining the classification level, periodical review, and delegation.
- **Custodian**: The custodian is the person delegated to maintain the information by the owner. A custodian's role includes the backup and restoration of the information and maintaining records.
- **User**: A user uses the information. A user may be an employee, an operator, or a third party. The role of the user is to exercise due care while handling the information by following the operating procedures. A user is responsible for using the information only for the authorized purpose.

Classification types in government

Governmental agencies classify information based on confidentiality requirements and on the damage that might be incurred if the information is disclosed or compromised. This classification schema enforces *need to know* principle for access.

The need to know principle establishes that one has to demonstrate specific need to know or access to information that is classified as sensitive. In other words, even if the primary clearance is available to the user to access the information, whenever such sensitive information is accessed, the user should establish the need to access the information.

For example, entering a data center may require an access card and also writing down the date, time, and reason for access in the log book. Another example could be: Joe has a secret clearance and works in IT. Joe has access to most secret material, but is restricted from accessing details of his companies latest aerospace project because his duties do not include aerospace engineering, therefore he does not need to know.

The United States information classification

Information classification in the United States government is based on the effect of compromise of the asset on national security. There is a specific classifications, such as **Core Secrets**, for information assets within the National Security Agency (NSA) besides others. They are:

- **Core Secrets** is the highest level of classification. In this classification, only select individuals from the NSA and government have access to the information.
- **Top Secret** is any information that will cause exceptional damage to national security if disclosed to unauthorized entities. This is level 5 or the highest level of classification after Core Secrets.
- **Secret** information has a potential to cause serious damage to national security if disclosed. This is one level down from Top Secret.
- **Confidential** information could cause certain damage to national security when disclosed to unauthorized entities. This is level 3 classification.
- **Public Trust** is a type of information that may require background clearance to access. This is neither confidential nor unclassified.
- **Unclassified** information does not compromise confidentiality and its disclosure will not have adverse impacts. This information is neither confidential nor classified.

Classification types in corporations

Private and public sector corporate entities classify information under four categories. These classifications are generic and vary between corporations and across countries. Some of the top classification types are follows:

- **Confidential**: This classification is used to denote that information is to be used strictly within the organization. Its unauthorized disclosure will have adverse effects. This is the highest level of classification in private sector or a corporation.
- **Private**: This information classification is applicable to personnel information and should be used strictly within the organization. Compromise or unauthorized disclosure will adversely affect the organization and will have legal and regulatory ramifications from privacy laws.
- **Sensitive**: This classification is used to ensure higher confidentiality and integrity requirements of the information asset. They are generally associated with competitiveness and corporate image.
- **Public**: This is an information classification applicable to all the information that can be disclosed to everyone. However, unauthorized modifications are not allowed. This is the lowest level of classification.

Data privacy

Information assets that contain personal details of people are classified as private or personal data. In other words, disclosure of personal data to third parties without the consent of the data owner is a breach of privacy requirements of such assets. The data owner is the individual associated with that data. The contents of data that can uniquely identify a person or group of persons is called **Personally Identifiable Information (PII)**. There are legal and regulatory requirements that pertain to the collection, storage, transmission, disclosure, retention, and destruction of personal information. References and online links to such requirements are provided in Chapter 5, *Day 5 – Exam Cram and Practice Questions*, of this book.

In information security, the requirement for data privacy is to share personal data in a secure manner to third parties depending on the need and as required. This requirement is to ensure that PII is not disclosed to unauthorized entities while sharing the information.

During data processing, various entities may access personal information, process, transmit, or store it. When personal details are grouped together, it is called a **record**.

For example, records that contain personal information may include the following:

- A health record that contains the physical and mental health of a person
- An education record that contains the marks and grades associated with a student
- An insurance record that contains information about the individual
- An employee record that contains the Employee ID and performance data
- A customer record that contains credit card numbers or social security numbers

When the previous records are accessed or available in an accessible location, then, as per data privacy requirements, there are limitations to who can access, process, modify, store, or transmit such information.

Within personal data, some of the information is considered to be sensitive. The term associated with this concept is sensitive personal data.

In the USA, the **Federal Trade Commission (FTC)** classifies the following as sensitive consumer data:

Financial data

Data about children

Health information

Precise geographic location information

Social security numbers

As per the Data Protection Act of the UK, the following are considered as sensitive personal data:

The racial or ethnic origin of the data subject

His/her political opinions

His/her religious beliefs or other beliefs of a similar nature

Whether he/she is a member of a trade union

His/her physical or mental health or condition

His/her sexual life

The commission or alleged commission by him/her of any offence, or any proceedings for any offence committed or alleged to have been committed by him/her, the disposal of such proceedings, or the sentence of any court in such proceedings

Data owners

Data owners that pertain to privacy are the people identified in that record. The owner can provide consent to process or share the personal information to others, such as corporations. In such cases, the entity that processes, stores, or transmits the information on behalf of the owner is called a licensee.

Data processors

When a third-party vendor is engaged by the licensee to create, receive, maintain, or transmit personal information, such entities are called business associates or data processors.

There are various privacy safeguard requirements pertaining to data processors in international laws.

For example, in the USA, all the companies that are strictly engaged in activities that are financial in nature are required to adhere to the **Gramm-Leach-Bliley Act (GLBA)** and the GLBA privacy and safeguarding rules.

All health care providers including health insurance companies and health care information clearing houses are subjected to the **Health Insurance Portability and Accountability Act of 1996 (HIPAA)** privacy and security rules. Similarly, all schools and institutions that receive funds from the department of education are subject to the **Family Education Rights and Privacy Act (FERPA)**.

In all the preceding laws, the legal obligations are passed on to the data processors as well.

Data remanence

Once the data is safely backed up or past its useful life, it needs to be deleted or purged from the digital media. However, such erasure actions may not completely wipe the data from the digital media. The possibility of residual data remains. Besides, in some systems, only the table entries for the data are removed and not the data itself until it is overwritten. Corporations regularly dispose of systems with digital media containing such residual data.

Data that remains even after erasing or formatting digital media is called residual data and the property to retain such data is called **data remanence**.

Data remanence is the residual data that remains when the data is not completely erased or destroyed. When the media is reused, this may result in the unauthorized disclosure of sensitive information. It is a good practice to prevent **media reuse** by physically destroying the media completely. In case of reuse, policies and procedures should be established to ensure that the data is destroyed completely.

Data collection limitations

Privacy laws stipulate data collection limitations pertaining to personal data. Safeguards include the following:

- Data should be collected by lawful and fair means
- Data should be collected with the knowledge and consent of the subject
- Personal data collected should be relevant for the purposes for which it is collected
- Collected data to be accurate and kept up to date
- Personal data should not be disclosed to other parties without the consent of the subject
- Personal data should not be used for other purposes than for what it was collected

- Personal data should be safeguarded against intentional or inadvertent access, use, disclosure, destruction, and modification

The following are some of the important privacy-related practices and laws across the world that provide frameworks and limitations pertaining to personal data.

Generally Accepted Privacy Principles (GAPP) is a best practices document jointly developed by the **American Institute of CPAs (AICPA)** and **Canadian Institute of Chartered Accountants (CICA)**.

OECD privacy principles are guidelines on the protection of privacy and transborder flow of privacy data. These principles were developed by the **Organization for Economic Co-operation and Development (OECD)**.

In the USA, there are a couple of Safe Harbor privacy laws to comply with European and Swiss data protection requirements.

Hence, from the information security perspective, data collection, use, retention, and destruction should be in accordance with established principles and best practices.

Data retention

Information in the form of data must be stored in digital media or in hard printed copies. Based on the requirements of the law and based on corporate policies, data needs to be retained even after its useful life. Data is also retained in media as a backup and used in business continuity and disaster recovery scenarios.

Data in media

Data security also concerns the physical protection of equipment as well as addressing security requirements pertaining to the media where the data is stored.

Storage media, such as hard disks, backup tapes, CDs, and diskettes, need additional security measures so as to ensure the security of the data they contain. Controls should ensure the prevention of data disclosure and modification by unauthorized entities.

The following controls need to be considered for media security:

Storage controls are the primary means to protect the data in storage media, such as hard disks, magnetic tapes, CDs, and so on. The primary consideration should be controlling access to the data, which is usually achieved by encrypted keys. Additional security considerations are required when the backup media is stored offsite.

Maintenance is a regular process to ensure that the data in the storage media is not corrupted or damaged. Media handling procedures are used to ensure this.

The users and operators should be provided with the proper **usage instructions** to handle the media.

Media usage should be in accordance with the established policies and procedures.

Data destruction is done by way of formatting the media. One time formatting may not completely delete all the data. Formatting the media seven times for complete data destruction is recommended by some of the standards.

Data in hardware

Theft is one of the most common threats that need to be addressed for personal computers, laptops, or media protection.

The following controls need to be considered for protection from theft:

- **Cable locks** are used to physically secure PCs and laptop computers. These locks prevent the computer or laptop being detached and taken away.
- **Port protection** is to ensure that media devices, such as CD-ROM, floppy drive, **Universal Serial Bus** (**USB**) devices such as memory sticks, **Wireless-Fidelity** (**Wi-Fi**) ports, printers, and scanners are not accessible by unauthorized personnel. The purpose of port protection is to prevent the download or transfer of confidential information and/or intellectual property by unauthorized users to a portable medium.
- **Switches** are used to prevent a malicious user to power on/off the systems.
- **BIOS checks** use password protection during the boot up process so that access to the operating system is controlled.
- **Encryption** is used to make the folders and files secure so that unauthorized disclosure and modification is prevented.

Data with personnel

The information people possess in their memories also needs to be controlled and data protection measures are applicable. Operational procedures, such as not discussing confidential or personally identifiable information in public places or transmitting information through publicly accessible mediums, should be discouraged.

Summary

This chapter has covered foundational concepts in asset security. In a nutshell, assets need protection from unauthorized or inadvertent disclosure, modification, or destruction. Hence, assets are classified based on factors, such as their value, useful life, and sensitivity, to establish protection requirements. Data privacy is a critical requirement as per laws and regulatory frameworks that are specific to safeguarding personal data. Data retention and data remanence can pose security challenges in protecting the information and were covered.

In the next chapter, **Data Loss Prevention (DLP)**-related terminologies, concepts, and techniques will be covered.

Sample questions

Q1. Which one of the following parameters is not applicable for asset classification?

1. Owner
2. Officer
3. User
4. Custodian

Q2. If an information disclosure does not affect confidentiality and may not cause adverse impacts, then such information is classified as:

1. Unclassified
2. Private
3. Confidential
4. Secret

Q3. Which statements, among the following, describe the need to know principle?

1. Information that can be disclosed unconditionally
2. Confidential information with proper authorization
3. Unclassified information
4. Sensitive information that requires a reason for access

Q4. Data that remains after erasure or formatting the media is known as:

1. Data remanence
2. Data classification
3. Residual data
4. Media sanitization

Q5. Which of the following criteria are widely used in asset classification (drag and drop the correct answers to the box on the right-hand side)?

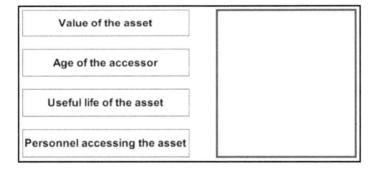

4

Day 4 – Asset Security - Data Security Controls and Handling

This chapter provides an overview of data security controls and data handling using a high-level illustration. Data can exist in different states in an organization. It can be in e-mails, stored on a USB stick, printed on paper, or spoken in conversations. Hence, in any of these states, appropriate security controls are necessary to protect such information assets.

The following topics are covered in this chapter:

- Overview of data security controls
- Overview of data handling
- Data security requirements in standards and regulatory compliance
- Data Loss Prevention-related concepts
- Data Loss Prevention strategies and controls

Overview of asset security – data security controls and handling

Critical data that may require CIA safeguards can exist in different states and reside in multiple locations in your corporation. Data can be in motion, as in e-mails, or data can be at rest, as in databases, or data can be in use, as in laptop or portable devices. Security controls are required to protect the data in any state or location. However, protection mechanisms vary depending on the data state.

Observe the following illustration:

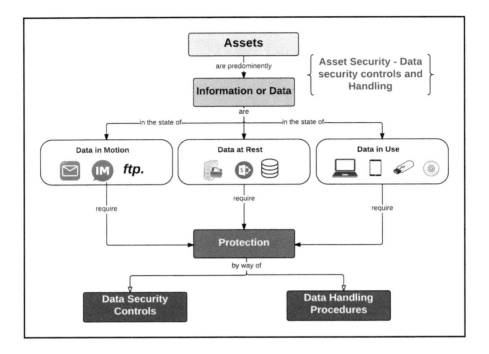

Data security controls

Logical assets such as data that are in a intangible form need various levels of protection based on the state they are in. Data protection requirements are based on the classification of the information assets and CIA requirements such as legal, regulatory, and privacy compliance.

Data security requirements

In the past decade, data in corporations has been growing exponentially. Some studies indicate that the compounded annual growth rate (CAGR) of data is 70% or above. Besides, an organization has to comply with various requirements during its operations. Compliance requirements pertaining to data security are based on the CIA requirements and privacy of data. Some of the following compliance requirements may be applicable to corporations.

Payment Card Industry Data Security Standard (PCI DSS)

PCI DSS is a standard that pertains to payment card-related security requirements. The PCI Security Standards Council is an open global forum that develops and maintains this standard. Any entity that is involved in the payment card processing chain needs to comply with the safeguards of this standard. There are six core objectives in this standard:

- Network security has to be robust. Hence, an entity has to implement and maintain a secure network and systems.
- Cardholder data has to be protected from fraudulent transactions.
- Vulnerability management program has to be maintained by the entities.
- Access control measures have to be strong.
- The monitoring and testing of the networks has to be regularly performed.
- A formal maintenance of information security policy is mandatory.

Sarbanes-Oxley Act (SOX)

This is the US federal law that mandates various administrative controls pertaining to the financial reporting of publicly traded companies in the United States. From an information security perspective, this law mandates the demonstration of internal controls over financial reporting systems. One of the key objectives of this act is to enforces *segregation of duties* to reduce the chances of committing financial fraud.

Segregation of duties or separation of duties is a security control measure to ensure that mutually exclusive roles are not assigned to a single user concurrently. In other words, if two roles are required to complete the job function and if one role ensures security, then they are mutually exclusive. Examples of such roles include system administrator versus security administrator, check signatory versus check approver, accounts receivable versus accounts payable, and so on.

Gramm-Leach-Bliley Act (GLBA)

This act in the United Sates mandates privacy rules for financial institutions, their customers, and their privacy rights. Various security safeguards are advised in the safeguards rules. As per this act, developing an information security plan and the protection of a client's nonpublic information are mandatory.

EU Data Protection Act (DPA)

This act is for the countries in the European Union and the primary focus is on data protection pertaining to the privacy information of client data.

In a nutshell, corporations are challenged with the explosive growth of data and with more and more regulations to protect the data and many channels of information exchange, where data can be compromised. Hence, appropriate strategies are required for Data Loss Prevention.

Data Loss Prevention (DLP)

Data can be traditionally grouped under three categories based on their criticality. They are as follows:

- **Personally Identifiable Information (PII)**: Examples include birth dates, employee numbers, Social Security Numbers, national identification numbers, credit card information, personal health information, and so on.
- **Intellectual Property (IP)**: Examples include product design documents, the source code of software, research information, patent applications, and customer data.
- **Non-Public Information (NPI)**: Examples include financial information, mergers—and acquisitions-related information and activities, corporate policies, legal and regulatory matters, executive communication, and so on.

Compromising any of the preceding data will have adverse impacts on corporations. Additionally, risk factors, such as employee behavior, customer treatment, and financial controls, will also have an effect on organizations.

Data, whether it is PII, IP, or NPI, can exist in three states. Protection requirements in each of the three states may vary based on the type and classification of the information.

The three states in which a data can exist are as follows.

Data in motion

This refers to information as it moves around the organization. Examples include e-mail, FTP, and messaging:

Data protection strategies for such information include the following:

- Secure login and session procedures for file transfer services.
- Encryption for sensitive data.
- Monitoring activities to capture and analyze the content to ensure that confidential or privacy-related information are is not transmitted to third parties or stored in publicly accessible file server locations.

Data at rest

This refers to the information that is stored within the organization. Examples include information stored in a file server and shared locations and information in databases:

Data protection strategies include secure access controls, the segregation of duties, and the implementation of need to know mechanisms for sensitive data.

Data in use

This refers to information that is used by staff, as in laptops or portable devices, and information that is being printed or copied to a USB stick. This is the data available in endpoints.

Data security controls for data in use would include port protection and whole disk encryption. Controls against shoulder surfing, such as clear screen and clear desk policies, are also applicable to data in use controls:

Data Loss Prevention strategies

In general, the compromise of data in any of the preceding three states is called *Data Loss* and the strategies to prevent such a loss are called **Data Loss Prevention (DLP)**.

Controls for Data Loss Prevention include the following:

- Security policy
- Data classification
- CIA requirements
- Risk assessment
- Devising suitable controls
- Implementing and monitoring the effectiveness of controls

DLP controls

Preventative controls for addressing data loss issues are generally in the form of monitoring activities and appropriate actions. For each of the data states, various types of controls are required to ensure security.

Data breach or loss can happen in any of the three states, that is, data in motion, data at rest, or data in use. Controls to prevent data loss can be either preventative or detective. Preventative controls include access restrictions based on the classification of the data. However, a 100% preventative environment is not feasible as the information technology components are heterogeneous in nature. Since different products and technologies from different vendors are used, a uniform policy to prevent data breach may be difficult to implement.

Data loss is an incident. An attempt, whether malicious or inadvertent, to steal data or cause data to be exposed should be identified through proper incident management controls and appropriate actions have to be taken based on the criticality of the data.

Generally, DLP controls are based on the following:

- What is the sensitivity or value of the information?
- Who is causing the incident?
- What actions were carried out by the individual to cause such an incident?
- Who else is involved and where?
- What action is taken?

For example, a user may be attaching a document containing confidential or PII to a web mail website or saving company confidential financial information to a USB stick. Such incidents require appropriate controls and actions to detect and prevent data loss or leakage:

Data in motion, such as e-mails or posting to the web, requires controls, such as blocking such an attempt, warning the user, alerting the monitoring team or the owner, and/or forcing encryption for sensitive data.

Additional controls, such as informing the security team, capturing the data for investigation, and redirecting the user to the appropriate training in data-handling requirements can also be considered. If the data is malicious, then quarantining such data may be necessary. Furthermore, and based on the incident's analysis, classifying the data and/or additional supervision based on user behavior would be necessary to ensure security.

Data at rest, such as files in file servers or records in databases, may require controls, such as copying the data for analysis, moving the data to a safer location, stubbing the data with a warning file, or reclassifying the data to prevent inadvertent or unauthorized access. Besides these steps, reviewing, deleting malicious files, or capturing the event are some of the additional actions that can be considered.

Data in use is data that is being printed or saved to external devices, such as USB or portable hard disks. Suitable controls include blocking such activities, supervising the activity, forcing encryption, and informing the monitoring team.

Furthermore, actions such as warning the user about the security policies, capturing the data being copied for further analysis, and reclassification can be used to strengthen the control environment.

Cryptographic methods to secure data

Data in native formats, such as texts, documents, or spreadsheets, may be easier to read using a suitable application software. For sensitive data, additional controls may be required to prevent unauthorized access or disclosure of such information. Cryptographic methods offer the best solutions for such requirements. By using cryptographic methods, confidentiality and integrity requirements can be addressed more effectively.

The following are some of the common cryptographic methods used in data security controls.

Encryption

When data is encrypted, it means that the data is scrambled or transformed into an unintelligible form with an appropriate key to unscramble it or, in other words, return it to its original form. Without the key, data cannot be read either by humans or other applications. The key is called the crypto variable. This method of data protection will ensure **confidentiality**.

Hashing

Data may be altered or modified by an unauthorized entity to commit fraud. In order to detect and prevent such unauthorized modifications, hashing or message digest methods are used.

In hashing, based on the contents of the document, a cryptographic value is computed. The computed value is called a **checksum**. By periodically recomputing the checksum and validating it with the original computed value, it is possible to detect whether the document is altered. This process helps ensure integrity.

Digital signatures

In digital communications, establishing the authenticity of the sender of the message is essential and is very important for integrity assurance requirements.

Establishing the identity of the receiver or sender can be accomplished through digital signatures. In other words, the authenticity of the data originating from the authorized sender and access only by the intended receiver can be achieved through digital signatures and encryption.

Note that cryptography and its concepts and methods are covered in detail in `Chapter 7`, *Day 7 – Security Engineering – Cryptography and Physical Security.*

Data handling requirements

Ensuring the confidentiality, integrity, and availability of requirements during various states that any data will pass through requires the secure handling of such data. Appropriate policies and procedures should be established for handling sensitive data.

Handling sensitive information

Sensitive data such as confidential files need special care. Some of the best practices to handle sensitive information include the following:

- **Secure disposal of media**: Media containing sensitive data has to be disposed off in a secure manner. Shredding in case of paper documents and pulverizing in case of digital media are some of the methods used in media disposal.
- **Labelling**: Appropriate labelling is important for sensitive data without disclosing the type of content.
- **Access restrictions**: The need to know principle is to be adopted while designing and implementing access restrictions to sensitive data.
- **Formal records of authorized recipients of data**: Recipients who are authorized to access the data should be documented and approved.
- **Storage of media**: Media storage should be as per manufacturers' specifications and industry best practices.
- **Data distribution**: Appropriate controls should be established to ensure that the data is distributed only to approved and authorized entities as per the authorized recipients list.
- **Clear marking**: Marking on sensitive data has to be clear and legible for appropriate identification and handling. Marking may use codes compare labelling that may only be used for identification purposes.

- **Review of distribution lists**: Periodic review of the distribution lists is necessary to ensure that the data is not shared with obsolete or unauthorized entities.
- **Control of publicly available information**: Suitable controls should be established to ensure that sensitive data is not disclosed or posted to publicly available repositories or websites.

Summary

This chapter has covered foundational concepts in data security and the data handling requirements of sensitive information. In a nutshell, data can exist in three states. They are data in motion, data at rest, or data in use. The protection of data in any of these states is called Data Loss Prevention. Sensitive data needs special handling requirements as the compromise of such data would have devastating consequences.

The next chapter is a revision chapter for the first four chapters. References and further study on the first four chapters is provided. An exam cram as well as a mock test consisting of about 10 questions is also provided.

Sample questions

Q1. Which one of the following is not a cryptographic method for securing data?

1. Encryption
2. Digital media
3. Hashing
4. Digital signature

Q2. Which one of following is not a commonly used data state definition?

1. Data at rest
2. Data in the cloud
3. Data in use
4. Data in motion

Q3. Drag appropriate statements to the box on the right-hand side that pertain to the data handling policy of sensitive information, such as PII.

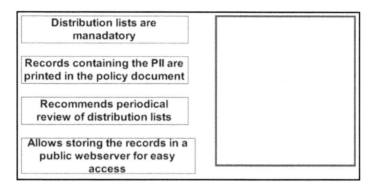

Q4. Which one of the following policies is the least secure? Place a tick mark on the appropriate circle.

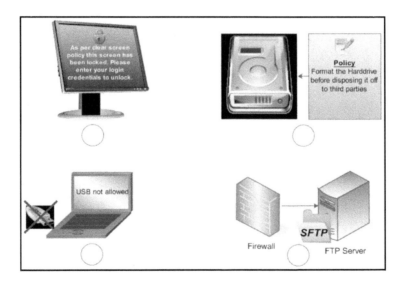

5
Day 5 – Exam Cram and Practice Questions

This chapter explains the concepts covered in the first two domains of CISSP CBK in a snippet format that will reinforce the topics learned, and it will serve as exam cram. A mock test consisting of 10 questions from the first two domains is provided. Finally, further reading and references are also provided.

This chapter covers the following:

- Important concepts from the first domain, security and risk management
- Important concepts from the second domain, asset security
- Mock test
- Further reading and references

An overview of exam cram and practice questions

Presented here is revision for the concepts discussed in the previous four chapters. They are provided in bullet points in the form of snippets that are easy to revise. These snippets are for a quick revision and the reinforcement of knowledge learned:

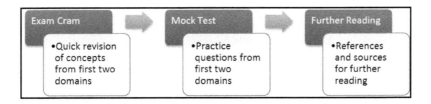

CISSP CBK domain #1 – security and risk management

The following information consists of some of the important concepts. They are presented as bullet points that will serve as exam cram for this first domain:

- Assets are tangible or intangible in nature.
- Assets are used by the organization for business processes.
- Assets have quantitative value such as monetary or qualitative value such as corporate image.
- Examples of assets are computers, operating systems, data, processes, products, infrastructure, and so on.
- Assets are grouped as physical, hardware, software, information, and personnel assets.
- Risk is defined as an exposure of the asset to loss, injury, and damage due to threats, vulnerabilities, and attacks.
- Risk to assets is from threat sources.
- Asset protection means identifying and implementing security controls.
- Asset protection requirements are identified through a structured method of risk analysis, evaluation, and assessment.
- Risk analysis, risk evaluation, risk assessment, and risk mitigation strategies are the components of risk management.
- Risk analysis provides risk values in numeric terms, such as monetary values are quantitative.
- Risk analysis provides risk values in non-numeric terms, such as high-low-medium are qualitative.
- Security controls are identified through risk mitigation strategies.
- Identifying threats and vulnerabilities, attacks, estimating potential impact, and establishing and implementing suitable controls to treat the risk are functional steps in risk management.

- Risk treatment includes accepting, transferring, reducing, or avoiding risk.
- Monitoring, reviewing, communicating the results, and improving the security posture are continual improvement processes in the risk management cycle.
- Security posture is an overall plan of the organization pertaining to its security. It includes security governance, policies, procedures, and compliance.
- Information security and risk management are analogous to each other.
- Information security is a preservation of the **Confidentiality, Integrity, and Availability (CIA)** of assets:
    - **Confidentiality**: Unauthorized users should not view the information
    - **Integrity**: Unauthorized users should not modify the information
    - **Availability**: Authorized users are able to access the information
- Threat is an event that could compromise information security by causing loss or damage to assets.
- A threat is predominantly external to organizational.
- The examples of threats are fires, floods, hacking, and so on.
- Vulnerability is a hole or weakness in the system. In other words, a vulnerability is susceptible to threat.
- Threat can exploit vulnerabilities through threat agents.
- The threat agent exploiting a vulnerability is called an attack.
- The end result of an attack could be a security violation.
- Security violation is a compromise of the Confidentiality, Integrity, and Availability requirement of the asset.
- Information has a life cycle that includes handling, processing, transporting, storing, archiving, and destroying.
- Information protection includes risk management, risk reporting, and accountability.
- Senior management and the board should provide strategic oversight for the implementation of security controls and they should ensure continual effectiveness.
- Aligning and integrating information security with enterprise and IT governance frameworks is called information security strategy.
- Information security strategy includes the definition of the current state of security, goals, and objectives that align with the corporate mission.
- The goal of an information security strategy is to understand protection requirements.

- The objectives of an information security strategy include estimating the value of the information, the expected outcomes of the information security program, the benefits that are quantifiable, and the methods used to integrate information security practices with organizational practices.
- An information security mission defines security requirements, its purpose, focus on risk management, commitment to continual maintenance, and the improvement of information security program.
- Organizational processes need to be aligned to the mission.
- Organization security processes include defining the roles and responsibilities, establishing monitoring mechanisms, reporting, reviewing and approving the processes and management support.
- Management control is indicated through a policy, which states the views of the management and their position on information security.
- Information security policy states management intent, support, and direction for security.
- Administrative controls are used to implement policies.
- Procedures, guidelines, and standards are administrative controls.
- Technical controls support management and administrative initiatives for information systems.
- Firewall, intrusion detection systems, antiviruses, and so on are examples of technical controls.
- Due diligence is understanding the risk and estimating the risk values.
- Due care is implementing security governance.
- Compliance is an example of due care activities.
- Security awareness and training is one of the core components of the due care exercise.
- Common law is a law that is developed based on the decisions of courts and tribunals.
- Statutory law is a legal system that is set down by the legislature or the executive branch of the government.
- Religious laws are legal systems based on religious principles.
- Civil law is a legal system based on codes and legislative statutes as opposed to common law.
- Privacy is the protection of Personally Identifiable Information (PII) or Sensitive Personal Information (SPI) of individuals.
- Privacy laws deal with protecting and preserving the rights of an individual's privacy.

- Intellectual property law is a legal domain that deals with Intellectual Property Rights (IPR).
- Copyright is an intellectual property right that grants exclusive rights to the creator of the original work.
- Patent is set of exclusive rights granted to the inventor of new, useful, inventive, and industry-applicable inventions.
- Trademark is a unique symbol or mark that is used by individuals or organizations to uniquely represent a product or a service.
- Trade secret is a formula, design, process, practice, or pattern that is not revealed to others.
- A computer crime is a fraudulent activity that is a crime committed using information technology assets.
- In computer crime, the term computer refers to the role it plays in different scenarios-crime committed against a computer, crime committed using the computer, and a computer incidental in the crime.
- Fraud is the manipulation of records for financial gain.
- Data diddling and Salami slicing are some examples of fraud.
- Hacking refers to discovering vulnerabilities, holes, or weaknesses in computer software and associated IT systems and exploiting them.
- Identity theft is to steal someone's identity.
- Intellectual property theft is stealing software code or designs for financial gain.
- Cyber stalking is to commit fraud by pretending as a legitimate entity.
- Malware is a malicious software.
- Viruses, worms, Trojan horses, and spyware, such as a Key logger, and so on, are examples of malware.
- Spyware is malicious code that tracks the user actions.
- Key loggers are a type of spyware that capture keystrokes and transmit them to an attacker's server.
- Cyber crimes are criminal activities that are perpetrated using communication networks, such as the Internet, telephone, wireless, satellite, and mobile networks.
- Cyber terrorism is a type of cyber crime perpetrated against computers and computer networks.
- Information warfare is a type of cybercrime used to destabilize the opponent, such as corporations and institutions, to gain competitive advantage.

- The **Denial-of-Service (DoS)** attack or **Distributed Denial-of-Service (DDoS)** attacks are cybercrimes where websites or the information systems of corporations are made inaccessible by way of multiple service requests to overload the web and application servers.
- Spamming is sending Unsolicited Commercial Email (UCE) and is called a cyber crime.
- Phishing is a type of cyber crime wherein a user is lured to an attacker-constructed illegitimate website that looks similar to the original website that a user intended to visit.
- Pharming is a type of cyber attack wherein a user is redirected to a malicious website constructed by the attacker.
- SMiShing is a type of cyber attack using mobile networks and is similar to phishing.
- Harassment is a crime that includes cyberstalking, cyber bullying, hate crime, online predating, and trolling.
- Transfer of computerized data across national borders or states or political boundaries called as transborder data flow.
- Data breach is a security incident in which sensitive, protected or confidential data is copied, transmitted, viewed, stolen, or used by an unauthorized entity.
- Laws concerned with data breaches are generally called security breach laws.
- Information security profession requires adherence to an ethically sound and consistently applied code of professional ethics.
- Code of ethics is based on the safety of the commonwealth, duty to principals, such as employers, contractors, and people whom a professional works for, and to each other.
- (ISC)^2 code of professional ethics includes four clauses. They are as follows:
    - Protect society, the commonwealth, and the infrastructure
    - Act honorably, honestly, justly, responsibly, and legally
    - Provide diligent and competent service to principals
    - Advance and protect the profession
- Security policies are high-level statements that provide management intent and direction for information security.
- Security standards provide prescriptive statements, control objectives and controls for enforcing security policies.
- Security procedures are step-by-step instructions to implement the policies and standards.
- Security guidelines provide best practice methods to support security controls, selection, and implementation.

- Personnel security policy concerns people associated with the organization, such as employees, contractors, consultants.
- Employment agreement and policies should include information security responsibilities and information handling procedures.
- Employee termination process has to be in accordance with the established security policies and practices.
- Third-party security includes screening, confidentiality, and non-disclosure agreements.
- Risk mitigation strategies to address risks in terms of the CIA of assets is addressed through business continuity management processes.
- An event that could impact regular operations for a prolonged period of time can be termed as a disruptive event.
- Business Impact Analysis (BIA) is a type of risk assessment exercise that tries to assess qualitative and quantitative impacts on the business due to a disruptive event.
- Addressing the risks by way of plans and procedures for the continuation of business operations during and after a disruptive event is called Business Continuity Planning (BCP.)
- The aim of BCP is to prevent interruptions to business operations.
- While designing BCP, availability should be considered the primary factor.
- BCP should be appropriate, adequate, and complete.
- Recovery Time Objective (RTO) is a timeframe within which the systems should be recovered.
- Recovery Point Objective (RPO) is the maximum period of time (or amount) of transaction data that the business can afford to lose during a successful recovery. In other words, with RPO the frequency of backups can be determined.
- Business continuity procedures consist of testing and updating plans.

CISSP CBK domain #2 – asset security

The following information is about some of the important concepts, presented as bullet points, that will serve as exam cram for this second domain:

- Asset security is based on asset classification and CIA values.
- Asset classification is used to identify the type of information based on its value, sensitivity, and the degree of assurance required.

- Asset value is based on the impact to the corporation in the event of unauthorized disclosure, alteration, or destruction.
- Asset classification helps to devise suitable security controls.
- The classification of assets is based on criteria such as value, age, useful life, and privacy.
- Assets have owners, custodians, and users.
- Governmental agencies classify information based on confidentiality requirements.
- The need-to-know principle establishes that one has to demonstrate a specific need to know or access to the information that is classified as sensitive. An individual will be granted access to the information only if it is required to perform the duties of their job.
- Information classification in the United States government is based on the effect of the compromise of the asset on national security.
- Core Secrets, Top Secret, Secret, Confidential, Public Trust, and unclassified are the types of information classifications in the US.
- Private and public sector corporate entities classify information under four categories: confidential, private, sensitive, and public.
- Information assets that contain personnel details of people are classified as private or personal data.
- In information security, requirement for data privacy is to share personal data in a secure manner to third parties on a need basis.
- In the USA, the Federal Trade Commission (FTC) classifies sensitive consumer data.
- In the UK, the Data Protection Act specifies sensitive personal data.
- Data owners that pertain to privacy are the personnel identified in the data.
- When a third-party vendor is engaged by the licensee to create, receive, maintain, or transmit personal information, such entities are called business associates or data processors.
- Data that remains even after erasing or formatting from digital media is called residual data and the property to retain such data is called data remanence.
- Privacy laws stipulate data collection limitations pertaining to personal data.
- Data collection, use, retention, and destruction should be in accordance with established principles and best practices.
- Storage controls are the primary means to protect data in storage media, such as hard disk, magnetic tapes, CDs, and so on.
- Theft is one of the most common threats that need to be addressed for personal computer, laptop, or media protection.

- PCI DSS is a data security standard pertaining to the payment of card transactions. PCI DSS is applicable to all the entities involved in payment card processing.
- Sarbanes-Oxley Act (SOX) is the US federal law that mandates the demonstration of internal controls over financial reporting systems.
- The segregation or separation of duties is a security control measure to ensure that mutually exclusive roles are not assigned to a single user concurrently.
- Gramm-Leach-Bliley Act (GLBA) is an act in the United Sates that mandates privacy rules for financial institutions.
- EU Data Protection Act (DPA) is an act in the European Union that mandates data protection pertaining to the privacy information of client data.
- Data can traditionally be grouped under three categories such as Personally Identifiable Information (PII), Intellectual Property (IP), and Non-Public Information (NPI).
- Data exists in three states: data in motion, data at rest, and data in use.
- Data in motion refers to the information as it moves around the organization.
- Information that is stored within the organization is considered to be data at rest.
- Data in use refers to the information that is used by the staff and the data that is available in endpoints.
- Strategies to prevent data loss are called Data Loss Prevention (DLP).
- Data Loss Prevention controls are based on who is causing the incident? What actions are carried out by the individual to cause such an incident? Who else is involved and where? What action is taken?
- Cryptographic methods are used in data security controls.
- Encryption means the data is scrambled with an appropriate key.
- Encryption is used for ensuring confidentiality.
- Hashing is a method in which cryptographic value is computed and periodically validated based on the contents of the document.
- Hashing is used for ensuring integrity. Hashes are generally one-way computed values.
- Establishing the identity of the sender in a digital communication is accomplished through digital signatures.
- Secure disposal of media, labeling, access restrictions, the formal record of authorized recipients, the storage of media, data distribution, marking, the review of distribution lists, and the control of publicly available information are a few of the data handling controls.

Sample questions

Q1. During a periodical review of information security controls and their effectiveness in a corporation, that a file was found to be containing privacy-related data in a publicly accessible location. Which one of the following is ultimately responsible for such a security violation?

1. Data user
2. Data custodian
3. Data owner
4. Data auditor

Q2. _____ is a cryptographic method in which plain text is scrambled to form a scrambled text that is not directly readable without unscrambling.

1. Hashing
2. Transposition
3. Transformation
4. Encryption

Q3. Which one of the following is a malicious threat?

1. Software weakness
2. Wrong configuration
3. Botnet
4. Weak encryption

Q4. Which one of the following is a Recovery Time Objective (RTO)?

1. Recovery of data that was processed up to last week
2. Recovery of statistical data for the past 12 months
3. Recovery of IT Systems within 4 hours
4. Recovery of people in the event of disaster

Q5. Which of the following represents Data in use? Drag and drop the correct examples to the red box.

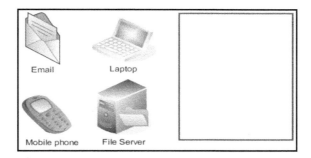

Q6. _____ is a type of cybercrime wherein an unsuspecting user is lured by way of emails or pop-up messages to visit attacker-constructed malicious websites.

1. Farming
2. Framing
3. Mishing
4. Phishing

Q7. A corporation establishes security policies and procedures based on proper risk assessment and compliance requirements. Such an activity is called_____.

1. Risk management
2. Risk mitigation strategy
3. Due diligence
4. Due care

Q8. Which of the following information classifications mandates the need to know principle?

1. Confidential
2. Sensitive
3. Public Trust
4. Non-Public

Q9. A cyber attack is perpetrated against a corporate network with the intention of destabilizing the systems and gaining competitive advantage. Such an attack can be referred as_____.

1. Cyberterrorism
2. Cyber bullying

3. Cyber stalking
4. Denial of Service

Q10. Which one of the following is not a best security practice?

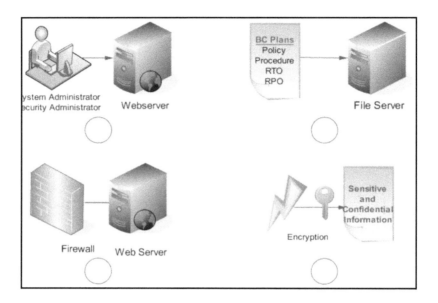

References and further reading

- **CISSP Candidate Information Bulletin (CISSP CIB):** https://www.isc2.org/
- **ISO/IEC 27001 and ISO/IEC 27002:** http://www.iso.org/iso/home/standar ds/management-standards/iso27001.htm
- **NIST Guide to Protecting Confidentiality of Personally Identifiable Information (PII) – Special Publication 800-122:** http://csrc.nist.gov/publ ications/PubsSPs.html
- **US Security and Exchange Commission (SEC) laws:** http://www.sec.gov/ab out/laws.shtml#sox2002
- **HIPAA:** http://www.hhs.gov/hipaa/index.html
- **Federal Trade Commission-GLBA:** https://www.ftc.gov/tips-advice/bus iness-center/privacy-and-security/gramm-leach-bliley-act

- PCI DSS:https://www.pcisecuritystandards.org/pci_security/
- **EU Data Protection Act**: https://www.gov.uk/data-protection/the-data-protection-act

Summary

This chapter covered some of the important concepts in the form of an exam cram from the first two domains of CISSP CBK. A mock test with a combination of questions in the first two domains was provided to test the knowledge gained. Further reading and references we provided to enhance the knowledge in these two domains.

In the next chapter, you will learn security engineering with a focus on security design principles and practices, security engineering models, and vulnerability mitigation strategies.

6

Day 6 – Security Engineering - Security Design, Practices, Models, and Vulnerability Mitigation

The security engineering domain consists of security design principles that are the building blocks of secure software, hardware, and networking products. This domain also addresses best practices, proven models, and processes that can be adapted during product design. The focus of this domain is to ensure good security implementation. This domain also deals with technical vulnerabilities and mitigation techniques. Additionally, cryptography and physical security principles and practices are also covered in this domain.

A candidate appearing for a CISSP exam is expected to have foundational concepts and knowledge in the following key areas of the **security engineering** domain:

- Secure design principles
- Security engineering practices
- Security organizational processes
- Information security models
- Systems security evaluation models
- Security capabilities in information systems
- Vulnerability assessment and mitigation in information systems
- Vulnerability assessment and mitigation in web-based systems
- Vulnerability assessment and mitigation in mobile systems

- Vulnerability assessment and mitigation in embedded and cyber-physical systems
- The fundamentals of cryptography
- The application of cryptography
- Physical security principles for sites and facilities
- Environmental security practices for sites and facilities

To get the most out this chapter, you need to understand and memorize subtle differences between vulnerability testing and mitigation actions, security engineering and organizational processes, and information security models and systems security evaluation models.

An overview of security design, practices, models, and vulnerability mitigation

Security engineering is based on design principles, practices, and models to ensure confidentiality, integrity, and the availability requirements of information assets. The end result could be the development of a product or supporting organizational processes. Further, the product could be hardware, software, or a combination of both.

Vulnerabilities are weaknesses in the process or product that might creep in during design stage, development, or in the end product. These weaknesses could be exploited for a myriad of reasons that include fraud, stealing trade secrets, the Denial-of-Services, and so on. Identifying vulnerabilities during design/development stage is critical to a secure an end product. Since the Information Technology environment is complex and diverse, it may not always be possible to foresee and identify all the possible vulnerabilities during the design/development stage itself. Hence, vulnerability identification remains essential even after the product or service roll-out. A robust security implementation needs mitigation plans and ongoing maintenance.

Observe the following illustration:

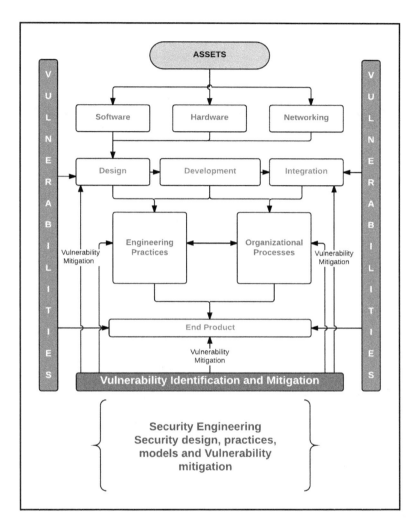

The following bullet points represent a brief overview of the preceding diagram. These points explain the overall structure of this chapter in a logical sequence:

- IT assets can be grouped as software, hardware, and networking related
- Software can be further grouped as operating systems, application software, embedded software, mobile applications, and web applications
- Hardware and networking systems may contain embedded software

- Security requirements should be addressed in a continual process through design, development, and integration phases
- Vulnerabilities might creep in during any of these phases
- By adhering to software development engineering practices and security organizational processes, vulnerability issues can be addressed

Secure design principles

System and application development consists of design, development, test, and deployment processes. Security has to be addressed at every step in the development cycle. However, addressing security in the design stage itself is most critical. Since prevention is better than cure, addressing security at the design stage itself can facilitate preventative controls to address security issues.

The computer architecture

The elements of a computer that are fundamental to its operations, together with the way the elements are organized, are referred to as the **computer architecture**.

A computer is a physical device consisting of physical components. These physical components are called **hardware**. The hardware components process the instructions and data presented to them. The set of instructions and data is called software.

Some of the fundamental elements in the computer architecture are the input/output systems, the CPU, and memory. A common plane connects the previous three and is called a **bus**.

The following are the functions of each of these elements:

- A **central processing unit (CPU)** is the heart and brain of a computer. Its primary function is to process the instruction and data presented to it by other systems such as application software through input/output systems. The process carried out by the CPU is called executing the program.
- An **input/output (IO)** systems interface with the CPU. Input/Output mechanisms and structures enable the supply of input instructions and data to the CPU, and they manage the output data from the CPU to appropriate interfaces.

  The function of memory is to store the instructions and data either permanently or temporarily. Computer memory can be categorized as primary memory and secondary memory.

 Primary memory refers to a storage area that is directly addressable by the CPU. The examples of such memory are cache, Random Access Memory (RAM), and Read Only Memory (ROM).
Secondary memory refers to permanent storage that is indirectly accessible by the CPU. Some examples are magnetic disks, tapes, and so on.

Computer system

Telecommunication and networking technologies enable computers to communicate with each other. A computer may act as a server or a client or both. Based on the role of a computer in a network, the network architecture is classified as a client-server or centralized model. Since interconnectivity is the primary goal, these models are generally called **distributed architecture**.

Sometimes, the collection of hardware and software is together referred to as a **computer system**.

A computer system can be categorized as an open system, a closed system, or a combination of both.

An **open system**, as the name implies, is open to interconnectivity with other systems. It can also be reviewed by independent third parties. This means an open system can be reviewed and evaluated by third parties. In contrary, a **closed system** is proprietary in nature, and the internal workings are not known; auditing such systems, such as code review or architecture review is not feasible. Such systems may not be compatible with other systems.

From an asset classification and information security perspective, a computer is a physical asset and the necessary physical security principles are applicable to it. The service provided by a computer is called **computing**. It is treated as a service asset.

Various computing methods are available to improve the instruction execution cycle. An instruction execution cycle is the time required to fetch the instruction and data from memory, decode the information, and execute it.

When many operations are performed per instruction, such a computing is known as **Complex Instruction Set Computing (CISC)**. When instruction sets reduce the cycle time to execute instructions, then the method is called **Reduced Instruction Set Computing (RISC)**. Instruction processing generally contains fetch, decode, and execute cycles.

When the fetch, decode, and execute cycles are overlapped by a set of instructions to reduce the time cycle, then such a method is called **pipelining**.

From an information security perspective, computer architecture should take into consideration the CIA aspects of computing services.

Trusted computing

In computer systems, establishing the level of assurance based on the defined security models so that the computer system can be trusted for use in critical infrastructure is called **trusted computing**.

The following are some of the concepts that relate to information security aspects of a trusted computing architecture:

- **Trusted computing base** is as follows:
    - The totality of protection mechanisms within it
    - It includes hardware, firmware, and software
    - It is responsible for enforcing a computer security policy
- **Trusted computer system** refers to systems that have a well-defined security policy, accountability, assurance mechanisms, and proper documentation.
- **Trusted Computer System Evaluation Criteria (TCSEC)** is a set of basic requirements to evaluate the effectiveness of computer security controls built into computer systems. TCSEC is the United States **Department of Defense (DOD)** standard and is popularly known as **orange book**.
- **Protection domain** is a security function used to control or prevent direct access by an insecure or lower-level entity to a secure higher-level entity. Software programs, such as operating systems or applications, run in either the user-protection domain or the kernel-protection domain.
- When the protection domains are organized in a hierarchical format, then they are called **protection rings**. The purpose of protection rings is to protect data and the computing system from malicious behaviors of programs. For example, sensitive and machine-critical data that is accessible to the operating system will be in the inner rings. They will be protected from access or modification by the programs that are on the outer-level ring.
- **Security perimeter** is an outer ring of a trusted computing base or, in simple terms, it is the outer ring of a protected domain or entity.
- **Trusted path** refers to secure paths provided by software to communicate with entities within trusted rings to eliminate unauthorized access.

- **Encapsulation** is a technique used to hide information from unauthorized entities. This is analogous to a capsule in medicine. The contents within the capsule are protected from environmental effects by the capsule shell.
- **Abstraction** is the process of hiding the details and exposing only the essential features of a particular concept or object that are encapsulated.
- **Reference monitor** is a secure module that controls access to trusted, protected entities in a trusted computing base.
- **Security kernel** is a computer architecture consisting of hardware and software elements that implement reference monitor.
- **Security label** is a classification mechanism used to indicate the security levels of entities. Examples of labels can be low, medium, or high or classified, secret, or sensitive and so on based on the sensitivity of the data and function.
- **Logical security guard** is a security mechanism to control the communication between entities that are labeled low sensitive and high sensitivity.
- Security modes are operating modes based on the operating level of the information systems and the sensitivity level or the security label. Some of the modes in which information systems operate are dedicated, compartmented, controlled, and limited access.

Assurance

In information security, the term assurance means the level of trust or the degree of confidence in the satisfaction of security needs. There are many standards and guidelines published by the government and commercial organizations to evaluate the assurance aspects of computer systems.

Common Criteria

Common Criteria (CC) is an assurance framework that is predominantly derived from the following three country specific standards:

- **Trusted Computer Security Evaluation Criteria (TCSEC)**
- **Information Technology Security Evaluation Criteria (ITSEC)**
- **Canadian Trusted Computer Product Evaluation Criteria (CTCPEC)**

CC basically defines a **Protection Profile (PP)** for computing systems.

The following are some of the concepts pertaining to CC:

- **Target of Evaluation (TOE)** is the target product or system that is to be evaluated.
- **Security Target (ST)** is principally a document that identifies the security properties of the TOE. This document contains **Security Functions Requirements (SFR)** that may be provided by the product or system.
- **Evaluation Assurance Level (EAL)** is a numerical rating based on the evaluation level. EAL is based on **Security Assurance Requirements (SAR)**. There are seven levels of EAL starting from EAL1 (Basic) to EAL7 (most stringent).

Trusted Computer Security Evaluation Criteria (TCSEC) is also called the orange book in a rainbow series published by the United States Department of Defense (DoD). The focus of TCSEC is on confidentiality while the DoD's other standard, **Trusted Network Interpretation (TNI)**, which is also called the **red book**, addresses confidentiality as well as integrity.

Information Technology Security Evaluation Criteria (ITSEC) is a European standard for IT security that specifies evaluation criteria for functionality and assurance. ITSEC divides evaluation parameters as follows:

- Functionality classes
- Assurance levels
- Correctness levels
- Security functions

There are two kinds of assurances specified:

- The correctness of security functions
- The effectiveness of the Target of Evaluation (TOE)

Canadian Trusted Computer Product Evaluation Criteria (CTCPEC) is a Canadian standard for security product evaluation published by the Communications Security Establishment.

Certification and accreditation

Information systems need to be evaluated and they may also need to be certified based on a set of defined parameters. There are many security certification and accreditation standards for security assurance. The following topics describe a few important ones.

DITSCAP

Department of Defense Information Technology Security Certification and Accreditation Process (DITSCAP) is the standardized approach designed to guide DoD agencies through the certification and accreditation process for a single information technology (IT) entity.

There are four phases to the DITSCAP process:

1. **Definition**: All the system requirements and capabilities are documented to include mission, function, and interfaces.
2. **Verification**: recommended changes to a system are performed and the resulting deliverable is a refined **System Security Authorization Agreement (SSAA)**.
3. **Validation**: This proceeds with a review of the SSAA.
4. **Post accreditation**: Here, system changes are managed, system operations are reviewed, acceptable risk is maintained, and the SSAA is updated.

 System Security Authorization Agreement (SSAA) is a document that details system specifications, such as the system mission, target environment, target architecture, security requirements, and applicable data access policies. SSAA is a basis on which certification and accreditation actions take place.

NIACAP

National Information Assurance Certification and Accreditation Process (NIACAP) is a process for the certification and accreditation of the computer systems that handle the US National Security information. It is derived from DITSCAP.

DIACAP

The **DoD Information Assurance Certification and Accreditation Process (DIACAP)** is a standard that supersedes DITSCAP. This standard was published in 2006.

Security engineering practices

System Security Engineering Capability Maturity Model (SSE-CMM) is a system security process maturity model that focuses on requirements pertaining to the implementation of security in a system or a group of systems specifically in the Information Technology security domain. It is a National Security Agency (NSA) sponsored effort.

There are 11 security engineering practices that are defined in SSE-CMM. They are as follows:

- **PA01**: Administer Security Controls
- **PA02**: Assess Impact
- **PA03**: Assess Security Risk
- **PA04**: Assess Threat
- **PA05**: Assess Vulnerability
- **PA06**: Build Assurance Argument
- **PA07**: Coordinate Security
- **PA08**: Monitor Security Posture
- **PA09**: Provide Security Input
- **PA10**: Specify Security Needs
- **PA11**: Verify and Validate Security

There are 11 more process areas and related project and organizational practices. They are as follows:

- **PA12**: Ensure Quality
- **PA13**: Manage Configuration
- **PA14**: Manage Project Risk
- **PA15**: Monitor and Control Technical Effort
- **PA16**: Plan Technical Effort
- **PA17**: Define Organization's Systems Engineering Process
- **PA18**: Improve Organization's Systems Engineering Process
- **PA19**: Manage Product Line Evolution
- **PA20**: Manage Systems Engineering Support Environment
- **PA21**: Provide Ongoing Skills and Knowledge
- **PA22**: Coordinate with Suppliers

Information security models

Computer security is based on the role of various entities within the system and their CIA requirement. Information security models address the CIA requirements in computing systems and data.

Take-grant model

This computer security model is also called the take-grant protection model and it specifies obtaining (taking) rights from one entity and giving them to another or the transferring (granting) of rights by one entity to another. There are two entities defined in this model: a *subject* and *object*. In simple terms, this model proposes a directed graph that represents the transfer of rights.

There are four rules in this model; they are as follows:

- **Take rule**: The subject takes rights of another subject
- **Grant rule**: The subject grants rights to another subject
- **Create rule**: The subject creates new nodes
- **Remove rule**: The subject removes its rights over an object

Bell-LaPadula model

This is a data-confidentiality model developed by David Elliot Bell and Len LaPadula. Since the focus is on confidentiality, this model prescribes access controls to classified or confidential information. This model specifies three security properties. The first two are related to **Mandatory Access Control (MAC)** and the last is **Discretionary Access Control (DAC)**:

- The **Simple Security property** states that a subject, at a given security level, may not read an object at a higher security level (**no read-up**)
- The ***-property (star-property)** states that a subject, at a given security level, must not write to any object at a lower security level (**no write-down**)
- The **Discretionary Security property** uses an access matrix to specify the discretionary access control

A simple way to remember this model is: **no read up and no write down**.

Biba model

This model focuses on data integrity. This model was developed by Kenneth J. Biba.

This model states the following two rules:

- **Simple integrity axiom** states that a subject, at a given level of integrity, may not read an object at a lower integrity level (**no read down**)

- *** (star) integrity axiom** states that a subject, at a given level of integrity, must not write to any object at a higher level of integrity (**no write up**)

A simple way to remember this model is: **no read down and no write up**.

Clark-Wilson model

This is an integrity model that was developed by David D. Clarke and David R. Wilson. This model aims to address multi-level security requirements in computing systems.

Vulnerability assessment and mitigation

IT components, such as operating systems, application software, and networks have many vulnerabilities. These vulnerabilities are open to compromise or exploitation. This provides a possibility of penetrating into systems that result in unauthorized access.

Vulnerability tests are done to identify vulnerabilities and penetration tests are conducted to check the possibility of compromising systems such that the established access control mechanisms may be defeated and the unauthorized access gained.

Otherwise, systems can be shutdown or overloaded with malicious data using techniques such as the denial of service attacks such that access by legitimate users or processes maybe denied.

The primary purpose of vulnerability and penetration tests is to identify, evaluate, and mitigate the risks of vulnerability exploitation.

Vulnerability assessment

Vulnerability assessment is a process in which IT systems, such as computers, networks, operating systems, and application software, are scanned for identifying the presence of known and unknown vulnerabilities.

Vulnerabilities in IT systems such as software and networks can be considered to be holes or errors.

Vulnerabilities creep into systems due to improper software design, insecure coding, or both. For example, buffer overflow is a vulnerability where the boundary limits for an entity, such as a variable and constants, are not properly defined or checked. Such a vulnerability can be compromised by supplying data that is much more than the entity can hold. This will result in data spill over other memory areas, which will corrupt the instructions or code that need to be processed by the microprocessor.

Vulnerabilities can be compromised and such an act is called the exploitation of vulnerabilities. When a vulnerability is exploited, it results in a security violation, which will result in a certain impact. A security violation may provide unauthorized access, give higher privileges, or stop some functions, which will result in the denial of service to IT systems.

Tools are used in the process of identifying vulnerabilities. These tools are called vulnerability scanners. A vulnerability scanning tool can be hardware based or a software application.

Generally, vulnerabilities can be classified based on the type of security error. A type is the root cause of such vulnerability.

Vulnerabilities may be classified into the following types:

- **Access control vulnerabilities**: This is an error due to lack of enforcement pertaining to users or functions that are permitted or denied access to an object or resource:
  - **Examples:**
    - Improper or no access control list or table
    - No privilege model
    - Inadequate file permissions
    - Improper or weak encoding
  - **Security violation and impact**:
    - File/object/process can be accessed directly without proper authentication or routing

- **Authentication vulnerabilities**: This is an error due to inadequate identification mechanisms, such that a user or a process is not correctly identified:
  - **Examples:**
    - Weak or static passwords
    - Improper or weak encoding, weak algorithms, or biometric errors

- **Security violation and impact**:
    - Unauthorized or less privileged users (e.g. Guest user) or a less privileged process gains higher privileges, such as administrative or root access to system or Denial-of-Service from authorized individuals being improperly denied.

- **Boundary condition vulnerabilities**: This is an error due to inadequate checking/validating mechanisms, so that the length of the data is not checked/validated against the size of the data storage or resource:
    - **Examples**:
        - Buffer overflow
        - Overwriting the original data in the memory
    - **Security violation and impact**:
        - Memory is overwritten with some arbitrary code so as to gain access to programs; or corrupting the memory, which will crash the operating system. An unstable system due to memory corruption may be exploited to get command prompt or shell access by injecting an arbitrary code.

- **Configuration weakness vulnerabilities**: This is an error due to improper configuration of system parameters or leaving the default configuration settings as it is, which may not be secure:
    - **Examples**:
        - Default security policy configuration
        - File and print access in Internet connection sharing
    - **Security violation and impact**:
        - Most of the default configuration settings of software applications are published and available in the public domain. For example, some applications come with standard default passwords, which, when not changed to a secure one, allow an attacker to compromise the system. Configuration weaknesses are exploited to gain higher privileges resulting in privilege escalation impacts.

- **Exception handling vulnerabilities**: This is an error due to improper setup or coding, such that the system fails to handle or properly respond to exceptional or unexpected data or conditions:
  - **Examples**:
    - **Structured Query Language (SQL)** Injection
  - **Security violation and impact**:
    - By injecting exceptional data, user credentials can be captured by an unauthorized entity
- **Input validation vulnerabilities**: This is an error due to lack of verification mechanisms to validate the input data or contents:
  - **Examples**:
    - Directory traversal
    - Malformed URLs
  - **Security violation and impact**:
    - Due to poor input validation, access to system-privileged programs may be obtained.

- **Randomization vulnerabilities**: This is an error due to a mismatch in random data used in the software process. Such vulnerabilities are predominantly related to encryption algorithms:
  - **Examples**:
    - Weak encryption key
    - Insufficient random data
  - **Security violation and impact**:
    - Cryptographic key can be compromised, which will impact data and access security
- **Resource vulnerabilities**: This is an error due to a lack of resources available for correct operations or processes:
  - **Examples**:
    - Memory getting full
    - CPU is completely utilized
  - **Security violation and impact**:
    - Due to lack of resources, the system may become unstable or hang. The impact could be Denial-of-Services to legitimate users.

- **State Error:** This is an error due to the lack of state maintenance because of an incorrect process flow:
  - **Examples:**
    - Opening multiple tabs in web browsers
  - **Security violation and impact**:
    - There are specific security attacks, such as cross-site-scripting, which will result in user-authenticated sessions being hijacked.

Information security professionals need to be aware of the processes involved in identifying system vulnerabilities and they need to devise suitable counter measures. Some such measures are applying patches supplied by application vendors and hardening systems.

Penetration testing

While vulnerability assessment and remediation is used to strengthen the computer system, it is also important to perform suitable **penetration tests** periodically to identify the possibilities of system compromise. The primary purpose of penetration tests is to identify the exploitation possibilities of an identified vulnerability.

Vulnerability assessment and the penetration testing process

The following diagram illustrates the process of Vulnerability Assessment and Penetration Testing (VAPT):

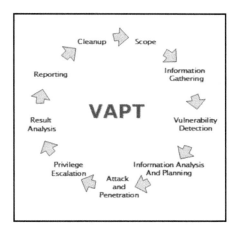

Vulnerability assessment and penetration testing contains the following processes:

- **Scope**: While performing assessment and testing, the scope of the assignment needs to be clearly defined. The following are the three possible scopes that exist:

    1. Testing from an external network with no prior knowledge of the internal networks and systems is referred to as **black box testing**.

    2. Performing the test from within the network is refereed to as internal testing or **white box testing**.

    3. Testing from an external and or internal network with the knowledge of internal networks and systems is referred to as **gray box testing**. This is usually a combination of black box testing and white box testing.

- **Information gathering**: The process of information gathering is obtaining as much information as the possible about the IT environment, such as networks, IP addresses, the operating system version, and so on. This is applicable to all three types of scope discussed previously.
- **Vulnerability detection**: In this process, tools such as vulnerability scanners are used and vulnerabilities are identified in the IT environment by way of scanning.
- **Information analysis and planning**: This process is used to analyze the identified vulnerabilities combined with the information gathered about the IT environment to devise a plan for penetrating the network and systems.
- **Penetration testing**: In this process, target systems are attacked and penetrated using the plan devised in the earlier process.

- **Privilege escalation**: After successful penetration into the system, this process is used to identify and escalate access to gain higher privileges such as root access or administrative access to the system.
- **Result analysis**: This process is used to perform a root cause analysis as a result of successful compromise of the system, leading to penetration and devising suitable recommendations, to make the system secure by plugging holes in the systems.
- **Reporting**: All the findings that are observed during the vulnerability assessment and penetration testing processes need to be documented, along with recommendations, to produce a testing report for the management for suitable actions.
- **Cleanup**: Vulnerability assessment and penetration testing involves compromising the system, and during the process, some files may be altered. The cleanup process is applied to ensure that the system is brought back to the original state before the testing, by cleaning up (restoring) the data and files used in the target machines.

CVE and CVSS

Many security groups, vendors and other organizations that are involved in vulnerability research identify vulnerabilities in systems almost daily. There are lots of variations in terms of these reported vulnerabilities by different vendors. Sometimes, it is difficult to identify whether a reported vulnerability by different vendors is the same or different.

To address this anomaly, many the security vendors, software vendors, and other similar business groups formed a worldwide effort and the outcome of this group is an online dictionary of vulnerabilities and exposures. This online dictionary is called **Common Vulnerabilities and Exposures (CVE)** and is sponsored by the **Department of Homeland Security (DHS)** of the USA.

CVE being an online dictionary of vulnerabilities, there is an effort by **National Institute of Standards and Technology (NIST)**, USA, as part of their **Information Security Automation Program (ISAP)**, provides a criticality rating or scoring for CVE listed vulnerabilities. This scoring is called the **Critical Vulnerability Scoring System (CVSS)** and it is contained in an online database called the **National Vulnerability Database (NVD)**.

Summary

This chapter covered foundational concepts in the security engineering domain. Hardware, software, or networking systems need to be secure, for which adherence to security best practices during design, development, and integration is essential. Security standards and models provide a baseline for developing and maintaining secure systems. During various stages of the information system life cycle, vulnerabilities may creep in. Hence, it is necessary to identify and assess vulnerabilities and mitigate them during development as well as during operations.

In the next chapter, we will understand the fundamentals of cryptography, its requirements in security, and its application in data security and communication security. Besides concepts and best practices that relate to the physical security of infrastructure and information systems are also covered in the next chapter.

Sample questions

Q1. Which one of the following is considered the BEST penetration testing method when the organization wants to ascertain the hacking possibilities from external networks to the internal systems?

1. Black box testing
2. Blue box testing
3. Grey box testing
4. White box testing

Q2. Vulnerabilities in IT systems are considered:

1. Holes or errors
2. Software functionality
3. Hardware functionality
4. None of the above

Q3. Which of the following step is not a vulnerability assessment and penetration testing process?

1. Scope
2. Result analysis

3. Software development
4. Reporting

Q4. Common Vulnerabilities and Exposures (CVE) is a:

1. Dictionary
2. Database
3. Software program
4. Vulnerability

Q5. The National Vulnerability Database (NVD) provides:

1. Common Software defects
2. Common Vulnerability Scoring System
3. Common Vulnerability Sorting System
4. Common hardware defects

Q6. If you need to address multi-level security requirements, which of the following models will you choose?

1. Take-Grant Model
2. Bell-LaPadula Model
3. Biba Model
4. Clark-Wilson Model

Q7. A boundary condition error results in:

1. Buffer overflow
2. Buffer reset
3. Segmentation fault
4. System reset

Q8. Which of the following statement about the Biba model is FALSE?

1. Data integrity model
2. No read up
3. No read down
4. No write up

Q9. Which of the following are used as evaluation parameters in Information Technology Security Evaluation Criteria (ITSEC)?

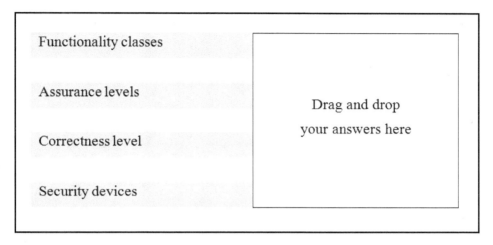

Q10. Which one of the following is a true representation of the protection domain in a Trusted Computer System (TCS)?

1. It is a function to control or prevent direct access by an insecure or lower-level entity to a secure or higher-level entity
2. It is a function to control or prevent direct access by an insecure or higher-level entity to a secure or higher-level entity
3. It is a function to control or prevent direct access by an insecure or higher-level entity to a secure or lower-level entity
4. It is a function to control or prevent direct access by an insecure or lower-level entity to an insecure or higher-level entity

7
Day 7 – Security Engineering - Cryptography

This chapter gives an overview of cryptography, its requirements, concepts, application, attacks, and management using a high-level illustration. Understanding and applying cryptography and its use in preserving the confidentiality and integrity of sensitive assets as well as attacks on cryptographic systems and cryptographic standards are some of the main topics covered in this chapter.

An overview of cryptography

Sensitive assets need protection from unauthorized disclosure or tampering. The sensitivity of assets is determined by confidentiality and integrity requirements and the impact of compromise on the corporation or national security. Cryptographic methods and solutions provide assurance to protect assets from compromise.

Observe the following illustration:

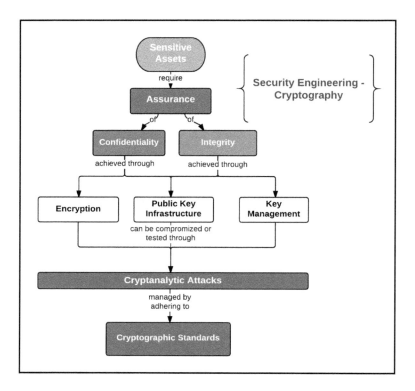

The following bullet points represent a brief overview of the preceding diagram. These points explain the overall structure of this chapter in a logical sequence:

- Sensitive assets require an additional level of security pertaining to confidentiality and integrity.
- Additional security requirements of confidentiality and integrity can be assured through the application of cryptographic methods.
- The fundamentals of cryptography are related to encryption and the methods of encryption.
- Various types of encryption methods are used in the cryptography domain based on their characteristics, such as the type of algorithm used, the key length, and the application.
- **Public Key Infrastructure (PKI)** is an industry standard framework, which enables the integration of various services that are related to cryptography.

- Key management techniques are important from the perspective of cryptographic key generation, distribution, storage, validation, and destruction.
- Cryptographic key can be compromised. Compromises can be due to a weak algorithm or weak keys. Many methods of cryptanalytic attacks exist to compromise keys.
- Cryptographic standards provide tools and best practice methods to secure information and keys from cryptanalytic attacks.

The rest of this chapter covers these concepts in detail.

The fundamentals of cryptography

Cryptography is an art as well as a science that involves the process of transforming plain text into scrambled text and vice versa. The purpose of cryptography is to conceal confidential information from unauthorized entities and ensure immediate detection of any alteration made to the concealed information. Concealing the original information that is in human or machine-readable format is achieved by a method called **encryption**.

The methods of encryption

A plain text in the cryptographic context is information that is in a human or machine-readable format that needs protection. For example, the password that you are typing is in plain text. Similarly, documents such as business agreements, MOU, and so on are in plain text.

Scrambled text in the cryptographic context is called a cipher text. A cipher text is the scrambled version of the plain text. Cipher text is not in a human or machine-readable format.

The functions of cryptography are to keep the plain text secret by way of scrambling and detecting unauthorized changes to such information. These functions are for the purposes of confidentiality and integrity.

The cryptographic process

The process of converting plain text into scrambled (cipher) text is called encryption. The process of encryption is also called enciphering. Hence, cipher text can be called encrypted text.

The process of converting scrambled (cipher) text into plain text is called decryption. The process of decryption is also called **deciphering**. The output of decryption is plain text or decrypted text.

Cryptographic algorithms

Encryption as well as decryption is based on algorithms. An algorithm, in cryptography, is a series of well-defined steps that provide the procedure for encryption/decryption. For example, if we use a scrambling method that substitutes the alphabets with the next alphabet, then we're using a type of substitution algorithm. In this type of algorithm A=B, B=C....Z=A. Hence, in this algorithm, a word such as WELCOME will be represented as XFMDPNF. As you can see, this example uses only one step, but complex algorithms use multiple steps with different mathematical formulae.

Julius Caesar used a type of shift3 cipher (substitution by third alphabet) to communicate military secret messages.
An example of a shift3 cipher is here:
WELCOME ~ shift by 3 letters would give ~ ZHOFRPH
The algorithm that is used for encryption as well as decryption is referred to as cipher.

A cryptographic key is also called a **Crypto variable**, and it is used on the operation for encryption and decryption of a text. This is analogous to the keys that we use in household padlocks. If you observe the physical key, you can find varying slots. These are called tumblers or levers. By adjusting the levers, different types of key combinations are obtained. Similarly, in cryptography, we use an electronic key (cryptographic key) to lock or unlock a plain text, document, or any electronic data.

The cryptographic method

A cryptographic method is a way of doing encryption and decryption in a systematic way. The following diagram illustrates a cryptographic method:

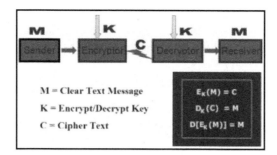

In the preceding process, message (**M**) from the sender is encrypted and results in the cipher text (**C**). A cryptographic key (**K**) is used in the encryption process. When cipher text is decrypted, it results in the original message. The same key (**K**) that was used for encrypting is required for decrypting (**D**) the cipher text. This process is represented as $E_K(M) = C$ and $D_K (C) = M$, where E is encryption, K is for key, M is for message, C is for a cipher text, and D is for decryption.

Decrypting an encrypted message (cipher text) will result in an original message. This process can be represented as $D[E_K(M)] = M$.

Types of encryption

Cryptography is based on algorithms and the keys that operate on them. Types of encryption or decryption are based on the combination of these two factors (algorithms and keys). There are two types of encryption predominantly used in government agencies as well as corporations. Either there is a single key or there are two keys:

- If only one key is used, then it is called symmetric key encryption
- If two keys are used, then it is called asymmetric key encryption

There is also a method in cryptography that uses no keys. If no key is used, then it is called **hashing**. It uses no keys and applies a one-way function of computing a hash value (sometimes called a checksum) from the original or scrambled text. Hashing is used for the assurance of integrity.

Symmetric key encryption

In symmetric key encryption, only one key is used. The name symmetric implies that the key used for encryption as well as for decryption is the same. This type of encryption is also called **Secret Key Cryptography (SKC)**.

Based on the algorithm used, this symmetric key encryption can be categorized into two types:

- **Stream cipher**: When the key stream algorithm operates on a single bit, byte, or a computer word such that the information is changed constantly, then it is called a stream cipher. For example, in a stream cipher, if we want to encrypt a word such as WELCOME, then each of the alphabets in the word will be encrypted using the algorithm. The Caesar shift3 algorithm is a stream cipher.
- **Block cipher**: If the algorithm operates on a block of text (as opposed to a single bit or byte), then it is known as a block cipher. In this case, the algorithm will encrypt the entire word.

The following are some of the examples of algorithms that are commonly used in the industry.

The examples of stream cipher is given here:

- The **Rivest Cipher (RC4)** algorithm uses about 40 to 256 bits and the key sizes are different. It is considered good for speed and is to be used in less-complex hardware. Some of the examples where RC4 is used are in protocols such as **Secure Sockets Layer (SSL)** and **Wireless Equivalent Privacy (WEP)**.

The examples of block cipher are given here:

- **Data Encryption Standard** (DES) is a block cipher that uses up to 56-bit keys and operates on 64-bit blocks. It was designed by International Business Machines (IBM) and adopted by the National Institute of Standards and Technology (NIST).
- **Triple-DES (3DES)**, as the name implies, uses three 56-bit keys that pass over the blocks three times.
- **Advanced Encryption Standard** (AES) is a 128-bit block cipher that employs 128, 192, or 256 bit keys. This is based on the NIST specifications and is the official successor to DES.

The present AES uses an algorithm known as Rijndael that uses a variable block as well as key lengths.

- **Blowfish** is an algorithm that uses variable key lengths of 32 to 448 bits that work on 64-bit blocks.
- **Twofish** is a block cipher that uses 128, 192, or 256-bit keys on 128-bit blocks. And is considered to be more secure.
- **International Data Encryption Algorithm** (**IDEA**) is a block cipher that uses 128-bit keys on 64-bit blocks.

The operation modes of block ciphers

The following are the different operational modes of block ciphers:

- When a cipher text block is formed by the application of a secret key to encrypt the plain text block, it is called **Electronic Code Book (ECB)**.
- When plain text is eXlusively-ORed (XORed) with the previous block of cipher text then the mode is called **Cipher Block Chaining (CBC)**.
- **Cipher FeedBack (CFB)** is a mode that allows encrypted data units to be smaller than the block unit size.
- **Output FeedBack (OFB)** uses an internal feedback mechanism such that the same plain text block cannot create the same cipher text block.
- **Initialization vectors** are a block of bits that allow either a stream cipher or a block cipher to execute on any of the previous modes. It is usually a random number that is applied to ensure that the cipher text is different when the same message is encrypted twice.

Asymmetric key encryption

In this type, there are two keys. The name asymmetric implies that the keys are not the same. This type of encryption is also called **Public Key Cryptography** (**PKC**):

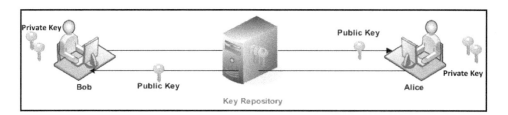

The two keys that are used in this type are called the **private key** and the **public key**. They are used in combination to encrypt and decrypt the message or text.

The following are important concepts in public key cryptography:

- There are two keys (private and public).
- The private key is kept secret.
- The public key is widely distributed.
- An entity's (a person or a software application) private and public keys are related by way of a mathematical algorithm.
- It is not possible to derive the private key from the public key.
- The body of the message is encrypted using the recipient's public key. Hence, only the recipient's private key can be used to decrypt the message. This **ensures the confidentiality** of the message. For example, if Bob wants to send a document to Alice and he does not want anyone to else be able to read this document, then Bob will encrypt the document using Alice's public key. Then, only Alice can open the document using her private key.

Digital signature is a type of public key cryptography where the message is digitally signed using the sender's private key. Digitally signing means encrypting the hash value. This can be verified using sender's public key. This is to verify the authenticity of the sender. For example, Bob will digitally sign the message that he is sending to Alice using his private key. Alice can verify the authenticity using Bob's public key.

One of the most important applications of public key cryptography is to ensure non-repudiation. **Non-repudiation** is a method by which the sender of the message can deny their actions.

 Asymmetric key encryption uses **one-way functions** that are easier to compute on one side and difficult to do the same on reverse.

The following are examples of algorithms that are commonly used in the industry:

- **Rivest, Shamir, and Adleman (RSA)** is an asymmetric key encryption algorithm named after its inventors. It uses a variable size encryption block as well as a variable size key. The algorithm uses a product of two large prime numbers to derive the key pairs.
- **Diffie-Hellman method** is used primarily for private-key exchange over an insecure medium.
- **ElGamel** is similar to Diffie-Hellman and is used for exchanging keys.
- **Elliptic Curve Cryptography (ECC)** is an algorithm that generates keys from elliptical curves.
- **Digital Signature Algorithm (DSA)** is specified by NIST under **Digital Signature Standard (DSS)**. This algorithm is primarily used for authentication purposes in digital signatures.

Hashing

Hashing or **hash functions** are a type of encryption where a key is not used. Instead, a hash value is computed based on the contents of the message. The computed value is called a **checksum**. The purpose of hashing is to provide **integrity checking** to the plain or encrypted text.

 Hashing is also called **message digest** or **one-way encryption** as there is no decryption but only validating the computed checksum.

The following are some of examples of algorithms that are commonly used in the industry:

- **Message Digest Algorithm** (MD) are series of hashing algorithms that produce 128-bit hash values from an arbitrary length message.
- **Secure Hash Algorithm** (SHA) is based on NIST's **Secure Hash Standard (SHS)**, which can produce hash values that are 224, 256, 384, or 512 bits in length.

The key length and security

In cryptography, the length of keys is not the only factor that indicates its strength or security. While short key means less secure, the same is not true for the reverse; that is, longer keys do not automatically translate into stronger security. The security of an encryption lies in the quality of the encryption algorithm and the entropy of the key.

The entropy of a key in cryptography means the uncertain portions of key combinations. In other words, entropy is related to the randomness of the key combinations. Hence, a 128-bit key may not have 128-bits of entropy. The more the entropy, the stronger the key and it requires more time and computing power to try the combinations.

The summary of encryption types

The following table summarizes the cryptographic algorithms, their key lengths, and other important details pertaining to the encryption types:

Encryption type	Algorithm	Key length	Application(s)
Symmetric key encryption	RC4	40 to 256 bits	Secure Sockets Layer (SSL) Wireless Encryption Privacy (WEP)
	Data Encryption Standard (DES)	Uses up to 56-bit keys and operates on 64 bit blocks	Secure Electronic Transaction (SET) Secure Sockets Layer (SSL) Transport Layer Security (TLS)
	Triple-DES (3DES)	Three 56-bit keys	Secure Electronic Transaction (SET) Secure Sockets Layer (SSL) Transport Layer Security (TLS)
	Advanced Encryption Standard (AES)	128, 192 or 256 bit keys	Secure Electronic Transaction (SET) Secure Sockets Layer (SSL) Transport Layer Security (TLS)

	Blowfish	32 to 448 bits that work on 64 bit blocks	Communication links Embedded file encryption
	Twofish	128, 192 or 256-bit keys on 128-bit blocks	Communication links Embedded file encryption
	International Data Encryption Algorithm (IDEA	128-bit keys on 64-bit blocks	Pretty Good Privacy (PGP)
Asymmetric key encryption	Rivest, Shamir, Adleman (RSA)	Variable key length	Communication links Embedded file encryption
	Diffie-Hellman	Variable key length	Communication links Embedded file encryption
	ElGamel	Variable key length	Secure Sockets layer (SSL)
	Elliptic Curve Cryptography (ECC)	Variable key length	Public Key Cryptography Smart cards
	Digital signature Algorithm (DSA)	Variable key length	Digital Signatures
Hashing	Message Digest Algorithm (MD)	Key not used. 128-bit hash value	For checking integrity of files such as MD5 hash SSL, TLS, IPSec
	Secure hash Algorithm (SHA)	Key not used. 224, 256, 384 or 512 bit hash value	SSL, TLS, IPSec

Applications and the use of cryptography

Cryptographic systems are the common implementations of standard algorithms. They may be used in applications and embedded systems.

The following are some systems that are popular:

- **Transport Layer Security (TLS)** and its predecessor **Secure Sockets Layer** (**SSL**) are protocols that provide communication security by encrypting sessions while using the Internet. They use many of the cryptographic algorithms discussed previously. Some of the activities that can be secured by TLS or SSL are web browsing, e-commerce transactions such as online shopping, banking, and more, and instant messaging or Internet chat.

- **Secure Electronic Transaction (SET)** is a set of standard protocols for securing credit card transactions over insecure networks. SET uses digital certificates and public key cryptography. One of the primary applications is to ensure security while using credit cards over the Internet.

- **IPSec** is a set of protocols to secure Internet communication. Authentication and encryption are the key functions. IPSec is primarily used in the implementation of **Virtual Private Networks** (**VPN**).

- **Pretty Good Privacy (PGP)** was developed by Zimmermann, is a software package that supports secure e-mail communications. Some of the security services provided by PGP include message encryption, digital signatures, data compression, and e-mail compatibility. PGP uses **International Data Encryption Algorithm** (**IDEA**) for encrypting the message and it uses RSA for key exchange and digital signature.

- **Secure Multi-Purpose Internet Mail Extensions** (**S/MIME**) uses public key cryptography to provide authentication for e-mail messages through digital signatures. This system uses encryption for the confidentiality of e-mail messages. This standard defines how both parts of e-mail (header and body) can be constructed. This standard is also called an extended Internet e-mail standard, as it defines the usage of multimedia content, such as picture, sound, video, and so on, in e-mail messages. MIME itself does not provide security. S/MIME is an encryption protocol and provides digital signature capabilities to e-mail messages. **S** here denotes secure.

- **Secure Hypertext Transfer Protocol** (**SHTTP**) is a protocol that introduces an authentication/encryption layer between the **Hyper Text Transfer Protocol** (**HTTP**) and **Transmission Control Protocol** (**TCP**) so as to secure the communications for the **World Wide Web** (**WWW**).

- **Secure Shell** (**SSH**) is a protocol that establishes a secure channel between two computers for communication purposes.

- **Kerberos** is an encryption and authentication service. Kerberos is designed to authenticate network resources and it does not provide any third-party verification (as opposed to digital signatures). Kerberos maintains a centralized server that performs the functions of key distribution and session authentication between two network resources. A single point of compromise would be the Kerberos server itself.
- **Steganography** refers to the art of concealing information within computer files, such as documents, images, or any multimedia content. This is opposed to obscuring information by encryption. Only the sender and receiver can know the presence of the hidden message.
- **Digital Watermarking** is a method by which copyright information is embedded in digital content, such as documents, images, and multimedia files.
- **SecureID** is a two-factor authentication system developed by Security Dynamics. This uses a randomly generated number along with a PIN or password for authentication purposes. This is used in local as well as remote access computers.
- **Wireless Application Protocol** (**WAP**) is a set of standards for wireless communications using devices such as mobile phones. The encryption technology is used in **Wireless Transport Layer Security** (**WTLS**).
- **IEEE 802.11** is a set of standards for **Wireless Local Area Networking (WLAN). Wired Equivalent Privacy (WEP)** and **Wireless (WI-FI) Protected Access** (**WPA**) are the commonly used protocols for encryption in this communication standard.

Public Key Infrastructure (PKI)

PKI is a framework which enables the integration of various services that are related to cryptography.

The aim of PKI is to provide confidentiality, integrity, access control, authentication, and most importantly non-repudiation.

Non-repudiation is a concept or a way to ensure that the sender of a message cannot deny in future the sending of such a message. This is the confirmation of the authenticity of the sender's message. Because it is encrypted with a private key, and only one person has the private key, it has to be this person who sent the message/e-mail. One of the important audit checks for non-repudiation is the time stamp. The time stamp is an audit trail that provides the information on the time the message was sent.

Encryption/decryption, digital signature, and key exchange are the three primary functions of a PKI.

RSS and Elliptic curve algorithms provide all three primary functions; that is, encryption/decryption, digital signature, and key exchange. The Diffie-Hellman algorithm supports key exchange while the **Digital Signature Standard (DSS)** is used in the digital signature.

Public Key Encryption is the encryption methodology used in PKI and was initially proposed by Diffie and Hellman in 1976. The algorithm is based on mathematical functions and it uses asymmetric cryptography; that is, it uses a pair of keys:

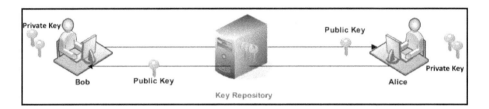

The preceding image represents a simple document-signing function. In PKI, every user will have two keys called a *pair of keys*. One key is called a private key and the other key is called a public key. The private key is never revealed and it is kept with the owner. The public key is accessible by everyone and is stored in a key repository.

A key can be used to encrypt or decrypt a message. The key pairs work together and, based on their function, they can either encrypt or decrypt (not both for the same info/function). Most importantly, a message that is encrypted with a private key can only be decrypted with a corresponding public key and, similarly, a message that is encrypted with a public key can only be decrypted with the corresponding private key.

In the preceding example image, Bob wants to send a confidential document electronically to Alice. Bob has four issues to address before this electronic transmission:

- To ensure that the contents of the document are encrypted such that the document is kept confidential.
- To ensure that the document is not altered during transmission and maintain integrity.
- Since Alice does not know Bob, he has to somehow prove that the document is indeed sent by him; that is, source authenticity.
- To ensure that Bob cannot deny sending it in the future.

PKI supports all four requirements by way of methods such as secure messaging, message digest, digital signature, and non-repudiation services.

Secure messaging

To ensure that the document is protected from eavesdropping and not altered during the transmission, Bob will first encrypt the document using Alice's public key. This ensures two things: one, that the document is encrypted, and two, only Alice can open it as the document requires the private key of Alice to open it. In summary, encryption is done using the public key of the receiver, and the receiver decrypts with his/her private key. In this method, Bob could ensure that the document is encrypted and the intended receiver (Alice) only can open it. However, Bob cannot ensure whether the contents are altered (Integrity) during transmission by just document encryption.

In summary, when confidentiality is required, the sender will use the receiver's public key to encrypt the message body.

Message digest

In order to ensure that the document is not altered during transmission, Bob performs a hash function on the document. The hash value is a computational value based on the contents of the document. This hash value is called **message digest**. By performing the same hash function on the decrypted document, the message digest can be obtained by Alice and she can compare it with the one sent by Bob to ensure that the contents are not altered.

This process will ensure the integrity requirement. However, the hash (message digest) will be encrypted using the public key of the receiver. Otherwise, without encrypting the hash (message digest), a hacker could simply alter the information and recompute a hash for the manipulated data. Because a digital signature is protected by the sender's private key, the encrypted hash could not be recreated.

Digital signature

In order to prove that the document is sent by him to Alice, Bob needs to use a digital signature. **Digital signature** means applying a sender's private key to the message, document, or to the message digest. This process is called **signing**. The message can only be decrypted using the sender's public key:

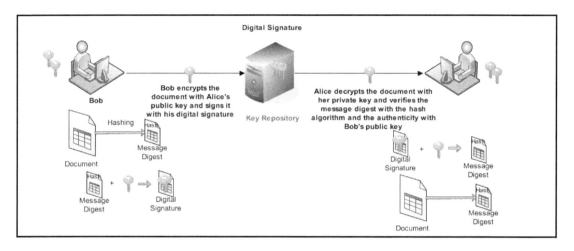

Bob will encrypt the message digest with his private key to create a digital signature. In this scenario, Bob will encrypt the document using Alice's public key and he will digitally sign it using his private key. This ensures that Alice can verify that the document was sent by Bob. She can do so by verifying the digital signature (Bob's private key) using Bob's public key (remember a private key and the corresponding public key are linked, albeit mathematically). She can also verify that the document is not altered by validating the message digest. She can also open the encrypted document using her private key.

 Message authentication is an authenticity verification procedure that facilitates verifying the integrity of the message as well as the authenticity of the source from which the message is received.

The digital certificate

By digitally signing the document, Bob has assured that the document was sent by him to Alice. However, he has not yet proved that he is Bob. To prove this, Bob needs to use a digital certificate. That is, digitally signing with the private key should prove Bob is genuine.

A **digital certificate** is an electronic identity issued to a person, system, or an organization by a competent authority after verifying the credentials of the entity. A digital certificate contains a public key that is unique for each entity. A certification authority issues digital certificates.

In PKI, digital certificates are used for authentic verification of an entity. An entity can be an individual, system, or an organization.

An organization that is involved in issuing, distributing, and revoking digital certificates is known as a **certification authority** (**CA**). A CA acts as a notary by verifying an entity's identity. A Certification Authority is a trusted third party. A CA digitally signs and publishes the public key of the user. This is done using the CA's private key. Hence, the trust of the user relies on the trust of the CA.

One of the important PKI standards pertaining to digital certificates is X.509. This is an **International Telecommunication Union (ITU)** published standard. It specifies, among other things, the standard format for digital certificates.

PKI also provides the key exchange functionality that facilitates a secure exchange of public keys so that authenticity of the parties can be verified. Hence, the significant function is for PKI to be used for the secure exchange of session (symmetric) keys.

Key management techniques

Cryptographic keys go through a life cycle. From the generation of keys, to their safe destruction, keys have to be managed according to the established policies and procedures.

Key management procedures

Key management consists of four essential procedures concerning public and private keys. They are as follows:

1. **Secure generation of keys**: Procedures to ensure that the private and public keys are generated in a secure manner.
2. **Secure storage of keys**: Procedures to ensure that keys are stored securely.
3. **Secure distribution of keys**: Procedures to ensure that keys are not lost or modified during distribution.
4. **Secure destruction of keys**: Procedures to ensure that the keys are destroyed completely once the useful life of the key is over.

Type of keys

NIST Special Publication 800-57, titled **Recommendation for Key Management – Part 1: General**, specifies the following nineteen types of keys:

- **Private signature keys**: They are private keys of public key pairs and are used to generate digital signatures. They are used to provide authentication, integrity, and non-repudiation.
- **Public signature verification key**: This is the public key of the asymmetric (public) key pair. It is used to verify the digital signature.
- **Symmetric authentication keys**: They are used with symmetric key algorithms to provide the assurance of integrity and source of the messages.
- **Private authentication key**: This is the private key of the asymmetric (public) key pair. It is used to provide assurance of the integrity of information.
- **Public authentication key**: This is a public key of an asymmetric (public) pair that is used to determine the integrity of information; and to authenticate the identity of entities.
- **Symmetric data encryption keys**: They are used to apply confidentiality protection of information.
- **Symmetric key wrapping keys**: They are key encryption keys in the sense that they are used to encrypt other symmetric keys.
- **Symmetric and asymmetric random number generation keys**: They are used to generate random numbers.
- **Symmetric master key**: This is a master key that is used to derive other symmetric keys.
- **Private key transport keys**: They are the private keys of asymmetric (public) key pairs that are used to decrypt keys, which have been encrypted with the associated public key.
- **Public key transport keys**: They are the public keys of asymmetric (public) key pairs that are used to decrypt keys that have been encrypted with the associated public key.
- **Symmetric agreement keys**: They are used to establish keys such as key wrapping keys, data encryption keys, and so on using a symmetric key agreement algorithm.
- **Private static key agreement keys**: They are the private keys of asymmetric (public) key pairs that are used to establish keys such as key wrapping keys, data encryption keys, and so on.

- **Public static key agreement key**: They are public keys of asymmetric (public) key pairs that are used to establish keys such as key wrapping keys, data encryption keys, and so on.
- **Private ephemeral key agreement keys**: They are private keys of asymmetric (public) key pairs that are used only once to establish one or more keys such as key wrapping keys, data encryption keys, and so on.
- **Public ephemeral key agreement key**: They are the public keys of asymmetric (public) key pairs that are used in a single key establishment transaction to establish one or more keys.
- **Symmetric authorization keys**: These keys are used to provide privileges to an entity using the symmetric cryptographic method.
- **Private authorization key**: This is a private key of an asymmetric (public) key pair that is used to provide privileges to an entity.
- **Public authorization key**: It is the public key of an asymmetric (public) key pair that is used to verify privileges for an entity that knows the associated private authorization key.

Key management best practices

The following are some of the best practices that are applicable to key management.

Key usage refers to using the key for a cryptographic process. This should be limited to using a single key for only one cryptographic process. This is to ensure that the security provided by the key is not weakened.

When a specific key is authorized for use by legitimate entities for a period of time or if the effect of a specific key for given system is only for a period of time, then the time span is known as a the **crypto period**. The purpose of defining a crypto period is to limit a successful cryptanalysis by a malicious entity.

 Cryptanalysis is the science of analyzing and deciphering codes and ciphers.

The following assurance requirements are a part of the key management process:

- **Integrity protection**: This assures the source and format of the keying material by verification
- **Domain parameter validity**: This assures the parameters used by some public key algorithms during the generation of key pairs and digital signatures and during the generation of shared secrets that are subsequently used to derive keying material
- **Public key validity**: This assures that the public key is arithmetically mathematically correct
- **Private key possession**: This assures that the possession of a private key is obtained before using the public key

The cryptographic algorithm and the **key-size selection** are two important key management parameters that provide adequate protection to the system and data throughout their expected lifetime.

Key states

Cryptographic keys go through different states from their generation to destruction. These states are defined as **key states**. When a cryptographic key moves from one state to another, it is known as **key transition**.

NIST SP800-57 defines the following six key states:

- **The pre-activation state**: The key has been generated, but not yet authorized for use
- **The active state**: The key may be used to cryptographically protect information
- **The deactivated state**: The crypto period of the key is expired, but the key still needs to perform cryptographic operations
- **The destroyed state**: The key is destroyed here
- **The compromised state**: The key is released or determined by an unauthorized entity
- **The destroyed compromised state**: The key is destroyed after a compromise or the compromise is found after the key is destroyed

Key management phases

The key states or transitions can be grouped under four **key management phases**. They are as follows:

- **The pre-operational phase**: The keying material is not yet available for normal cryptographic operations
- **The operational phase**: The keying material is available for normal cryptographic operations and is in use
- **The post-operational phase**: The keying material is no longer in use, but access to the material is possible
- **The destroyed phase**: Keys are no longer available

Cryptanalytic attacks

Cryptanalytic attacks mean compromising keys by way of decipherment to find out the keys. The goal of cryptanalysis is to decipher the private or secret key. The amount of information provided to the analyst as well as the type of information provided determines the type of attacks possible.

The methods of cryptanalytic attacks

The following six are the possible attack scenarios. Candidates are advised to understand the key differences between the different types of attacks:

- **The cipher text only attack**: This refers to the availability of the cipher text (encrypted text) to the cryptanalyst. With large cipher text data, it maybe possible to decipher the cipher text by analyzing the pattern.
- **The known-plain text attack**: When a cryptanalyst obtains cipher text as well as the corresponding plain text, then this type of attack is known as the known-plaintext attack. In this scenario, even if the data is small, it is possible to understand the algorithm.
- **The chosen-plain text attack**: This refers to the availability of corresponding cipher text to the block of plain text chosen by the analyst.
- **The adaptive-chosen-plain text attack**: If the cryptanalyst can choose the samples of plain text based on the results of previous encryptions in a dynamic passion, then this type of cryptanalytic attack is known as an adaptive-chosen-plain text attack.

- **The chosen-cipher text attack**: This is a type of attack used to obtain the plain text by choosing a sample of cipher text.
- **The adaptive-chosen-cipher text attack**: This is similar to the chosen cipher text, but the samples of cipher text are dynamically selected by the cryptanalyst; and the selection can be based on the previous results as well.

Cryptographic standards

Cryptography standards are related to the following:

- Encryption
- Hashing
- Digital signatures
- Public key infrastructure
- Wireless
- Federal standards

We've covered different cryptographic standards pertaining to encryption, hashing, digital signatures, and public key infrastructure in the previous sections. In this section, we'll cover the wireless standards and the Federal standard FIPS-140 for cryptographic modules.

Wireless cryptographic standards

Wireless protocols and services are predominantly governed by IEEE 802.11 standards. These standards are basically for Wireless Local Area Networking (WLAN) for computer communications.

The following are some of the cryptographic standards that are used in WLAN:

Wired Equivalent Privacy (WEP) is an algorithm that uses the stream cipher RC4 encryption standard for confidentiality protection and CRC-32 for integrity assurance. This algorithm is now deprecated as it was breached easily.

Wi-Fi Protected Access (WPA) is a security protocol developed by the Wi-Fi alliance that replaces WEP. This protocol implements majority of the advanced requirements in IEEE802.11i standard released in 2004. WPA is backward compatible with WEP.

WPA2 is an advanced protocol certified by the Wi-Fi alliance. This protocol fulfills the mandatory requirements of IEE 822.11i standard, and it uses the AES algorithm for encryption.

IEEE 802.11 is a set of standards that govern wireless networking transmission methods. IEEE 802.11a, IEEE 802.11b, and 802.11g are different standards based on the throughput or bandwidth and the frequency band.

IEEE 802.11i is an amendment to the original 802.11 standards.

Wi-Fi implementations are based on IEEE standards, an international organization known as, Wi-Fi alliance promotes Wi-Fi standards.

Wi-Fi alliance is a non-profit organization that supports IEEE wireless standards. Here is the information about the Wi-Fi alliance as published on their website.

The Wi-Fi Alliance is a global, non-profit industry association of more than 300 member companies devoted to promoting the growth of Wireless Local Area Networks (WLANs). With the aim of enhancing the user experience for wireless portable, mobile, and home entertainment devices, the Wi-Fi Alliance's testing and certification programs help ensure the interoperability of WLAN products based on the IEEE 802.11 specification.

Bluetooth is a wireless protocol for short-range communications of fixed or portable computers and mobile devices. It uses 2.4GHz short-range radio frequency bandwidth for communication between mobile devices, computers, printers, GPS and more. Bluetooth uses custom block ciphers for confidentiality and authentication.

The Federal Information Processing Standard

We'll cover one of the most important federal standards, titled **Security Requirements for Cryptographic Modules**, FIPS-140 series, in the this section.

As per the published information, the **Federal Information Processing Standards Publication Series of the National Institute of Standards and Technology (NIST)** is the official series of publications relating to standards and guidelines, adopted and promulgated under the provisions of Section 111(d) of the Federal Property and Administrative Services Act of 1949, as amended by the Computer Security Act of 1987, Public Law 100-235. These mandates have given the Secretary of Commerce and NIST important responsibilities for improving the utilization and management of computer and related telecommunications systems in the Federal Government. NIST, through its Computer Systems Laboratory, provides leadership, technical guidance, and coordination of government efforts in the development of standards and guidelines in these areas.

The core structure of FIPS140 recommends four security levels for cryptographic modules that protect sensitive information in federal systems, such as computer and telecommunication systems that include voice systems as well. These levels are qualitative in increasing order-level 1 being the lowest and level 4 the highest.

The following are brief descriptions of the FIPS140 levels:

- **FIPS140 Security Level 1**: This is a basic or the lowest level of security that prescribes basic security requirements for a cryptographic module, such as using at least one approved cryptographic algorithm. This level does not emphasize physical security.
- **FIPS140 Security Level 2**: Tamper evidence mechanisms is the requirement in this level. This enhances the physical security of the device. Tamper-evident seals or coatings should be used to physically protect the device or storage that contains the cryptographic module. This level also emphasizes the implementation of role-based authentication as a minimum requirement.
- **FIPS140 Security Level 3**: The primary requirement is preventing an intruder from gaining access to the cryptographic modules and the **Critical Security Parameters (CSP)** contained within. This level prescribes high probability of detection and response mechanisms for physical attacks. This level emphasizes identity-based authentication.

- **FIPS140 Security Level 4**: This is the highest level and physical security mechanisms provide a complete envelope of protection around the cryptographic module with the intent of detecting and responding to all unauthorized attempts at physical access. This level requires a two-factor authentication. This level also requires the control of environmental conditions, such as preventing damage to cryptographic modules due to temperature, heat, and voltage.

Summary

This chapter has covered foundational concepts in Cryptography. In a nutshell, cryptography is an art and science to conceal information. Encryption methods are used to ensure the confidentiality of information as well as authenticity verification. Additionally, hashing methods are used to ensure the integrity of the information. Public key cryptography and public key infrastructure provide methods to assure confidentiality, integrity, source authentication, and non-repudiation during digital communications. Cryptanalysis consists of methods used to validate the strength and security of cryptographic algorithms and keys.

In the next two chapters, we will cover Communication and Network security, which forms the basis for the selection and implementation of technical and administrative controls for networked communication systems.

Sample questions

Q1. Cryptographic algorithms would include all of the these *except?*

1. Data Encryption Standard
2. Advanced Encryption Standard
3. Transport Layer Security
4. Message Digest Algorithm

Q2. Which one of the following is called a crypto variable?

1. Plain Text
2. Cipher Text
3. Cipher
4. Cryptographic Key

Q3. Identify the *best* explanation from the following for a digital signature?

1. Applying senders private key to the message
2. Applying senders public key to the message
3. Applying receivers private key to the message
4. Applying receivers public key to the message

Q4. When a specific key is authorized for use by legitimate entities, and that usage is based on time, it is known as what?

1. Cryptanalysis
2. Cryptography
3. Crypto period
4. Key usage

Q5. Which one of the following is a type of cryptanalytic attack?

1. Chosen image
2. Chosen plaintext
3. Adaptive image parameter
4. Adaptive plain-cipher text

Q6. Which one of the following is an application of IPSec?

1. Wireless Application Protocol
2. Virtual Private Networking
3. S/MIME
4. Social engineering

Q7. An image file downloaded from the Internet conceals a secret code. Such a method of concealing information is known as what?

1. Message hiding
2. Message docking
3. Steganography
4. Watermarking

Q8. A birthday attack is a cryptographic attack and is used to guess a random input data. Which one of the following mathematical probability theories provides basis for such an attack?

1. There is a chance that more than 50% of randomly chosen people in a group of 23 may have the same birthday
2. There is a chance that less than 50% of randomly chosen people in a group of 23 may have the same birthday
3. There is a chance that 50% of randomly chosen people in a group of 23 may have the same birthday
4. There is a chance that more than 80% of randomly chosen people in a group of 23 may have the same birthday

Q9. Which of the following encryption standards is proposed as an official successor of the Data Encryption Standard (DES)?

1. Triple-DES
2. Advance Encryption Standard (AES)
3. Blowfish
4. Twofish

Q10. Which of the following choices are true statements pertaining to cryptographic algorithms?

Encryption and decryption are based on algorithms

An algorithm is called as cipher

An algorithm is a series of well-defined steps

An algorithm defines procedure for encryption and decryption

Drag and drop
your answers here

8

Day 8 – Communication and Network Security - Network Security

This and the next chapter will cover foundational concepts in network architecture and network security. IP and non-IP protocols, their application, threats, attacks, vulnerabilities, and countermeasures are covered with suitable examples. Wireless networks and the security requirements are also covered. The application of cryptography in communication security is covered with illustrations. Concepts related to securing network components are also covered.

An overview of communication and network security

The communication and network security domain deals with the security of voice and data communications through local area, wide area, and remote access networking. The focus here is to understand the networking models, such as Open System Interconnect (OSI) and TCP/IP as well as the security mechanisms for Internet/Intranet/Extranet, such as firewalls, routers, and intrusion detection/protection systems. Candidates are expected to have knowledge in the areas of secure communications, securing networks, threats, vulnerabilities, attacks, and countermeasures to communication networks and protocols that are used in remote access.

Observe the following illustration. It gives an overview of communication and network security in the entity-relationship model, and it represents the topics covered in this chapter:

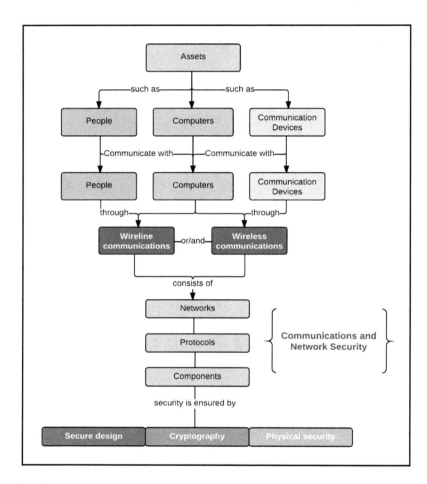

The following bullet points represent a brief overview of the preceding diagram. These points explain the overall structure of this chapter in a logical sequence:

- Applying secure design principles to network architecture
- Understanding IP and non-IP protocols and security weaknesses
- Understanding wireless networks and security requirements

- Getting an overview of application of cryptography in communication security
- Understanding the security requirements in network components

Network architecture, protocols, and technologies

Security in communication and networks is based on the architecture type, protocols, and the technologies used. Secure network design forms the baseline for the network's resilience against attacks. Generally, network architecture consists of layered independent communication channels. Security has to be understood and applied in each and every layer for an overall communication and network protection. In a nutshell, networks are architected like roads, and protocols are architected like cars. Each car can be different but must follow constraints of the roads.

Layered architecture

Layered architecture is a technique that is used to design communication networking in the form of layers. Each layer is independent and communicates with its immediate upper and lower layers. This technique allows the isolation of network components without affecting others in other layers.

Open System Interconnect (OSI) model

Open System Interconnect (**OSI**) is an International Organization for Standardization (ISO) layered architecture standard that defines a framework for implementing protocols in seven layers.

A **protocol** is a communication standard that defines rules pertaining to syntax, semantics, and synchronization for communications.

The seven layers in the OSI model are represented as a top-down list in the following illustration:

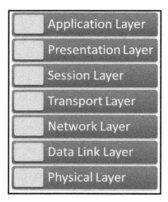

Layers 7, 6, 5, and 4 work at the host (computer) level and are sometimes called **host layers**, whereas layers 3, 2, and 1 are related to transmission through the media and are called **media layers**:

- **Layer 7**: This is the **application layer** that provides application services that are required for application processes. Interaction between the user and the host application is facilitated in this layer. All functionalities in this layer are oriented toward applications.
- **Layer 6**: This is the **presentation layer** that manages the way information or data is encoded or represented. Hence, this layer transforms the data for applications.
- **Layer 5**: This is the **session layer**, and the primary purpose of this layer is to manage communications between two computers.
- **Layer 4**: This is used to maintain the integrity and validity of the data that is being transported, and it is known as the **transport layer**.
- **Layer 3**: This is called the **network layer**, and it ensures that the proper route is established for transporting the data.
- **Layer 2**: This is the **data link layer** that ensures node-to-node validity of the data that is being transmitted.
- **Layer 1**: This deals with electrical and mechanical characteristics of the data and is called the **physical layer**.

OSI mnemonics are used to remember the order of the seven layers. The following are a couple of the most popular OSI mnemonics:

- **Top to bottom**: **A**ll **P**eople **S**eem **T**o **N**eed **D**ata **P**rocessing
- **Bottom to top**: **P**lease **D**o **N**ot **T**ake **S**ales People's **A**dvice

Transmission Control Protocol / Internet Protocol (TCP/IP)

Transmission Control Protocol / Internet Protocol (TCP/IP) is an **Internet Protocol** suite on which most of the Internet and commercial networks run. There are two important protocols in it, Transmission Control Protocol (TCP) and Internet Protocol (IP) based on which this suite is named.

The original TCP/IP reference model consists of four layers that are purely related to Internet communications. These four layers are the application layer, the transport layer, the network/internet layer, and the data link layer.

The following diagram illustrates the four-layered TCP/IP model:

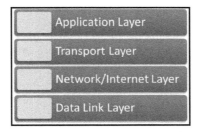

OSI layers and security

The upcoming section covers some important protocols in OSI layers. Application layer protocols, presentation layer protocols, session layer protocols, and their security are covered in this chapter. The remaining layers are covered in the next chapter.

This section also gives an overview of security weaknesses in such layer/protocols as well as security measures to mitigate such weaknesses.

Application layer protocols and security

In the application layer, some of the important protocols are **Domain Name System (DNS)**, **Dynamic Host Configuration Protocol (DHCP)**, **Hyper Text Transfer Protocol (HTTP)**, **File Transfer Protocol (FTP)**, **TELNET**, **Post Office Protocol (POP3)**, **Internet Message Access Protocol (IMAP)**, **Simple Mail Transfer Protocol (SMTP)**, and **Simple Network Management Protocol (SNMP)**.

Domain Name System (DNS)

DNS works at the application layer. DNS translates domain names into IP addresses. DNS's main purpose is to resolve host names to matching numeric IP addresses, as well as maintaining resource records for e-mail and other services where end-to-end delivery needs to be assured.

Threats, attacks, and countermeasures

A common threat to DNS is **spoofing**. It is a terminology used in computer security to refer to the successful masquerading of one entity as another. An entity can be a person or program. Masquerading refers to disguising, impersonating, or masking.

Many spoofing attacks exist. Some of them are as follows:

- **Man-in-the-Middle-Attack**: This refers to spoofing the systems in order to listen to the network traffic between two computers and capture data packets. In other words, attackers insert themselves in the communication path between hosts.
- **URL spoofing**: Uniform Resource Locator (URL) is the method by which a web page or website is identified by the browser. This is also called the website or webpage address. In URL spoofing, a web browser is led to believe that it is accessing the requested legitimate website. However, the browser accesses the attacker-directed website due to spoofing.
- **Phishing**: This is a spoofing technique used by fraudsters to capture sensitive information, such as user name, password, credit card details, and more. In Phishing, URL spoofing is used to redirect a user to the attacker-constructed illegitimate website, and e-mail spoofing is used to lure the user to open an illegitimate spoofed URL.
- **E-mail spoofing**: This is a technique used to masquerade as a legitimate source address (such as a bank) of the e-mail. Due to this, the user is led to believe that the e-mail is from a trusted source.

- **SMS spoofing**: This is similar to e-mail spoofing, but in this case, the mobile number of the source is masqueraded by a malicious entity to send a spoofed text message.
- **DNS cache poisoning**: This relates to altering the DNS cache data with illegitimate entries. A cache data is the information stored in the host memory. Since DNS resolves IP addresses, a poisoned data would redirect a legitimate address request to an illegitimate address.

Countermeasures provide methods to address security threats. A countermeasure can be a technical solution or a kind of best practice. Some of the countermeasures for the common security threats and attacks include.

Domain Name System Security Extensions (DNSSEC): They are a set of extensions that provide origin authentication, data integrity, and the authenticated denial of existence. The primary purpose of DNSSEC is to prevent Zone Enumeration.

Zone enumeration: The practice of discovering the full content of a zone via successive queries. Zone enumeration was non-trivial prior to the introduction of DNSSEC.

Source: RFC5155 – DNS Security (DNSSEC) Hashed Authenticated Denial of Existence

Dynamic Host Configuration Protocol (DHCP)

In an Internet Protocol (IP) network, client devices obtain necessary network parameters from a centralized server(s) using this protocol. One of the primary parameters obtained is the IP address itself. DHCP helps in reducing manual configurations.

DHCP is primarily used for assigning IP addresses to servers and clients. This protocol also uses **Point-to-Point Protocol (PPP)** and **Network Address Translation (NAT)** for assigning IP addresses to on-demand hosts such as dialup and broadband.

The IP address allocation is either automatic or manual depending upon the level of user intervention required. The address allocation method used is called as **Discover, Offer, Request, Acknowledge (DORA)**.

Threats, vulnerabilities, attacks, and countermeasures

This protocol has similar threats as DNS, such as cache poisoning and masquerading.

Vulnerabilities are generally in the form of misconfigured DHCP and DNS server (misconfiguration), and lack of session authentication and encryption.

Few unique attacks exist in the protocol such as birthday attack and DNS forgery:

- **Birthday attack**: This is a cryptographic attack to guess a random input data. It works on a mathematical probability theory that there is a chance that more than 50% of randomly chosen people in a group of 23 may have the same birthday. The probability increases to 99% when the group is more than 57.
- DHCP exhaustion due to DOS attacks or Man-in-the-Middle-Attacks to access alt gateways.
- **DNS Forgery**: This is a type of DNS cache poisoning. Countermeasures for the preceding security threats, vulnerabilities, or attacks include:
- **Transport Layer Security** (**TLS**) and **Secure Sockets Layer** (**SSL**): These are cryptographic protocols. The purpose of these protocols is to provide a secure communication by way of encryption.
- **Secure Shell** (**SSH**): This is a network protocol that facilitates secure encrypted communications between two computers.
- **Digital Signature**: This is used in a public key cryptography where the message is digitally signed using the sender's private key. The purpose here is to authenticate the sender.

Hyper Text Transfer Protocol (HTTP)

The Internet web pages on the World Wide Web (WWW) are coded in the Hyper Text Markup Language (HTML). HTTP is a communication protocol that enables retrieval and transfer of hypertext pages. HTTP uses Transmission Control Protocol (TCP) for connections.

HTTP works in the application layer of the TCP/IP model, and HTTP is the default protocol for serving web pages. Hence, the primary delivery mechanisms for web pages use this protocol.

Threats, vulnerabilities, attacks, and countermeasures

Some of the common threats for HTTP include spoofing, unauthorized disclosure, and path traversal; and vulnerabilities include weaknesses in coding header information and weak encoding of get methods.

Path traversal: This relates to unauthorized access to the web server directory structure. Generally, the server should return an HTTP web page; instead of this, the directory structure is revealed.

DNS spoofing attacks exist for HTTP as well. Besides attacks such as Denial-of-Service (DoS) and Eavesdropping are also popular attacks to HTTP.

 Eavesdropping is a type of attack, and it is used to listen to the communication between the client and the server in a surreptitious manner.

Countermeasures include strict validation techniques and using HTTPS protocol during sensitive information transmission. For example, **Secure Hyper Text Transfer Protocol (S-HTTP or HTTPS)** uses **Secure Sockets Layer (SSL)** for encrypting the session between the server and the client.

FTP and TELNET

FTP is a network protocol and is used to transfer files from one computer to another over a TCP/IP network. The main application of FTP is to transfer files between computers. FTP is not suitable for executing programs in the target servers.

TELNET stands for TELecommunication NETwork and is used to access remote computer resources using a communication shell. The purpose of TELNET is to log into the remote server and perform maintenance works in the system from a remote location.

Threats, vulnerabilities, attacks, and countermeasures

Some of the common threats for FTP and TELNET include unauthorized data capture including the password capture. Vulnerabilities that aid such a threat include sending passwords in clear text as well as the clear text transmission of sensitive information.

Similar to HTTP, eavesdropping attacks are possible on FTP and TELNET. Sniffing is another common attack on these protocols.

 Sniffing is used to capture the data that flows through the network and analyze it in order to obtaining sensitive information.

Adapting to Secure File Transfer Protocol (SFTP) and using Secure Shell (SSH) for sensitive information transmission will act as a countermeasure to such attacks. Hence, countermeasures are using SFTP instead of FTP and using SSH instead of TELNET.

 Secure File Transfer Protocol (SFTP) uses SSH for transmitting the files and session data. This ensures that the session is encrypted end to end.

Post Office Protocol (POP3) and Internet Message Access Protocol (IMAP)

POP3 and IMAP protocols are used to retrieve e-mails from the e-mail servers over the TCP/IP connection.

The POP3 protocol is used by e-mail clients to download e-mail messages from the remote e-mail server. Unless configured, this protocol is designed to delete the e-mails after download.

IMAP is used to view the e-mail messages in the server. Unless offline mode is enabled, the messages are not stored in the local machine, and the messages in the server are not deleted.

Threats, vulnerabilities, attacks, and countermeasures

Some of the common threats to POP3 and IMAP include the non-delivery of e-mails and Unsolicited Commercial E-mail (UCE), which is popularly known as SPAM. Vulnerabilities are generally related to the misconfiguration of the e-mail servers.

 Unsolicited Commercial E-mail (UCE) is also known as **spam**. Due to vulnerabilities in Mail Transport Agents (MTA), a commercial mail that is spam is relayed to many e-mail accounts.

Attacks include e-mail relay and spoofing. Countermeasures are implementing strong authentication such as two-factor solutions as well as source-verification methods.

Simple Network Management Protocol (SNMP)

As the name implies, this network protocol is used for managing administrative tasks in the network. Managing the uptime of the network, network query, and measuring throughput are some of the primary applications of this protocol/service

Threats, vulnerabilities, attacks, and countermeasures

Some of the common threats to SNMP include unauthorized data capture and the disclosure of sensitive information such as community strings. Vulnerabilities are related to the misconfiguration of SNMP servers and using default values for community strings and other data.

Common attacks to SNMP include packet sniffing, brute force and dictionary attacks, as well as IP spoofing.

 Brute force and **dictionary attacks** use a combination of words in dictionary and numeric and special characters to crack the encrypted password hashes.

Enforcing stronger passwords and a secure configuration of servers are some of the countermeasures for such attacks. Using SNMP3 is also a countermeasure as this version addresses many of the security issues.

Presentation layer protocols and security

In the presentation layer, some of the important protocols are **Multi-Purpose Mail Extensions (MIME), Secure Shell (SSH),** and **Transport Layer Security (TLS).**

 In the TCP/IP reference model, the preceding protocols are grouped under the application layer. TCP/IP combines the application, presentation and session layers into a single layer as the application layer.

Transport Layer Security (TLS) and Secure Sockets Layer (SSL)

TLS is used to ensure the confidentiality and integrity of data while being transmitted. SSL is a predecessor of TLS. This protocol is used in encrypting sessions and transported data. Both these protocols are cryptographic protocols.

Threats, vulnerabilities, attacks, and countermeasures

The most common threat for TLS and SSL is unauthorized information access, and software vulnerabilities help such threats to materialize.

A common attack is the replay attack. It uses a session or data capture to replay the data to the server such that a software vulnerability can be exploited to gain unauthorized access to the system or data.

Validating the session data and source authenticity verification are some of the common countermeasures against Replay attacks.

Session layer protocols and security

Session layer sockets are primarily used for a session establishment of protocols, such as TCP. This layer is responsible for a session between applications. Some of the functions pertaining to sessions include the opening/closing of connections, maintaining the sessions, and managing request/response mechanisms between end-user applications.

Some of the important protocols in this layer are **Network Basic Input Output System (NetBIOS)**, **Network File System (NFS)**, and **Server Message Block (SMB)**.

Threats, vulnerabilities, attacks, and countermeasures

The most common threats for the session layer are hijacking and unauthorized information disclosure.

There are many vulnerabilities that are present in the session layer protocols. Weaknesses in session management and weak access mechanisms are common vulnerabilities of the same.

A common attack is session hijacking. Specifically, when NetBIOS is used over TCP/IP, attacks on the vulnerabilities will allow the exposure of a network or file share information to the attackers.

SMB signing and limiting NetBIOS to intranet are some of the countermeasures for the attacks.

Summary

In this chapter, we covered some of the concepts in telecommunications and the network security domain.

We've revised Open System Interconnect (OSI) and the TCP/IP protocol suite. OSI forms the baseline for other models such as TCP/IP. There are seven layers in an OSI model, with the layers stacked. Each layer has a communication mechanism using protocols. A protocol or an implementation of it may have vulnerabilities that can be exploited by threat agents. Countermeasures have to applied to improve the security.

In the next chapter, we will cover the next four layers in the OSI model, the application of cryptography in communication security, and concepts related to securing network components.

Sample questions

Q1. Media Access Control (MAC) is a:

1. Addressing scheme
2. Internet protocol
3. Hardware model
4. Network Interface card address

Q2. A protocol is a:

1. Data Encryption Standard
2. Layered architecture
3. Communication standard
4. Data link

Q3. Spoofing is a type of:

1. Vulnerability
2. Masquerading
3. Protocol
4. Layer in a TCP/IP model

Q4. The purpose of using Secure Shell (SSH) over TELNET is:

    1. SSH provides shell access to the target system
    2. SSH is faster than Telnet
    3. SSH encrypts the session and Telnet does not encrypt the session
    4. SSH is less expensive than Telnet

Q5. An attack is a:

    1. Threat
    2. Vulnerability
    3. Technique
    4. Protocol

Q6. Transport Layer Security and Secure Sockets Layer are *not:*

    1. Protocols
    2. Use cryptographic algorithms
    3. Vulnerability Use encryption

Q7. Replay attacks are used to:

    1. Gain unauthorized access to the application systems
    2. Resolve domain names
    3. Break cryptographic keys
    4. Setup secure connections

9

Day 9 – Communication and Network Security - Communication Security

This chapter covers foundational concepts in the communication security domain. Security in communication channels—security requirements in voice, data, multimedia, and remote access—and virtualized networks are covered. An overview of attacks on communication networks, prevention and mitigation of such attacks, including widely used security controls, is also covered.

An overview of communication security

Communication and the network security domain deals with the security of voice and data communications through local area, Wide area, and Remote access networking. Candidates are expected to have knowledge in the areas of secure communications: securing networks, threats, vulnerabilities, attacks, and countermeasures to the communication networks and protocols that are used in remote access.

Observe the following illustration. We have already covered the application, presentation, and session layer in the OSI model. In this chapter, we will cover transport, networks, data links, and the physical layers of the OSI model:

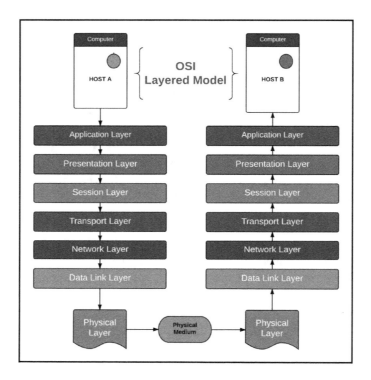

Transport layer protocols and security

Transport layer does two things. One is to package the data given out by applications to a format that is suitable for transport over the network, and the other thing is to unpack the data received from the network and then format it suitable for applications.

In the transport layer, some of the important protocols are **Transmission Control Protocol (TCP)**, **User Datagram Protocol (UDP)**, **Stream Control Transmission Protocol (SCTP)**, **Datagram Congestion Control Protocol (DCCP)**, and **Fiber Channel Protocol (FCP)**.

The process of packaging the data packets received from the applications is called **encapsulation**, and the output of such a process is called a **datagram**.

Similarly, the process of unpacking the datagram received from the network is called **decapstulation**.

When moving from layer 7 down to 4, when the layer 4 header is placed on the *data*, it becomes a *datagram*. When the datagram is encapsulated with a layer 3 header, it becomes a *packet*; the packet encapsulated becomes a *frame*, and it is put on the wire as *bits*.

The upcoming section describes some of the important protocols in this layer along with the security concerns and their countermeasures.

Transmission Control Protocol (TCP)

This is a core Internet protocol that provides reliable delivery mechanisms over the Internet. TCP is a connection-oriented protocol. A protocol that guarantees delivery of datagram (packets) to the destination application by way of a suitable mechanism (for example, a three-way handshake of SYN, SYN-ACK, and ACK in TCP) is called a **connection-oriented protocol**. The reliability of the datagram delivery of such a protocol is high due to the acknowledgment part of the receiver.

This protocol has two primary functions. The primary function of TCP is the transmission of datagrams between applications; and the secondary one is in terms of the controls that are necessary to ensure reliable transmission.

Applications where the delivery needs to be assured, such as e-mail, World Wide Web (WWW), file transfer and more, use TCP for transmission

Threats, vulnerabilities, attacks, and countermeasures

One of the common threats to TCP is a service disruption. A common vulnerability is half-open connections exhausting the server resources.

Denial of service attacks, such as TCP SYN attacks as well as connection hijacking as IP Spoofing attacks, are also possible.

A[1] half-open connection is a vulnerability in the TCP implementation. As discussed earlier, TCP uses a three-way handshake to establish or terminate connections. Refer to the following illustration:

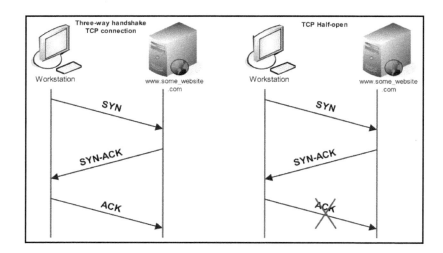

In a three-way handshake, first the client (workstation) sends a request to the server (for example, `www.some_website.com`). This is called an **SYN request**. The server acknowledges the request by sending a SYN-ACK, and in the process, it creates a buffer for this connection. The client does a final acknowledgement by ACK. TCP requires this setup, since the protocol needs to ensure the reliability of the packet delivery.

If the client does not send the final ACK, then the connection is called **half open**. Since the server has created a buffer for this connection, a certain amount of memory or server resource is consumed. If thousands of such half-open connections are created maliciously, then the server resources may be completely consumed, resulting in Denial-of-Service to legitimate requests.

TCP **SYN attacks** technically establish thousands of half-open connections to consume the server resources. There are two actions that an attacker might perform. One is that the attacker or malicious software will send thousands of SYN attacks to the server and withheld ACK. This is called **SYN flooding**. Depending on the capacity of the network bandwidth and server resources, in a span of time, the entire resources will be consumed, resulting in denial-of-service. If the source IP were blocked by some means, then the attacker or the malicious software would try to spoof the source IP addresses to continue the attack. This is called **SYN spoofing**.

SYN attacks, such as SYN flooding and SYN spoofing, can be controlled using **SYN cookies** with cryptographic hash functions. In this method, the server does not create the connection at the SYN-ACK stage. The server creates a cookie with the computed hash of the source IP address, source port, destination IP, destination port, and some random values based on an algorithm. Then, the source sends it as SYN-ACK. When the server receives an ACK, it checks the details and creates the connection.

 A **cookie** is a piece of information that is usually in the form of a text file sent by the server to the client. Cookies are generally stored in client computers and are used for purposes such as authentication, session tracking, and management.

User Datagram Protocol (UDP)

UDP is a connectionless protocol and is similar to TCP. However, UDP does not provide the delivery guarantee of data packets. A protocol that does not guarantee the delivery of datagram (packets) to the destination is called a **connectionless protocol**. In other words, the final acknowledgment is not mandatory in UDP.

UDP uses one-way communication. The speed of the delivery of the datagram by UDP is high. UDP is predominantly used where a loss of intermittent packets is acceptable, such as with video or audio streaming.

Threats, vulnerabilities, attacks, and countermeasures

Service disruptions are common threats, and validation weaknesses facilitate such threats.

UDP flood attacks cause service disruptions; and controlling the UDP packet size acts as a countermeasure to such attacks.

Internet Control Message Protocol (ICMP)

ICMP is used to discover service availability in network devices or servers. ICMP expects response messages from devices or systems to confirm the service availability.

Threats, vulnerabilities, attacks, and countermeasures

Service disruptions are common threats. Validation weaknesses facilitate such threats.

ICMP flood attacks, such as the Ping of Death, causes these service disruptions; and controlling ICMP packet size acts as a countermeasure to such attacks.

Pinging is a process of sending an **Internet Control Message Protocol** (**ICMP**) ECHO_REQUEST message to servers or hosts to check whether they are up and running. In this process, a server or host on a network responds to a ping request, and such a response is called an echo. **Ping of death** refers to sending large numbers of ICMP packets to the server to crash the system.

Other protocols in the transport layer

- **Stream Control Transmission Protocol** (**SCTP**): This is a connection-oriented protocol similar to TCP, but it provides facilities such as multi-streaming and multi-homing for better performance and redundancy. It is used in UNIX-like operating systems.

- **Datagram Congestion Control Protocol** (**DCCP**): As the name implies, this is a transport layer protocol that is used for congestion control. Applications here include Internet telephony and video/audio streaming over the network.

- **Fiber Channel Protocol** (**FCP**): This protocol is used in high-speed networking. One of the prominent applications is Storage Area Network (SAN).

Storage Area Network (**SAN**) is a network architecture used to attach remote storage devices, such as tape drives, disk arrays, and more, to the local server. This facilitates using storage devices as if they are local devices.

The network layer protocols and security

The Network or Internet layer in the TCP/IP model is used for internetworking. This layer has a group of methods, functions, and protocols to facilitate communication between different networks. In this layer, communication between networks is achieved through mechanisms called **gateways**.

In the Network layer, some of the important protocols are Internet Protocol (IP), Internet Communication Message Protocol (ICMP), Internet Group Management Protocol (IGMP), and Internet Protocol security (IPsec).

Protocols in this layer carry out the following functions:

- Passing the outgoing packets through gateways to the next layer (the data link layer)
- Passing the incoming packets to the transport layer
- Providing error detection and diagnostics for incoming and outgoing packets

Internet Protocol (IP)

IP is a connectionless protocol and is used in packet-switched networks such as the Internet. The primary function of this protocol is to send data from one computer to another. IP works in the network layer of OSI and the Internet layer of the TCP/IP model.

The primary function of this layer is to send data packets across the network to the destination computer. The computers, in such networks, are called hosts. IP tries the best effort method of delivery for packets, but it does not guarantee it. Transmission Control Protocol (TCP) manages the reliability of the transmission.

Two versions are being used in the Internet. One is Internet Protocol version 4 (IPv4) and the other is Internet Protocol version 6 (IPv6).

Threats, vulnerabilities, attacks, and countermeasures

Some of the common threats in this layer are the non-delivery of packets or some corrupted data. Vulnerabilities that these threats could exploit include lack of validation mechanisms and a lack of sequencing procedures and processes.

The most common attack on this layer is data theft. Information or data packets can be captured during transmission and decoded. Unauthorized access and privilege escalation entry points are possible in this layer.

Countermeasures is by way of using appropriate security features in Transmission Control Protocol, Address Resolution Protocols (ARP), IPv6 security controls, and most importantly Internet Protocol Security (IPSec).

 Internet Protocol version 4 (IPv4) is a widely deployed protocol on the Internet. As the name implies, it is the fourth iteration of the protocol. It uses 32 bits for the length of the address and is limited to 2^{32} addresses. The number of publicly available IPv4 addresses is more or less consumed, and the Internet is moving toward IPv6.

Internet Protocol version 6 (IPv6) is designed as a successor to the IPv4 address space. This protocol uses 128 bits for the IP addresses and has an address space of 2^{128} IP addresses.

IPsec protocols

IPsec is a suit of protocols that is created to secure Internet Protocols (IP). They provide authentication, integrity, and encryption functions. Compared to the upper-layer security protocols, such as SSL or TLS, IPsec is an independent application, and it can be used to protect the application and transport layer protocols as a whole.

IPsec uses the following three protocols for various security functions:

- **Internet Key Exchange (IKE)**: This is used to negotiate protocols, algorithms, and generate keys for encryption and authentication
- **Authentication Header (AH)**: This is used to provide the data origin authentication to datagrams and integrity assurance
- **Encapsulation Security Payload (ESP)**: This is used to support encryption-only and authentication-only configurations

Threats, vulnerabilities, attacks, and countermeasures

Threats such as spoofing and unauthorized connections materialize due to weak authentication and a lack of connection checks in this protocol. Such vulnerabilities are exploited through Man-in-the-Middle attacks. These attacks can be countered by proper IPsec policies and by deploying additional IPsec connection checks. Using Virtual Private Networks (VPN) enables a secure communication in this layer.

 Virtual Private Network (VPN) is a virtual network that is set up to use a larger public network, such as the Internet. VPN uses a concept called tunneling to route the data, and IPsec protocols are used for an end-to-end encryption.
A **tunnel** in a computer network, such as VPN, is a secure path, or route for the datagram to pass through an insecure or un-trusted network. Protocols such as IPsec, Point-to-Point Tunneling Protocol (PPTP), and Layer2 Tunneling Protocol (L2TP) are some of the examples of **tunneling protocols**.

Data link layer protocols and security

The methods, protocols, and specifications that are used to link hosts or nodes in a network are grouped as a data link layer. The link layer operates close to the physical layer components.

In data link layer some of the important protocols are **Point-to-Point Protocol** (PPP), **Address Resolution Protocol** (ARP), and **Serial Line Internet Protocol** (SLIP). Fiber channel and Ethernet also work in this layer.

Link layer protocols

The following protocols operate on the link layer:

- **Address Resolution Protocol** (ARP): This is used to resolve the hardware address (Layer 2, MAC address, 48 bits, 12 HEX characters) for a given IP address
- **Reverse Address Resolution Protocol** (RARP): This is used to obtain IP addresses based on the hardware address
- **Neighbor Discovery Protocol** (NDP): This is used to find neighbor nodes in an IPv6 network

Address Resolution Protocol (ARP)

This protocol is a standard method of finding hardware addresses from network layer addresses, such as **Internet Protocol (IP)**. The primary application of ARP is to translate IP addresses to ethernet **Media Access Control (MAC)** addresses.

The primary purpose of this protocol is to resolve hardware addresses such that communication can be established between two computers within the same network or over the Internet. This is necessary because as you go down the OSI model stack from 7 -> 1, you know that IP address 1 is trying to send to IP address 2. But to encapsulate this at layer 2, you need to know the MAC address of IP address 2.

Threats, vulnerabilities, attacks, and countermeasures

Some of the common threats in this layer include sniffing and spoofing. Unsolicited ARP reply is a common vulnerability. Attacks such as ARP poisoning, ARP poison routing, and Denial-f-Service (DOS) are prevalent in this layer. Countermeasures include MAC to IP-mapping processes.

ARP poisoning refers to overwriting the existing entry in the ARP table with a malicious address. The primary purpose of this is to perform a MIIM attack.

Media Access Control (MAC) is a unique hardware address that is assigned to **Network Interface Cards** (**NIC**) or network adapters.

Border Gateway Protocol

This is a type of *routing protocol* that is being used on the Internet. The primary purpose is to decentralize the Internet routing. **Internet Service Providers** (**ISP**) predominantly use this protocol for routing the data and information between them.

Routing protocols exist so that routers can *tell* each other about the routes they own (otherwise, having to manually insert routes in *ever* router for EVERY network, that is static routes). Interior routing protocols called RIP, OSPF, EIGRP, and ISIS are used inside the organizations. They are fast but don't scale to the Internet size. Exterior protocols, such as BGP, are used to *tell* backbone routers where all the routes on the Internet are. BGP is very slow, but it can obviously scale to the entire Internet.

Threats, vulnerabilities, attacks, and countermeasures

Some of the common threats include the misuse of network resources, network congestion, packet delays, and the violation of local routing policies. Another issue with BGP is that it advertises networks that are not its own.

Vulnerabilities that help these threats to materialize include misconfigured routers and software flaws. Such vulnerabilities are exploited through spoofing and message-injection attacks.

Message or **data injection** refers to injecting arbitrary code into the system. This is to compromise input validation techniques.

Multi Protocol Label Switching (**MPLS**) is often referred to as layer 2.5 protocol, as it lies between layer 2 and 3 of the OSI model. It provides more reliability and support for T1, ATM, the Frame relay, and DSL.

Ethernet

This is a family of frame-based networking technologies that is used in **Local Area Network** (**LAN**). Ethernet operates in the Link layer as well as the Physical layer of the TCP/IP model. Ethernet initially used coaxial cables for networking. However, the present-day technologies include switches and twisted pair cabling.

Present-day switches can provide layer 3 functions such as support for routing protocols as well.

Ethernet technologies have predominantly replaced other LAN standards such as token ring, FDDI, and ARC net.

Threats, vulnerabilities, attacks, and countermeasures

Threats in this layer include spoofing, while a common vulnerability is the reuse of frame buffers. Attacks such as eavesdropping and Denial of Service (DOS) are possible due to the vulnerabilities. Segmentation, filtering, and encryption methods act as countermeasures to such attacks.

The physical layer and security

The physical layer is the lowest layer in the OSI stack. It is concerned with the transmission of bits from one computer to another. The components in the physical layer are concerned with a physical connection between the computers. The transmission and receiving of signals in bit stream is the primary function.

Some of the important components in this layer include RS-232, RJ45, and 802.11a/b/g/n, Universal Serial Bus (USB), and Bluetooth.

Security in the physical layer is predominantly used to deal with physical disconnections, damage of the physical components, and theft.

Security in communication channels

Communication channels facilitate the transmission of information across users or devices. The increasing adoption of mobile communication systems with smart technologies have blurred the isolation of communication and computing devices to Unified Information and Communication systems. This rapid progression and unification of communication and computing technologies have also opened multiple vectors for attacks, numerous threats, and vulnerabilities. Hence, it is essential for a security professional to understand and apply suitable security controls to address modern-day threats and vulnerabilities in communication technologies, such as voice, multimedia, remote access, data communications, mobile communications, and virtualized networks.

Security requirements in voice, multimedia, remote access, data communications, and virtualized networks

In **Information and Communication Technology** (**ICT**), which is a convergence of data communication and voice communication technologies, security requirements focus primarily on data integrity, service availability, and identity assurance. The traditional circuit-based telephony networks are being rapidly replaced with packet-switching-based data networks. Thus, end-to-end protection for devices, communication channels, and operator networks from unauthorized access and compromise from external networks become a priority requirement while designing and implementing communication networks.

The following are some of the common security requirements in ICT systems:

- Prevention of unauthorized access and modification of the data at devices, data in transmission, and the data being processed
- Service assurance such as availability of communication channels and devices, including the operator side equipment
- Assurance from theft or the leakage of service such as the diversion of data or calls and operator and business side revenue theft

Attacks on communication networks

Increasing the convergence of data and voice communication technologies has brought into focus many cyber-based attacks on communication. Some common attacks can be broadly classified under the following:

- Snooping/eavesdropping
- Theft of services
- Denial-of-Service (DoS)

Preventing or mitigating communication network attacks

Security services for communication networks should take into consideration the following security services for preventing and mitigating attacks:

- Authentication
- Access control
- Non-repudiation
- Confidentiality
- Integrity
- Key management

We've covered most of these concepts in earlier chapters.

Security controls in communication networks

Some of the common security controls used in the communication networks include the following:

- HTTP digest authentication: In the digest authentication, there are two request/response pairs to enhance the authentication security.

- Secure Multipurpose Internet Mail Extensions (S/MIME): This provides extensions for using public key cryptography for encryption and signing messages, thereby enhancing the security.
- Secure Real Time Protocol (SRTP): This protocol provides security functions such as encryption, message authentication, integrity, and replay protection to Real Time Transport protocol (RTP).
- Transmission Layer Security (TLS) (covered earlier in this chapter).
- Internet Protocol Security (IPSec) (covered earlier in this chapter).
- Authenticated Identity Body (AIB): This method is generally used in Session Initiation Protocols (SIP), and allows authenticated identity to be shared across the network.
- Authenticated Identity Management (AIM).
- Stateful Firewall: This is a firewall that dynamically inspects the packets. To allow/disallow the packets is called stateful.
- Network Address Translation (NAT)) (covered earlier in this chapter).
- Application Level Gateways (ALG): These are Gateway applications that work in the firewall and act as an application proxy.
- Session Border Controllers (SBC): This provides controls for Voice Over IP (VOIP) communications.
- Virtual Private Networks (VPN)) (covered earlier in this chapter).

Summary

In this chapter, we covered some of the concepts in telecommunications and the network security domain.

Security requirements in voice, data, multimedia, remote access, and virtual networks are based on service availability, data confidentiality, and theft/leakage. Security requirements are addressed through prevention and mitigation strategies and communication controls.

The next chapter is a revision chapter for chapters six through nine. References and further study on these four chapters are provided. An exam cram as well as a mock test consisting of about 15 questions is also provided in the next chapter.

Sample questions

Q1. Spoofing is a type of:

    1. Vulnerability
    2. Masquerading
    3. Protocol
    4. Layer in a TCP/IP model

Q2. An attack is a:

    1. Threat
    2. Vulnerability
    3. Technique
    4. Protocol

Q3. Transport layer security and secure sockets layer are *not:*

    1. Protocols
    2. Cryptographic algorithms
    3. Vulnerabilities
    4. Use encryption

Q4. Replay attacks are used to:

    1. Gain unauthorized access to the application systems
    2. Resolve domain names
    3. Break cryptographic keys
    4. Setup secure connections

Q5. Internet Protocol (IP) operates in:

    1. Physical layer
    2. Network layer
    3. Application layer
    4. Communication layer

Q6. Border Gateway Protocol is a:

1. Physical layer protocol
2. Address Resolution Protocol
3. Routing Protocol
4. LAN technology

Q7. Multi Protocol Label Switching (MPLS) is often referred to as:

1. Application Layer Protocol
2. Layer 2.5 protocol
3. Layer 3 protocol
4. Layer 3.5 protocol

Q8. IPsec is a set of protocols that are used to secure Internet communications. Which of the following is not a key function of the protocol?

1. Authentication
2. Encryption
3. Key exchange
4. Key modification

10

Day 10 – Exam Cram and Practice Questions

This chapter offers concepts covered in the first two domains of CISSP CBK in a snippet format that will reinforce the topics already learned, and it will serve as an exam cram. A mock test consisting of 10 questions from the second two domains is provided. Finally, further reading and references are also provided.

An overview of exam cram and practice questions

This chapter starts with an exam cram that consists of some quick revision points from the third domain of CISSP CBK **security engineering** and from the fourth domain of **communication and network security**. This is followed by a mock test from these two domains. The last topic of this chapter provides additional references for further reading:

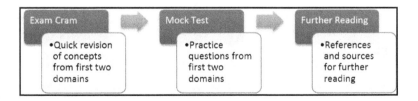

The exam cram

Presented here is a revision of the concepts discussed in the previous four chapters, namely, chapters six through nine. They are provided in bullet points as snippets that are easy to revise. These snippets are for quick revision and the reinforcement of the knowledge that has been learned.

CISSP CBK Domain #3 â□□ security engineering

The following bullet points are presented in an exam cram format for quick revision. They cover important points from the security engineering domain. The covered topics include security design principles; best practices and proven models that are adapted during product design as well as in processes; technical vulnerabilities and mitigation techniques; cryptography; and physical security concepts:

- Security engineering is based on design principles, practices, and models to ensure confidentiality, integrity, and the availability requirements of information assets.
- CIA is the commonly used acronym for Confidentiality, Integrity, and Availability.
- The elements of a computer that are fundamental to its operations together with the way in which the elements are organized are referred to as computer architecture.
- A **central processing unit (CPU)** is the heart and brain of a computer. The process carried out by the CPU is called executing the program.
- **Input/output (IO)** systems interface with the CPU.
- The function of **memory** is to store instructions and data either permanently or temporarily.
- **Primary memory** refers to a storage area that is directly addressable by the CPU.
- **Secondary memory** refers to the permanent storage that is indirectly accessible by the CPU. Some examples of this are magnetic disks, tapes, and so on.
- Telecommunication and networking technologies enable computers to communicate with each other or act as a server, client, or both.
- The collection of hardware and software together is sometimes referred to as a **computer system**.
- A computer system can be categorized as an open system, a closed system, or a combination of both.

- An **open system**, as the name implies, is open to interconnectivity with other systems. It can be reviewed by independent third parties.
- Various computing methods are available to improve the instruction execution cycle. An instruction execution cycle is the time required to fetch the instruction and data from the memory, decode the information, and execute the same.
- When many operations are performed per instruction, then such a computing is known as **Complex Instruction Set Computer (CISC)**.
- When instruction sets reduce the cycle time to execute instructions, then the method is called **Reduced Instruction Set Computer (RISC)**.
- From an information security perspective, computer architecture should take into consideration the CIA aspects of computing services.
- **Trusted Computer System** refers to the systems that have a well-defined security policy, accountability, assurance mechanisms, and proper documentation.
- **Trusted Computer System Evaluation Criteria (TCSEC)** is a set of basic requirements used to evaluate the effectiveness of computer security controls built into computer systems. TCSEC is the United States **Department Of Defense (DoD)** standard and is popularly known as **Orange book**.
- **Protection Domain** is a security function used to control or prevent direct access by an insecure or lower-level entity to a secure higher-level entity.
- When protection domains are organized in a hierarchical format, then they are called **Protection Rings**.
- **Security Perimeter** is an outer ring of a trusted computing base; or in simple terms, it is the outer ring of a protected domain or entity.
- **Trusted Path** refers to a secure path provided by a software to communicate with entities within the trusted rings to eliminate unauthorized access.
- **Encapsulation** is a technique used to hide information from unauthorized entities.
- **Abstraction** is the process of hiding the details and exposing only the essential features of a particular concept or object that are encapsulated.
- **Reference Monitor** is a secure module that controls access to trusted, protected entities in a trusted computing base.
- **Security Kernel** is a computer architecture consisting of hardware and software elements that implement the reference monitor.
- **Security Label** is a classification mechanism used to indicate the security levels of entities.
- **Logical Security Guard** is a security mechanism used to control the communication between entities that are labeled lower and high sensitive.

- Security Modes are operating modes based on the operating level of the information systems based on the sensitivity level or the security label.
- In information security, the term assurance means the level of trust or the degree of confidence in the satisfaction of security needs.
- **Common Criteria** (**CC**) is an assurance framework that is predominantly derived from **Trusted Computer Security Evaluation Criteria** (**TCSEC**), **Information Technology Security Evaluation Criteria** (**ITSEC**), and **Canadian Trusted Computer Product Evaluation Criteria** (**CTCPEC**).
- In Common Criteria, a **Target of Evaluation** (**TOE**) is the target product or system that is to be evaluated.
- **Security Target** (**ST**) is principally a document that identifies the security properties of TOE.
- **Evaluation Assurance Level** (**EAL**) is a numerical rating based on the evaluation levels. There are seven levels of EAL starting from EAL1 (Basic) to EAL7 (most stringent).
- **Trusted Computer Security Evaluation Criteria** (**TCSEC**) is also called Orange Book in the rainbow series. It is published by the United States Department of Defense (DOD).
- **Information Technology Security Evaluation Criteria** (**ITSEC**) is a European standard for IT security that specifies the evaluation criteria for functionality and assurance.
- **Canadian Trusted Computer Product Evaluation Criteria** (**CTCPEC**) is a Canadian standard for security product evaluation published by Communications Security Establishment.
- **Department of Defense Information Technology Security Certification and Accreditation Process** (**DITSCAP**) is a standardized approach designed to guide DoD agencies through the certification and accreditation process for a single information technology (IT) entity.
- **System Security Authorization Agreement** (**SSAA**) is a document that specifies system specifications such as the system mission, target environment, target architecture, security requirements, and applicable data access policies. SSAA is the basis on which certification and accreditation actions take place.
- **National Information Assurance Certification and Accreditation Process** (**NIACAP**) is a process used for the certification and accreditation of the computer systems that handle the US National Security information.
- **DoD Information Assurance Certification and Accreditation Process** (**DIACAP**) is a standard that supersedes DITSCAP.

- **System Security Engineering Capability Maturity Model (SSE-CMM)** is a system security process maturity model that focuses on the requirements pertaining to the implementation of security in a system or a group of systems, specifically in the Information Technology Security domain. It is a **National Security Agency (NSA)** sponsored effort.
- There are 11 security engineering practices that are defined in SSE-CMM.
- There are 11 process area-related projects and organizational practices in SSE-CMM.
- Computer security is based on the role of various entities within the system and their CIA requirement.
- A computer security model known as the take-grant protection model specifies obtaining (taking) rights from one entity to another or transferring (granting) rights from one entity to another.
- The Bell LaPadula security model focused on confidentiality; this model prescribes access controls to classified or confidential information. A simple way to remember this model isâ◉◉**no read up** and **no write down**.
- The Biba model focuses on data integrity. A simple way to remember this model isâ◉◉**no read down** and **no write up**.
- The Clarke Wilson model focuses on integrity, and it aims to address multilevel security requirements in computing systems.
- IT components such as operating systems, application software, as well as networks have many vulnerabilities.
- The primary purpose of vulnerability and penetration tests is to identify, evaluate, and mitigate the risks due to vulnerability exploitation.
- Vulnerabilities in IT systems such as software and networks can be considered as holes or errors.
- While vulnerability assessment and remediation is used to strengthen the computer system, it is also important to perform suitable **penetration tests** periodically to identify the possibility of system compromise.
- Testing from an external network with no prior knowledge of the internal networks and systems is referred to as **black box testing**.
- Performing the test from within the network is referred to as internal testing or **white box testing**.
- Testing from an external and/or internal network with knowledge of internal networks and systems is referred to as **gray box testing**. This is usually a combination of black box testing and white box testing.
- **Common Vulnerability and Exposures** (**CVE**) is an online dictionary of vulnerabilities.

- Cryptography is an art as well as a science that involves the process of transforming a plain text into a scrambled text and vice versa.
- The process of converting plain text into scrambled or unintelligible (cipher) text is called encryption.
- The process of converting scrambled or unintelligible (cipher) text into plain text is called decryption.
- An algorithm in cryptography is a series of well-defined steps that provide the procedure for encryption/decryption.
- A cryptographic method is a way of doing encryption and decryption in a systematic way.
- Cryptography is based on algorithms and the keys that operate on them.
- If only one key is used, then it is called symmetric key encryption; if two keys are used, then it is called asymmetric key encryption; and if no key is used, then it is called hashing.
- When the key stream algorithm operates on a single bit, byte, or computer word such that the information is changed constantly, then it is called stream cipher.
- If the algorithm operates on a block of text (as opposed to a single bit or byte), then it is known as block cipher.
- The **Rivest Cipher (RC4)** algorithm uses about 40 to 256 bits, and the key sizes are different. RC4 is a stream cipher.
- **Data Encryption Standard** (**DES**) is a block cipher that uses up to 56-bit keys and operates on 64-bit blocks.
- **Advanced Encryption Standard** (**AES**) is a 128-bit block cipher that employs 128, 192, or 256 bit keys.
- When a ciphertext block is formed by the application of a secret key to encrypt the plaintext block, this is called **Electronic Code Book** (**ECB**).
- When a plaintext is **exclusively-ORed(XORed)** with the previous block of ciphertext, then the mode is called **Cipher Block Chaining** (**CBC**).
- **Cipher FeedBack (CFB)** is a mode that allows the encrypted data units to be smaller than the block unit size.
- **Output FeedBack(OFB)** uses an internal feedback mechanism such that the same plaintext block cannot create the same ciphertext block.
- **Initialization vectors** are a block of bits that allow either a stream cipher or a block cipher to execute any of the preceding modes.
- **Digital signature** is a type of public key cryptography where the message is digitally signed using the sender's private key.
- Hashing is called **message digest** or **one-way encryption** as there is no decryption, only validating the computed checksum.

- **Transport Layer Security (TLS)** and its predecessor **Secure Sockets Layer** (SSL) are protocols that provide communication security by encrypting the sessions while using the Internet.
- **Secure Electronic Transaction (SET)** is a set of standard protocols for securing a credit card transaction over insecure networks.
- **IPSec** is set of protocols used to secure Internet communication.
- **Pretty Good Privacy (PGP)** is a software package that supports secure e-mail communications.
- **Secure Multi-Purpose Internet Mail Extensions** (**S/MIME**) uses public key cryptography to provide an authentication for e-mail messages through digital signatures. S/MIME can also provide non-repudiation and confidentiality.
- **Secure Hypertext Transfer Protocol** (**SHTTP**) is a protocol that introduces an authentication/encryption layer between the Hyper Text Transfer protocol (HTTP) and Transmission Control Protocol (TCP), to secure communications for the World Wide Web (WWW).
- Secure Shell (SSH) is a protocol that establishes a secure channel between two computers for communication purposes.
- **Kerberos** is an encryption and authentication service.
- **Steganography** refers to the art of concealing information within the computer files such as documents, images, or any multimedia content.
- **Digital Watermarking** is a method by which copyright information is embedded in a digital content such as documents, images, and multimedia files.
- **SecureID** is a two-factor authentication system.
- **Wireless Application Protocol** (**WAP**) is a set of standards for wireless communications using devices such as mobile phones.
- IEEE 802.11 is a set of standards for **Wireless Local Area Networking** (**WLAN**). **Wired Equivalent Privacy** (**WEP**) and **Wireless (WI-FI) Protected Access** (**WPA**) are the commonly used protocols for encryption in this communication standard.
- **Public Key Infrastructure** (**PKI**) is a framework that enables the integration of various services related to cryptography.
- The aim of PKI is to provide confidentiality, integrity, access control, authentication, and most importantly non-repudiation.
- Key management includes a secure generation of keys, a secure storage of keys, a secure distribution of keys, and secure destruction of keys.
- **Key Usage** refers to using the key for a cryptographic process. This should be limited to using a single key for only one cryptographic process.

- When a specific key is authorized for use by legitimate entities for a period of time, or the effect of a specific key for a given system is for a period of time, then the time span is known as a **Crypto period**.
- **Cryptanalysis** is the science of analyzing and deciphering codes and ciphers.
- **Cryptographic algorithm** and **key size selection** are two important key management parameters that provide adequate protection to the system and data throughout their expected lifetime.
- The **Cipher-text only attack** refers to the availability of the cipher-text (encrypted text) to the cryptanalyst.
- When a cryptanalyst obtains cipher text as well as the corresponding plain text, then this type of attack is known as the **known-plaintext attack**.
- **Chosen-plaintext attack** refers to the availability of corresponding cipher text to the block of plain text chosen by the analyst.
- If a cryptanalyst can choose the samples of plaintext based on the results of previous encryptions in a dynamic passion, then this type of cryptanalytic attack is known an as **adaptive-chosen-plaintext attack**.
- **Chosen-cipher text attack** is a type of attack used to obtain the plaintext by choosing a sample of cipher text by the cryptanalyst.
- **Adaptive-chosen-cipher text attack** is similar to the chosen-cipher text, but the samples of cipher text are dynamically selected by the cryptanalyst and the selection can be based on the previous results as well.
- **Wired Equivalent Privacy (WEP)** is an algorithm that uses stream cipher RC4 encryption standard for confidentiality protection, and it uses CRC-32 for integrity assurance.
- **Wi-Fi Protected Access (WPA)** is a security protocol developed by the Wi-Fi alliance that replaces WEP.
- **WPA2** is an advanced protocol certified by the Wi-Fi alliance. This protocol fulfills the mandatory requirements of IEE 822.11i standard, and it uses the AES algorithm for encryption.
- **Bluetooth** is a wireless protocol for short-range communications for fixed or portable computers and mobile devices.
- The core structure of FIPS140 recommends four security levels for cryptographic modules that protect sensitive information in the federal systems, such as computer and telecommunication systems that include voice system as well.

CISSP CBK Domain #4 â□□ communication and network security

The following bullet points presented in an exam cram format for quick revision cover important points from the Communication and Network Security domain. The covered topics include foundational concepts in network architecture and network security; IP and non-IP protocols and their applications; threats, attacks, vulnerabilities, and countermeasures to communication and network security; security requirements in wireless networks; the application of cryptography in communication security; and securing network components:

- Security in Communication and Networks is based on the architecture type, protocols, and the technologies used.
- Layered architecture is a technique used to design communication networking in the form of layers. Each layer is independent and communicates with its immediate upper and lower layers.
- **Open System Interconnect (OSI)** is an International Organization for Standardization (ISO) layered architecture standard that defines a framework for implementing protocols in seven layers.
- **Layer 7** or the **Application layer** provides application services that are required for application processes.
- **Layer 6** is the **Presentation layer** that manages the way in which the information or data is encoded or represented.
- **Layer 5** is the **session layer**, and the primary purpose of this layer is to manage communication between two computers.
- **Layer 4** is used to maintain the integrity and validity of the data being transported, and is known as the **transport layer**.
- **Layer 3** is called the **network layer**, and it ensures that the proper route is established for transporting data.
- **Layer 2** is the **data link layer** that ensures node-to-node validity of the data being transmitted.
- **Layer 1** deals with the electrical and mechanical characteristics of the data and is called the **physical layer**.
- **Transmission Control Protocol/Internet Protocol (TCP/IP)** is an Internet Protocol suit on which most of the Internet and commercial networks run.
- The original TCP/IP reference model consists of four layers that are purely related to the Internet communications.
- The four layers are application layer, transport layer, network/Internet layer, and data link layer.

- DNS works at the application layer. DNS translates domain names into IP addresses.
- A common threat to DNS is **spoofing.**
- **Domain Name System Security Extensions (DNSSEC)** are a set of extensions that provide origin authentication, data integrity, and authenticated denial of existence.
- In an Internet Protocol (IP) network, client devices obtain necessary network parameters from a centralized server(s) using DHCP.
- HTTP is a communication protocol that enables the retrieval and transfer of hypertext pages. HTTP uses Transmission Control Protocol (TCP) for connections.
- Common threats for HTTP include Spoofing, Unauthorized disclosure, and Path traversal.
- Transport layer in the TCP/IP model does two things. One job is to package the data given out by applications to a format that is suitable for transport over the network, and the other one is to unpack the data received from the network to the format suitable for applications.
- The process of packaging the data packets received from the applications is called **encapsulation**, and the output of such a process is called a **datagram**.
- Similarly, the process of unpacking the datagram received from the network is called **abstraction**.
- **Transmission Control Protocol (TCP)** is a core Internet protocol that provides reliable delivery mechanisms over the Internet. TCP is a connection-oriented protocol and is represented in Layer 4 of the OSI model.
- **User Datagram Protocol (UDP)** is a protocol similar to TCP but is a connectionless protocol, and it is represented in Layer 4 of the OSI model.
- TCP **SYN attacks** establish thousands of half-open connections to consume the server resources. It works by spoofing different source IPs and not replying to SYN/ACK.
- Network or the Internet layer in the TCP/IP model is for internetworking. This layer has a group of methods, functions, and protocols to facilitate communication between different networks.
- IP is a connectionless protocol and is used in packet-switched networks such as the Internet.
- The primary function of IP is to send data from one computer to another. IP works in the Network Layer of OSI and Internet layer of the TCP/IP model.
- IPsec is a suite of protocols that are created to secure Internet Protocols (IP). They provide authentication and encryption functions.

- A **tunnel** in a computer network, just as VPN is a secure path or route for the datagram, which is used to pass through an insecure or un-trusted network. This is achieved using additional encapsulation.
- In communication security, the prevention of unauthorized access and modification of data at the devices, data in transmission, and the data being processed is a primary requirement.
- Service-assurance requirements are the availability of communication channels and devices including the operator-side equipment.
- Assurance from theft or leakage of service, such as the diversion of data or calls and operator side and business side revenue theft, are assurance requirements.
- Snooping/eavesdropping, theft of services, and Denial-of-Service (DoS) are common attacks on communication systems.

Sample questions

Q1. Testing from an external network with no prior knowledge of the internal networks and systems is referred to as _____.

1. Penetration Testing
2. Gray box testing
3. Black box testing
4. Vulnerability assessment

Q2. The transport layer in the TCP/IP model does two things. One is to package the data given out by applications to a format that is suitable for transport over the network, and the other is to:

1. Unpacking the data received from the network
2. Transposition of data for networks
3. Transformation data to binary format
4. Encryption of data

Q3. The network or the internet layer in the TCP/IP model is for internet working. This layer has A group of:

1. Methods
2. Functions

3. Protocols
4. All of the above

Q4. Which one of the following services does Domain Name System Security Extensions (DNSSEC) not provide?

1. Origin authentication
2. Non-repudiation
3. Data integrity
4. Authenticated denial

Q5. Which check does Wired Equivalent Privacy (WEP) use for integrity assurance?

1. CRC-12
2. CRC-14
3. CRC-28
4. CRC-32

Q6. Kerberos provides which of the following:

1. Authentication and authorization
2. Authentication and encryption
3. Authentication and accountability
4. Authentication and availability

Q7. Biba model focuses on data integrity. A simple way to remember this model is:

1. No read down and no write down
2. No read up and no write up
3. No read down and no write up
4. No read up and no write down

Q8. A security mechanism to control the communication between entities that are labeled lower sensitive and high sensitive is known as what?

1. Local security system
2. Logical security guard
3. Security tunnel
4. Security rings

Q9. One of the popular methods to authenticate the sender using sender's public key is known as what?

1. Public Key cryptography
2. Digital certificate
3. Digital signature
4. Non-repudiation

Q10. Which one of the following is not a Denial-of-Service (DoS) attack?

1. Teardrop
2. Smurf
3. SYN
4. Sniffing

Q11. In a Trusted Computer System (TCS), which one of the following is a security mechanism that controls the communication between entities that are labeled as low sensitive and high sensitive?

1. Security label
2. Logical Security Guard
3. Protection ring
4. Security mode

Q12. Secret Key Cryptography is denoted as what?

1. Asymmetric key encryption
2. Symmetric key encryption
3. Public Key Cryptography
4. Private Key Cryptography

Q13. Domain Name System (DNS) maintains records to resolve host names to IP addresses. For faster resolving of addresses, the browser stores data of the resolved IP addresses in a temporary memory. Which of the following attacks could most likely compromise such a mechanism to redirect user request to illegitimate addresses?

1. Spoofing
2. Sniffing
3. Cache poisoning
4. Request forging

Q14. Identify the correct statements pertaining to the primary purpose of cryptography?

Conceal the confidential information from unauthorized users	
Ensuring immediate detection of any alteration made to the concealed information	Drag and drop your answers here
Ensuring availability of confidential information all the time	
Converting a plain text to a cipher text	

Q15. When a plaintext is Exclusively-ORed (XORed) with the previous block of ciphertext, then the mode is called what?

1. Electronic Code Block
2. Electronic Code Book
3. Cipher Block Chaining
4. Cipher Feedback

References and further reading

- **Common Vulnerabilities and Exposure (CVE)**: https://cve.mitre.org/
- **Common Vulnerabilities Scoring System (CVSS)**: https://nvd.nist.gov/cvss.cfm
- **FIPS 140 standards**: http://csrc.nist.gov/groups/STM/cmvp/standards.html
- **Trusted Computing Security Evaluation Criteria (TCSEC)**: https://fas.org/irp/nsa/rainbow/std001.htm

Summary

This chapter covered some of the important concepts in the form of an exam cram from the third and fourth domains of CISSP CBK. A mock test with a combination of questions in the two domains is provided to test the knowledge already learned. Further reading and references are provided to enhance the knowledge in these two domains.

In the next chapter, you will learn Identity Management with a focus on provisioning and managing identities, along with the access used in the interaction between humans and information systems.

11

Day 11 – Identity and Access Management - Identity Management

This chapter covers provisioning and managing identities, and the access used in the interaction between humans and information systems. The core concepts of identification, authentication, authorization and accountability are covered in detail here. Concepts related to identity as a service or cloud based third-party identity services are covered; and security requirements in such services are covered with illustration.

A candidate for the CISSP exam is expected to have foundational concepts and knowledge in the following key areas of the identity and access management domain:

- Physical and logical access to assets
- Identity management principles and implementation
- Identity as a service
- Third-party identity services
- Access management
- Authorization mechanisms
- The identity and provisioning life cycle
- Preventing or mitigating access control attacks

An overview of identity and access management

An asset, such as data, is accessed through systems and applications. Similarly, access to facilities such as data centers and operational areas are facilitated through access control mechanisms. Hence, physical or logical access to assets needs to establish the identity of the person or process scripts before determining the access permission.

Observe the following illustration. Users need access to data or physical facilities. Similarly, scripts or programs need access to data for processing and execution. Essentially, one type of asset needs access to another type of asset. The overall process of facilitating and managing identities of such assets, and controlling access while ensuring information security, is termed as **Identity and Access Management (IAM)**:

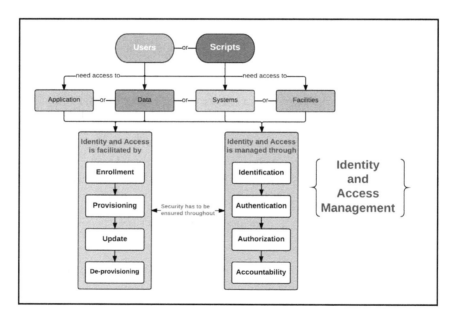

In this module you will understand the following:

- Physical and logical access to assets and security controls
- Identification and authentication
- Managing people to device interactions
- Integrating identity as a service and third-party identity services

Physical and logical access to assets

In information technology, physical access includes access to physical assets such as facilities, operational areas, and data centers. Logical access includes access to computing assets such as operating systems, application programs, and networks that include the Internet/intranet, information, and data.

Access to physical or logical assets is attempted by entities such as people, programs, or scripts. From the perspective of access, every entity that is trying to access physical or logical assets through any method is considered to be anonymous before some sort of method is used to determine the identity of the entity, and subsequently the access permission. The information security domain that deals with such activities is called identity and access management—in short, **IAM.**

The IAM domain can be further subdivided into two interrelated management activities: identity management and access management. Generally, they are called layers in this domain. There are distinctive principles and practices that govern processes in these layers. The layers are known as identity layers and access layers.

This chapter covers principles and practices in the identity layer, or in other words, it covers identity management principles and practices. In the next chapter, we will cover access management principles and practices that pertain to access layers.

Identity management principles and implementation

Identity and access management consists of four distinctive principles and practices. They are Identification, Authentication, Authorization, and Accountability. Sometimes, the last three are together referred to as access control. In centralized access control systems, such as radius and TACACS, they are identified as the Triple A of access control based on the starting letter of each practice.

Observe the following illustration. The core principles and practices in identity and access domains are layered into three groups. The first layer is called the Identity layer and consists of identification principles and practices. The subsequent layer is called the access layer and consists of authentication and authorization principles and practices. The third and the last layer consists of accountability principles and practices such as auditing, audit trail, and monitoring.

Accountability is common and applicable to identity as well as the access layer:

The identity layer consists of distinctive principles and practices termed as identity management. Consider the following example. John Edwards requires multiple identities in an organization. While his core identity, in other words his principle identity, is **John Edwards**, he needs access to other systems such as a directory system, a database, and web applications.

Observe the following illustration:

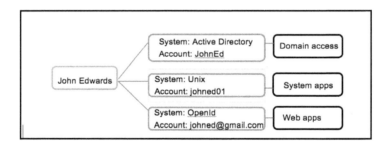

John has multiple identities.

Each identity may have one or more credentials associated with it. For example, a combination of passwords and a digital certificate.

Hence, managing identities requires few processes in the identity management domain.

All the activities are to be performed in accordance with corporate security policies, such that identity is not misused to commit fraud or unauthorized access to systems.

In the preceding illustration, a single primary identity (John Edwards) spans to multiple identities in different systems; and the requirement of each identity for access to applications is also different. For example, an `active` directory account may be used for a domain logon, while Unix system access is through a specific terminal.

Hence, identity management includes some or all of the following:

- Enrollment of user identifiers
- Provisioning of user identities to different systems
- Whenever there is a change in user information, updating all or some of the associated accounts
- If the user no longer needs access, retire, and then deprovisioning accounts

Identity as a service

The traditional methods of software implementation and access from a local installation at standalone servers are slowly and steadily migrating to centralized cloud-based service models. Furthermore, application hosting and access from cloud-based models are available as subscription services. When software is delivered as a service through the Internet cloud, then it is generically termed as **Software as a Service (SaaS)**.

Some of the popular cloud-based services include Google cloud, which provides Platform as a Service. Amazon AWS provides PaaS and Infrastructure as a Service (IaaS) and Salesforce provides SaaS.

Similarly, identity and access management applications and associated services are delivered through subscription-based cloud models. Such services are termed as **Identity as a Service (IDaaS)**. While such services provide flexibility and cost effectiveness, there are security concerns due to the open nature of the Internet.

Security concerns

The following are some of the security concerns pertaining to Software or Identity as a Service:

- Due to the open nature of the Internet, cloud-based identity services are subject to higher scrutiny in regard to security. One important concern is identity theft. During the login process to the cloud application, it may be possible that the communication can be intercepted (eavesdropping) and the credential details can be captured.
- The security of data at rest, such as the credentials stored in the database. Systems can be compromised and the credentials may be captured from the databases.

- When using software as a service, one important security concern is privacy. The amount of personal information that the cloud software application can access from the local computer is a concern.
- The compromise of passwords using brute force or other password attacks on the identity systems.
- Cookies are generally used by identity services to store session information. Some systems are susceptible to cookie replay attacks. In such a scenario, an attacker may be able to gain access to the system without knowing the credentials.

 Cookies are temporary files that may contain the user logon session information and other data necessary for personalization purposes. They may be stored in the user's browser disk or on the hard disk. A cookie may not contain a password.

- Data may be tampered during the communication, which would compromise the integrity of the identity data during the communication.
- Identity services may be unavailable due to denial-of-service (DoS) type of attacks, thereby affecting access and compromising the availability requirements.
- The spoofing of identities and forgery or cloning attacks.
- Phishing attacks on the users to gain identity information.

 Security concerns and attacks listed previously are covered in Chapters 8, *Day 8 – Communication and Network Security – Network Security,* and Chapter 9, *Day 9 – Communication and Network Security – Communication security.*

Security solutions for many of the security concerns pertaining to **Identity as a Service (IDaaS)** are based on strong authentications, such as multifactor authentication; cryptographic methods, such as encryption; and robust monitoring.

 Cryptographic controls are covered in Chapter 7, *Day 7 – Security Engineering – Cryptography and Physical security.*

Third-party identity services

Identity as a service is predominantly provided by third-party service providers. It may include all the processes, such as identification, authentication, authorization, and accountability, or some of them. Similarly, such services may include activities such as enrollment, provisioning, and deprovisioning.

Some of the identity services that may be offered by third-party service providers include the following:

- **Single Sign-on services**: When a user needs to access many different resources that have similar authentication requirements and varying authorization polices, then Single Sign-On (SSO) services provide seamless access to such additional resources, without the user needing to provide credentials at each of the resource access. For example, assume that a user is first authenticated in a website called abc.com, and then he traverses to another website called xyz.com. Since xyz.com also requires user authentication, the site may ask for user credentials again. With SSO, it is possible to trust the earlier authentication at abc.com and check only authorization policies to allow the user to access xyz.com resources without asking for the credentials again.

- **Federated identity provider services**: A federation is based on standards and works on the identity layer. In a federation, there are two entities. One is called (**Asserting Party (AP)** or **Identity Provider (IdP)**. The other one is **Relying Party (RP)** or **Service Provider (SP)**. A user tries to access service-provider website resources, then the service provider requests the identity provider to assert about the identity of the user. The identity provider authenticates the user and asserts about the identity to the service provider. A federation provides a centralized identity service for many consuming service provider websites.

- **Password management services**: Password management services provide a centralized password vault for safe storage and credential transmission facilities for users.

- **User provisioning services**: Provisioning of user identity is required for access. User-provisioning services provide automatic or dynamic provisioning capabilities of user accounts to different systems, based on the access requirements.

- **Access certification services**: Third-party access certification services provide digital identity information, such as digital certificates during electronic transactions.

Summary

This chapter has covered foundational concepts in the Identity and Access Management (IAM) domain. The core of identity management is enrolling user identities and provisioning. An important concern related to identities is Identity Theft. All core services of identity and access are also offered by third-party service providers on a subscription model and are delivered as a service from cloud.

Continued in the next chapter are the topics of this domain pertaining to access management with a focus on access control concepts, methods, attacks, and countermeasures.

Sample questions

Q1. Which one of the following is not an Identity and Access Management (IAM) process?

1. Authorization
2. Accountability
3. Identification
4. Allocation

Q2. A user is trying to access an application. During the process, the user fills in a user name and password, and he submits the same to the application. Which one of the following represents such an activity?

1. Identification
2. Authentication
3. Authorization
4. Accountability

Q3. Which statements, among the following, are a part of the Identity and Access Management facilitation process (this is a drag and drop type of question. Here you can draw a line from the list of answers from the left to the empty box on the right)?

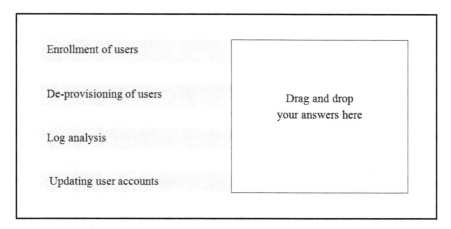

Q4. Identity theft is what?

1. Stealing one's money
2. Stealing one's property
3. Stealing one's credentials
4. Stealing one's computer

Q5. The following statements pertaining to Single Sign On (SSO) are true *except*.

1. SSO is an accountability mechanism to monitor user logon activities
2. SSO is an access control mechanism that allows multiple web resource access with a single credential
3. SSO works on the access layer
4. SSO allows one authentication and multiple authorizations

Q6. Identity federation-related services and terminologies from the following list (this is a drag-and-drop type of question. Here, you can draw a line from the list of answers from the left to the empty box on the right).

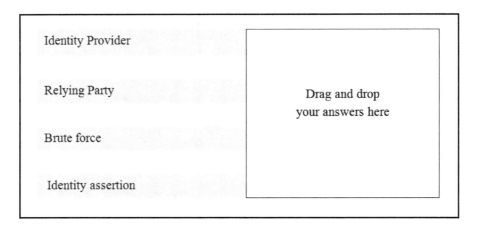

Q7. Listening to communications surreptitiously between a client and a server is called what?

1. Eavestailing
2. Eavesdropping
3. Tailgating
4. Forgery

Q8. The Triple A of access control consists of what?

1. Identification, Authentication and Authorization
2. Identification, Authentication and Accountability
3. Identification, Authorization and Authorization
4. Authentication, Authorization and Accountability

12

Day 12 – Identity and Access Management - Access Management, Provisioning, and Attacks

This chapter covers foundational concepts in the access and accountability layers of the **Identity and Access Management (IAM)** domain.

A candidate appearing for the CISSP exam is expected to understand the foundational concepts and have knowledge of the following key areas of the identity and access management domain:

- Access management
- Authorization mechanisms
- The identity and provisioning lifecycle
- Preventing or mitigating access control attacks

An overview of access management

Observe the following illustration. Access management is facilitated through authentication and authorization processes. Each of these processes consists of various concepts and techniques. From an information security perspective, there are process-centric threats, vulnerabilities attacks, and counter measures that need to be understood:

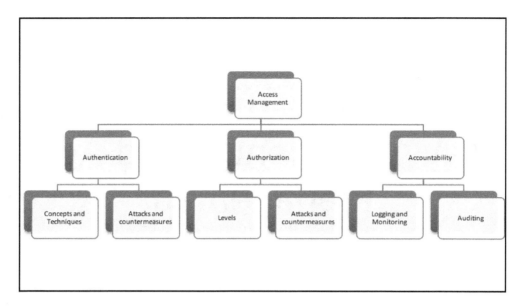

In this module, you will understand the following:

- Access control concepts, methodologies, and techniques
- Authorization mechanisms
- The identity and provisioning lifecycle
- Preventing or mitigating access control attacks

Access management concepts, methodologies, and techniques

The access management layer consist of access control mechanisms, such as authentication and authorization. This layer also consists of accountability mechanisms such as logging and monitoring activities.

Basic concepts

One of the primary concepts in access control is that of **subject** and **object**.

A subject maybe a person, process, or technology component that either seeks access or controls the access. A physical entry to a data center and login to a system are examples of access. Hence, an employee trying to access their business e-mail account is a subject; similarly, the system that verifies the credentials, such as the user name and password, is also termed as subject.

An object can be a file, data, a physical equipment, or premises that needs controlled access. For example, the e-mails stored in the mailbox are an object that a subject is trying to access is data.

Controlling access to the object by a subject is the core requirement of an access control process and its associated mechanisms. In a nutshell, a subject either seeks or controls access to an object.

An access control mechanism can be classified broadly into the following two types:

- If access to an object is controlled based on certain contextual parameters such as location, time, sequence of responses, access history, and more, then it is known as context-dependent access control. In this type, the value of the asset being accessed is not a primary consideration. The following are the examples of such an access control mechanism:
  - Providing username/password combination followed by a challenge/response mechanism such as CAPTCHA
  - Filtering access based on a MAC address in wireless connections
  - Firewall filtering the data based on packet analysis

 Completely Automated Public Turing test to tell Computers and Humans Apart (CAPTCHA) is a challenge-response test used to ensure that the input to an access control system is supplied by humans and not machines. This mechanism is predominantly used by websites to prevent Web roBots (WebBots) from accessing the controlled section of the website by brute force methods.

- Here is an example of CAPTCHA:

- If access is provided based on the attributes or content of an object, then it is called content-dependent access control. In this type, the value and attributes of the content that is being accessed determines the control requirements. The following are few examples of content-dependent access control mechanisms:
  - Hiding or showing menus in an application
  - Views in databases
  - Controlling access to confidential information

Access control models

Access control models define methods by which a system controls the access to an object by a subject. The upcoming headings are some of the models that are predominantly used in the access control domain.

Discretionary access control

Discretionary access control employs an access control scheme where the subject has some authority to specify the objects that are accessible to them. In simpler terms, access to an asset is based on the discretion of the owner of the asset.

Access control list (**ACL**) is an example of discretionary access control, wherein users and privileges are mapped. The following is a simple example of an access control list that allows or denies a connection from a specific IP addresses by a router:

```
10 permit 10.1.1.1
20 permit 10.1.1.2
30 permit 10.1.3.0, wildcard bits 0.0.0.255
```

In the preceding example, the router allows connections from 10.1.1.1, 10.1.1.2, and all the IP addresses in the 10.1.3.0 to 10.1.3.255 range, and denies any other connections. ACLs implicitly deny anything not defined in the list.

Identity-based access control is a form of discretionary access control in which the control is based on an individual's identity. For example, biometrics-based access control systems are based on this type.

Non-discretionary access control

When the access to an object is based on certain rules, then it is called **Rule-Based Access Control** (**RBAC**). For example, the clearance level of the subject and the classification level of the object determines the access levels. Some practical examples include your college providing Internet access during specific hours of the day (the rule here is based on time).

When access is controlled based on mandatory rules, then it is known as **Mandatory Access Control** (**MAC**). This type of access control is based on security labels. The security label is applicable to a subject as well as an object. A subject should have an equal or higher security label than the object to access it. For example, most of the modern-day operating systems, such as Vista or certain Linux variants, restrict the permissions of applications to access certain processes, based on integrity or sensitiveness labels.

> The acronym MAC is also used in computer networking, and it denotes Media Access Control. This is an addressing scheme that provides a unique hardware number to the network interface card.

If a centralized authority controls access based on a specific policy, then this is referred to as **non-discretionary access control**.

Centralized access control is a facility in which all the core functions of access, such as **Authentication, Authorization and Accountability** (**AAA**), are performed from a centralized location.

Role Based Access Control (**RBAC**) is a type of non-discretionary access control based on the subject's role or position in the organization. The majority of applications, such as **Enterprise Resource Management** (**ERP**) and **Manufacturing Execution Systems** (**MES**), use this control as a default or a preferred option. For example, an Active Directory setup may contain *server admins*, *domain admins*, and so on. Hence, people put in groups the permissions assigned to groups based on the role.

> Rule Based Access Control (RBAC) and Role based Access Control (RBAC) share the same acronym RBAC.

Task-based access control is based on a subject's responsibilities in the organization. A role may contain multiple tasks. For example, a role may contain tasks such as creating a user record, and then provisioning the user to a specific system. In task-based access control, the access is allowed only for specific tasks within a role and not all of them.

Lattice-based access control is one where there is a pair of values that determine the access rights. The pair of values are related to least upper bound and the greatest lower bound in the lattice model. This is another type of non-discretionary access control. This model is usually represented in a grid-like setup where a subject and object are mapped.

In the following example, user levels and file levels are mapped in a lattice model to represent access levels:

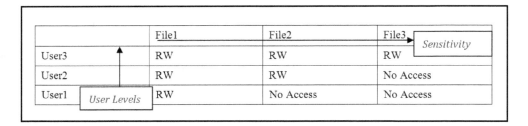

	File1	File2	File3 *Sensitivity*
User3	RW	RW	RW
User2	RW	RW	No Access
User1 *User Levels*	RW	No Access	No Access

Decentralized access control or **Distributed access control** is such that the core functions of the access are distributed over a network. A distributed database is an example of such a system. In a distributed access control mechanism, authentication may be handled by a centralized server, such as an **Active Directory**, and authorization may be handled by a different source, such as a database.

Authentication and authorization

Identity and access management consists of two distinctive activities. One is related to the *identification* of the subject by the system. The other is *authentication* and *authorization*, which is the system's ability to validate the credential supplied by the subject and determine access levels.

The authentication process may require more than one type of credential to validate the identity. This type of validation is called **factoring**. Access security is enhanced when more than one factor of authentication is used.

When an entity (subject) is validated against a single credential, then it is called a **one-factor authentication**. For example, providing a user name and password to the system is a single-factor authentication. Generally, the user name/password combination authenticates the credentials from the principle of **what you know** (the user name and password).

When an entity (subject) is validated against two different credentials, then it is called a **two-factor authentication**. For example, providing a PIN along with the ATM or smart card to the system is a two-factor authentication. In this scenario, the system authenticates the credentials from the principle of *what you have* (a smart card) and *what you know* (a PIN)

When an entity (subject) is validated against two or more different credentials, then it is called a **multi-factor authentication**. For example, providing a PIN along with the ATM or smart card and also swiping your finger on the fingerprint (biometric) reader is a multi-factor authentication. In this scenario, the system authenticates the credentials from three factors, such as *what you are* (fingerprint), *what you have*, and *what you know*.

 Biometric authentication validates biological characteristics to authenticate the entity (user). This follows the principle "what you are". Some of the biometric authentication methods are: fingerprint scanning, retina scanning, hand geometry, and face geometry.

Hence, strong authentication includes more than one factor. The more factors of authentication using different mechanisms, the stronger the security is.

Authorization

Authorization is a process of determining the levels of access a subject may have on the object. For example, when an employee accesses an intranet portal, based on the employee type such as manager, administrator, or an ordinary employee, then the functions and sections that are accessible to them may vary.

Authentication determines *whether a user identification is valid and whether the user can have access to the resource*, whereas authorization determines *what the user can access or which resource the user can access*.

From an information security perspective, attacking and compromising authorization mechanisms gives higher privileges of access to the attacker. Such types of attack are called privilege escalation attacks.

Identity and provisioning life cycle

In an identity and provisioning life cycle, there are two distinctive activities. One is user management and the other is system or application access. Furthermore, the life cycle consists of the assignment of privileges through roles and delegation.

Observe the following illustration, a typical identity and provisioning life cycle consists of these things:

- Enrollment of users, which is creating and/or registering user accounts
- Determining roles, privileges, and access requirements to systems and applications
- Provisioning user accounts to systems
- Ongoing updates based on changes in roles, privileges, and access requirements
- Deprovisioning in the case of user retirement or termination

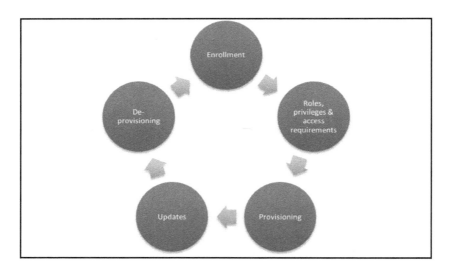

Access control attacks and countermeasures

There are many attacks that can be attributed to the compromise of access control systems and processes to gain unauthorized access. The following are some of the most prominent ones.

Port scanning and compromise

Backdoors are the unauthorized open ports created by malicious programs that allow an unauthorized entity to gain access into the system. An important countermeasure is to periodically check these open ports in the system and close the ports that are not used by programs. Port scanning tools will help in this process. While port scanning helps security tests to identify open ports, the scanners can also be used by attackers to find the entry points to system.

Denial-of-Service (**DoS**) is a type of attack wherein the availability of the system is compromised, and the legitimate users of the system are prevented from accessing their desired resources. A **Distributed Denial-of-Service** (**DDoS**) is a type of attack where multiple systems attack a single resource from distributed locations. SYN attacks, Teardrop attack, and Smurf are some examples of Denial-of-Service attacks. A countermeasure to DoS attacks is regularly monitoring the network activities. Also, firewall and **Intrusion Protection Systems** (**IPS**) have robust mechanisms to protect against such attacks.

Hijacking

Hijacking is an attack in which the session established by the client to the server is taken over by a malicious person or process. A strong session management and encryption is the countermeasure for such attacks.

The **Man-in-the-Middle attack** (**MIIM**) is a type of attack where an attacker hijacks the established session to the server by substituting his public key instead of the client. MIIM attacks are also used to surreptitiously listen to network communications.

TCP hijacking is a type of attack in which the TCP session of the trusted client to the server is hijacked by an attacker.

Malicious codes

Malicious codes are prevalent in the information technology environment and are varied in use and purpose. The basic functionality of malicious code is to execute itself in the client machine and compromise security. Important countermeasures are to use and update antivirus systems, firewalls, and intrusion detection systems.

A **trojan horse** is a type of malicious code that comes disguised inside a trusted program. Once installed, this malicious code can open ports, create backdoors to the system, and do innumerable security breaches. When the Trojan horse is activated on a particular event (such as a particular date), then it is called a **logic bomb**.

Malicious mobile codes are the ones that are executed in the client system through the network from a remote server.

Password attacks

Password guessing is a type of attack that uses various methods to obtain user passwords. The use of strong password with a combination of alpha, numeric, and special characters is a countermeasure. Besides, adhering to strict password policies, such as frequent change of passwords, length of passwords, and history of passwords, are effective against such attacks.

Dictionary attacks are a type of password-guessing attack that checks the encrypted password database with words found in a dictionary.

Brute force attacks are the means by which the password database is attacked with every possible character combination.

Hybrid attacks combine the dictionary as well as brute force attacks.

Replay attacks are ones in which the session (such as authentication) is captured and replayed against the system. In such attacks, valid authentication tokens are played back at a later time by an unauthorized user. These authentication tokens are commonly obtained through MIIM attacks.

Vulnerability compromises

Scanning is an attack to probe the network and system to identify the vulnerabilities for planning a possible attack to compromise.

Vulnerability exploitation is a way of attacking systems by compromising the holes or errors in the operating system or application software to gain access or bypass security controls.

Spoofing is a type of attack to imitate a trusted entity, thereby making the system trust this imitated entity. IP spoofing is an example of such an attack.

Social engineering is a type of attack to obtain credential information, such as passwords, pin numbers, and so on, using social skills such as impersonation or fake e-mails. Generally, social-engineering attacks exploit human nature, such desires to please or be helpful to others, as well as ignorance.

An important countermeasure for the vulnerability compromise of systems is to periodically scan and fix the vulnerabilities in the IT systems using vendor-supplied patches, along with other means of filtering and protection using suitable vulnerability management tools.

Accountability

In identity and access management, accountability aspects play a major role in establishing preventative, detective, and corrective controls to access control attacks. Accountability, in simple terms, can be defined as *monitoring activities of the authorized user*. In other words, it is used for ensuring that the authorized users access the systems and perform activities for legitimate purposes.

When an attacker compromises a system, then the primary step for such an attack would be escalating privileges to get an authorized administrator level of access. Hence, it is important to establish strong accountability mechanisms to mitigate privilege-escalation attacks. Similarly, accountability measures provide audit data to validate available identity and access management controls and improve them.

Some of the common accountability measures in this domain are as follows:

- Logging
- System monitoring
- Session recording
- Keystroke monitoring
- Auditing

Summary

This chapter has covered some foundational concepts in access management. In a nutshell, the access management layer consists of authentication and authorization as key processes. Access control is facilitated by way of access control models and mechanisms. Accountability aspects such as logging, monitoring, and audits play a vital role in ensuring security.

In the next two chapters, we will cover security assessment concepts and security testing methods.

Sample questions

Q1. Which one of the following is not a mandatory access control?

1. Rule-based access control
2. Role-based access control
3. Lattice based access control
4. Discretionary access control

Q2. If access to an object is controlled based on parameters such as location, time, and so on, then this type of access control is known as what?

1. Content-dependent access control
2. Context-dependent access control
3. Character-dependent access control
4. Class-dependent access control

Q3. Which one of the following is also called as a logic bomb?

1. Spoofing
2. Trojan horse getting activated on an event
3. Vulnerability exploitation by an attacker
4. Virus

Q4. Dictionary attack is a type of?

1. Denial-of-Service attack
2. Spoofing

3. Password guessing attack
4. Social engineering

Q5. Basic functionality of the malicious code is to_____.

1. Upgrade the operating system
2. Execute itself in the client system
3. Spoof
4. Denial-of-Service

Q6. CAPTCHA is one of the popular mechanisms used by websites to control input to the access control system is supplied by humans and not machines. This mechanism is called Completely Automated Public Turing test to tell Computers and Humans Apart (CAPTCHA). Which type of machines is this access control system predominantly concerned with?

1. WebDots
2. BotNets
3. WebBots
4. WebNets

Q7. The Man-in-the-middle attack is an example of_____.

1. Sniffing
2. Spoofing
3. Eavesdropping
4. Cache poisoning

Q8. Hiding or showing menus in an application depending on the access permissions of a user is known as_____.

1. Context-dependent access control
2. Content-dependent access control
3. Mandatory access control
4. Role based access control

13

Day 13 – Security Assessment and Testing - Designing, Performing Security Assessment, and Tests

This chapter covers tools, methods, and techniques used for identifying and mitigating risks due to architectural and developmental issues in information assets and associated infrastructure, by systematic security assessment and testing. The requirements pertaining to security controls and measures to assess their continued effectiveness are covered in detail here.

A candidate appearing for a CISSP exam is expected to understand the foundational concepts and possess knowledge of the following key areas of the **security assessment and testing** domain:

- Security assessment and test strategies
- Security control testing
- Designing and validating assessment and test strategies
- Understanding security testing and tools, methods, and techniques
- Understanding the effectiveness of controls

An overview of security assessment and testing

Risk management involves assessment and testing pertaining to security. Controls such as preventive, detective, or corrective measures require appropriate design and implementation. During the design, development, implementation, and operational phases of security controls, assessment and testing need to be performed on periodical basis to ascertain the effectiveness of security controls and their continued suitability for protecting the assets.

Generally, security assessment and testing is carried out on the basis of suitably designed assessment and test strategies. Such strategies include the application of suitable testing tools, methods, and techniques. It is also important that the outcome of the test results provide the data pertaining to the effectiveness of the implemented security control.

Observe the following illustration. IT assets, such as computers, contain operating systems, databases, and applications. They are used in business in day-to-day operations, transaction processing in e-commerce, in universities, and so on. Security issues in such systems could provide unauthorized access or denial of service. Security assessment and testing methods and tools provide the identification of security issues and mitigate them:

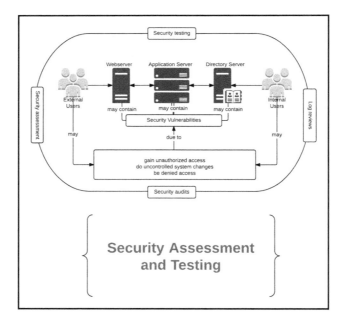

In this module, you will understand the following:

- Designing and validating assessment and test strategies
- Security testing and tools, methods, and techniques
- The effectiveness of controls

Security assessment and test strategies

Information technology infrastructure consists of heterogeneous combinations of software, hardware, networking, and communication-related assets. Such a combination is used in design, development, production, and business operations. Risk assessments on IT infrastructure provide an area of risk on the assets and the impact to business that it would have if the assessed risk materializes. However, risk is a function of probability and consequence. Hence, both the probability and consequence of a risk to business needs to be adequately ascertained in order to design suitable security controls. Such controls have to be effective in mitigating the risk. In this context, proper security assessments and test strategies are required to ascertain the suitability of controls to mitigate the assessed risk, and their continued effectiveness if the risk value changes.

Security assessment and test strategies are administrative controls that provide processes and procedures to operate and continually assess the effectiveness of controls. This chapter provides some of the assessment and testing strategies that are recommended in best practices, standards, or are emphasized in regulatory or other frameworks.

Designing and validating assessment and testing strategies

Security assessment and testing strategies are based on risk to assets. They play a pivotal role in providing inputs while assessing the risk and the validation of risk mitigation actions. Hence, while designing assessments and tests, and during the validation of such assessment and tests, it is important to consider the risk assessment results and the identified or implemented controls. For example, a two-factor authentication system may be implemented as part of a risk mitigation strategy for password compromises.

A security assessment and test on such a control should include technical tests, such as dictionary-attack simulations, as well as social engineering like phishing or calling techniques to ascertain the control effectiveness. Similarly, a technical vulnerability assessment in an operating system may focus on the identification of such a vulnerability and the effectiveness of administrative controls, such as patch management.

In essence, security assessment is a combination of security tests and the validation of security control effectiveness based on the test results. A security assessment strategy is based on the requirements from the information security policy, generic and domain-specific business requirements, and risk management processes.

Security controls

Risk mitigation strategies involve the security controls that address one or more risk areas. For example, preventative controls are designed and implemented to prevent a *security violation* from happening. Similarly, detective controls are designed and rolled out to detect a security violation; reactive and recovery controls assist in business continuity in the event of a disaster or disruptions to business processes.

This security violation can stem from either an inadvertent or malicious breach of a security policy. For example, a security policy may state that **Non-Public Information (NPI)** *such as internal communications between board members or internal project information should not be exposed to general public.* If an employee posts such kind of information in a public blog, or if he sends out such information to an external entity through e-mail, then this will constitute a security violation. Such an act by an employee may be inadvertent. However, if an employee sends out such information to an external entity for a monetary benefit, then such an act is malicious.

Regardless of the intent of the act by the employee, the violation has to be identified and categorized as an incident for suitable remedial action. Any control that captures a security policy violation is an example of a security control.

Security controls can target a specific domain as well as combinations of domains. For example, preventive-physical controls are preventative controls that address physical security requirements. Similarly, an **Intrusion Detection System (IDS)** is a detective control that is available for IT networks as well as physical infrastructure.

Identifying suitable security controls is based on the security assessment, which in turn is a part of the risk management process. Once a suitable security control is identified, then its integration with the systems, associated processes, and the operations they perform should be a controlled activity. Besides, the data that is used for testing and the output of testing also needs to be a controlled activity.

Information-security standards, legal-regulatory frameworks and best practice recommendations provide baseline requirements for security assessments and expected test outcomes. However, a specific security control for an assessed risk depends on the risk mitigation strategy and is sometimes specific to the type of business.

For example, a bank may require a different type of security control compared to a research organization for the similar types of IT operations. Hence, security assessment and testing draw methods that are based on a combination of baseline standard requirements and domain-specific control needs.

The following sections describe various standard security assessments and test strategies, along with the expected outcomes of such security control testing. The expected outcomes can also be termed as the performance metrics for a security control.

Conduct security control testing

Generally, security control testing involves testing for the effectiveness of the control. In other words, whether the implemented control is performing as expected. A couple of examples of measurements of performance for a control would be the relevancy and adequacy of the control.

For example, to identify technical vulnerabilities in an off-the-shelf software product, relevant technical tools are required. Such tools are called scanners. However, such a tool may be inadequate for identifying vulnerabilities for logical implementation errors, which may require a different type of approach.

Vulnerability assessments

Vulnerability tests and assessments are performed to ascertain the presence of technical vulnerabilities or weaknesses in a system. It could be an IT system or any other automation product. Vulnerability in IT systems such as operating systems, an application software, or a network implementation can be considered as a hole or an error. Being technically an error, a vulnerability may allow a security violation to happen.

In the parlance of security, a security violation that happens due to a vulnerability is called a vulnerability compromise or vulnerability exploitation. Such exploitation may affect the confidentiality, integrity, or availability requirement of an organization's IT assets. For example, a buffer overflow vulnerability exploit may allow unauthorized access to the system or result in Denial-of-Service to legitimate users.

Vulnerability types, attacks and impacts are covered in detail in `Chapter` `6`, *Day 6 – Security Engineering – Security design, practices, models and Vulnerability mitigation.*

Vulnerability tests are performed to ascertain the presence of vulnerabilities that are published either by the application vendor or by an unknown one. When an identified vulnerability is not published by the application vendor, then it is called a *zero-day vulnerability*. Sometimes, an exploit code may be published by security or malicious groups. Such an exploit code is called *zero-day exploits*.

Hence, periodical vulnerability tests have to be performed to identify known and unknown vulnerabilities. Such tests reveal the effectiveness of security controls such as patch management; and for zero-day vulnerabilities, such tests reveal the effectiveness of compensating controls. Some of the areas where vulnerability tests are performed include the following:

- Operating system software
- Application software including web applications
- Firmware
- SCADA systems
- Industrial control systems

Compensating controls are security controls that compensate for the lack of actual security control. In a zero-day vulnerability scenario, if a patch is not available for an identified vulnerability then additional monitoring may act as a compensating control for attack detection.

Penetration testing

Penetration testing is often performed to ascertain break-in possibilities to systems. In other words, penetration tests are done to ascertain the exploitation possibilities of identified or unidentified vulnerabilities that are present in the software but are yet to be identified or published.

An identified vulnerability may be exploited; in other words, the vulnerability here is tested by trying to get unauthorized access possibilities to the application or system. A penetration test simulates an attack scenario. The scenario could be from the perspective of an internal authorized user such as an employee, an external entity, or a combination of both.

The tests are performed using different attack scenarios. The scenarios are based on the level of information available to the tester or an attacker. The following section lists some of the most common test or attack scenarios.

Black box testing

In black box testing, the network and application details are unknown to the tester. This is to simulate an external attacker trying to compromise the network or application from external locations, without the knowledge of internal configurations and the application's infrastructure.

White box testing

In white box testing, the network and application infrastructure is provided to the tester including configuration details. Hence, the test is performed to simulate the possibility of an attack by an internal user, who is an employee with in-depth knowledge about the infrastructure.

Grey box testing

A grey box testing can be considered as a combination of black box and a white box. In this scenario, some information about the infrastructure is known. For example, vendors may need to be provided access to internal applications. However, they may access the systems from external networks or connect to the corporate networks using technologies such as VPN. This test will simulate the possibility of an attack from such a setup.

Log reviews

Log reviews are a part of monitoring activities. Logs reveal a trail of transactions or activities that have taken place in real-time monitoring scenarios, while the activities are going on. Generally, a log review is a part of the accountability domain wherein the activities of the authorized users are monitored.

A log is a **Write Once Read Many** (**WORM**) type of data. The protection of log data itself is an important security control. If the integrity of the log data is lost, then the log review mechanism itself will produce erroneous results. Hence, an important security control such as "segregation of duties" is enforced for such data.

The segregation of duties and other security controls are described in the earlier chapters.

Synthetic transactions

These are generally used for performance monitoring, and hence, they are directly associated with the availability tenet of the information-security triad. Such kind of transaction testing is sometimes referred to as a real process or user monitoring. While log monitoring or reviewing can be used for checking all the three tenets of the information security, synthetic transaction tests focus mainly on the availability of systems and processes during different use case scenarios. Generally, a use case scenario in this type of test is stress or load testing.

Some of the tests in synthetic transactions are mentioned here.

Stress tests

While software or hardware is built to certain operational limits, stress tests are performed to test the robustness of the operational capabilities. For example, how much physical memory the application requires under certain test conditions, such as the number of transactions per hour, can be ascertained through stress tests.

Denial-of-Service tests

Denial-of-Service (**DoS**) is a type of test used to check the availability of a service under different conditions such as multiple and simultaneous requests. Using such tests involves flooding the application or network with many requests and checking the application or network-response times. If such a test is simulated from multiple networks to a single-targeted system, then it is called a **Distributed Denial-of-Service** (**DDoS**) test.

Load tests

Load tests are performed to simulate the performance of an application under load. For example, peak office hour loads versus non-business hour operations. The outcome of load tests will assist in defining or enhancing the capacity of the infrastructure or devising appropriate business-continuity plans.

Concurrency tests

This test is performed to test the application with a concurrent user activity. Generally, applications may not be accessed concurrently by all users. However, when an application is accessed concurrently by multiple users, then the request processing may get delayed. For example, the opening of a reservation window in a web application for a popular sports activity. Many users may try to book tickets at the same time, which increases the stress or load.

Latency test

Any request to a network or an application may involve a round trip of data—from the user, to application, and the resultant data back to the user. A latency test is used to check the round-trip time. The more time it takes for the request to reach the application, results in more time for the response to the user and vice-versa.

Code review and testing

Code review and testing involves testing the source code of an application for the presence of technical vulnerabilities as well as performance and logical issues. The following types of tests are applicable for code review.

Manual code review

A manual review of code is performed to check for any logical errors based on the application structure. Besides, such a review is conducted to check adherence to coding standards. Manual code reviews are generally done by the peer group of software developers or selected reviewers.

Dynamic code review

In dynamic code reviews, or the testing of a program, the software is executed in a simulated system or a virtual processor. In such tests, the program is fed with the required input values as well as malicious data to test the operational efficiency and security effectiveness.

Static code review

Contrary to dynamic code review, in a static review a software code is analyzed without executing the program code. This process is also called static code analysis. Unlike a manual review, a static review is mostly performed using automated tools to check for security, performance, and logical issues in an application code.

Fuzz code review

When random data is fed to an application as input values (sometimes, a large amount of random data as well) to test for application performance and security, then such a test is called a **fuzz test**. The purpose of a fuzz test is to test for application resilience in the event of unknown or unrelated data streams.

Misuse case testing

In this type of test, the reverse of use case is tested. In other words, doing a malicious act against a system is the misuse case of a normal act. For example, if an application is designed to perform a mathematical calculation and provide an input, such as an image data, then this is a **misuse case**. Generally, a security attack itself is a misuse case, which deviates from the purpose for which the application was actually built, and it is done to compromise the system.

Test coverage analysis

Generally, a software or an application code may not be completely taken up for code analysis due to the time-consuming process. Hence, the sample coverage of code is taken up for analysis. There may be security issues due to lesser test coverage. Similarly, all types of code reviews or other tests may not be conducted on the application. Hence, based on the security requirements, metrics have to be evaluated to identify the required tests, and the optimum level of code samples are required for testing. An analysis performed to identify such metrics is called a test coverage analysis.

Interface testing

User interfaces are gateways between man-machine interactions. Such interactions can be through the simple text methods of interaction—which are sometimes referred to as command-line interfaces—**Graphical User Interfaces** (GUI) and **Application Programming Interfaces** (API). Interface testing is done to ascertain the security during interactions between user to interfaces and interface to modules. For example, a user may be accessing a web application that requires a login. This is an example of a user interacting with an interface to provide an input. After the user provides the input (for example, the username/password), the application passes this to an authentication module for verification; and based on the feedback from the module, it allows the user to access the application. This is an example of an interface application to the module interaction.

The API

An API is a method to interact with applications through request-response calls rather than through a graphical user interface. API's are generally published by the application vendor with available methods and parameters to interact with the application. An API test involves the testing of functionality, performance, and security.

The UI

A **User Interface (UI)** testing can include **Command-Line Interface (CLI)** or Graphical User Interface (GUI) testing. The focus of such tests include the operations that can be performed through user interfaces. The performances of such user interfaces and the security of data during the interactions are the focus of such tests. Besides, the usability aspects of the interface are also tested.

Physical

Physical interfaces are generally used in instruments where operating parameters can be adjusted using physical buttons, switches, rotating units, and so on. Human interaction to computing devices using touch interactions can also be grouped under physical interfaces. For example, a biometric reader is a physical input from the user. Tests such as pressure, temperature, and environmental conditions are relevant for such interfaces.

The effectiveness of controls

In security, the effectiveness requirements of tools take precedence over efficiency. For example, a 100% efficient antivirus software that allows 10% of critical viruses to go undetected is an ineffective application. Similarly, systems that have high false-positive and false-negative rates are ineffective as well.

Summary

This chapter has covered foundational concepts in security assessment and testing strategies. Designing and validating security assessment and test strategies are important parts of the security profession. Conducting security tests provides information about vulnerabilities in the systems and can also be used to test the effectiveness of security controls. Depending on the type of IT asset, a suitable test method has to be adopted. Vulnerability assessment and penetration tests are generally conducted on networks and servers. Software tests including load tests and code reviews are conducted on application programs.

Continued in the next chapter are topics in this domain pertaining to the collection analysis of security test data, which include reporting internal and third-party auditing requirements.

Sample questions

Q1. Which one of the following is not a security testing method?

1. Vulnerability assessment
2. Penetration testing
3. Risk mitigation strategy
4. Gray box testing

Q2. A user is trying to access a web server that requires authentication and authorization. However, the system has given access to the web application without the user entering the password? This type of security issue is known as what?

1. Accountability error
2. Vulnerability
3. Penetration testing
4. Access control

Q3. Which type of tests, among the following, are a part of the software code review process? (This is a drag-and-drop type of a question. Here, you can draw a line from the list of answers from the left to the empty box to the right.)

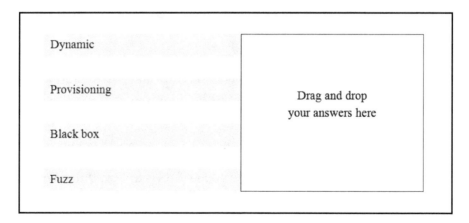

Q4. Test coverage analysis provides what?

1. Metrics needed for the code coverage
2. Authentication errors

3. Code review timelines
4. Interface design

Q5. Which one the following BEST describes a synthetic transaction?

1. Vulnerability testing
2. Penetration testing
3. Concurrency testing
4. API testing

Q6. When a threat event exploits a vulnerability, it results in which one of the following?

1. Security measure
2. Security improvement
3. Security violation
4. Security process

Q7. Code review and testing includes all of these *except:*

1. Fuzz
2. Dynamic
3. Load
4. Static

Q8. Denial-of-Service (DoS) is a type of test to check the availability of a service under different conditions, such as_____.

1. Logical security failure
2. Relevancy of controls
3. Multiple and simultaneous requests
4. Authentication failure

14

Day 14 – Security Assessment and Testing - Controlling, Analyzing, Auditing, and Reporting

This chapter covers management and operational controls pertaining to security process data. Analyzing and reporting test outputs either automated or through manual methods, and conducting or facilitating internal and third party audits are covered in detail.

A candidate appearing for the CISSP exam is expected to understand the foundational concepts and have knowledge in the following key areas of **controlling, analyzing, auditing, and reporting security tests** from the security assessment and testing domains:

- Management and operational controls on security process data
- Disaster recovery and business continuity
- Analyzing and reporting test outputs
- Internal and third-party security audits

An overview of controlling, analyzing, auditing, and reporting security test data

Security controls can be grouped as administrative and technical. The physical verification of an employee badge is a procedural administrative security control. Similarly, an access control system, such as a card reader that automates such a verification, is a technical security control. The function of a security control is based on data.

There are two types of applicable data pertaining to security controls. One is the data that is provided to the control for processing, in other words, the input data to the control. The other is security process data, in other words, the output data. For example, during a vulnerability scan on systems, lots of process data is available. Similarly, monitoring systems, such as intrusion prevention or detection systems, generate process data during control operations.

The input and output data of a security process has to be secured for analysis and establish an audit trail. Besides, such process data may need to be preserved for a longer period of time based on legal and regulatory requirements:

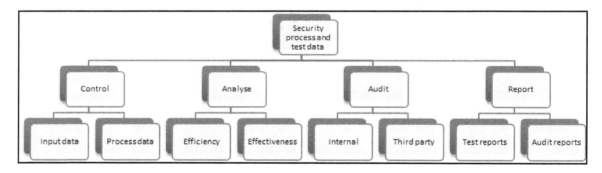

In this module, you will learn the following:

- Understanding the collection of security process data
- Understanding key performance and risk indicators
- Understanding disaster recovery and business continuity
- Getting an overview of automated and manual test results analysis and reporting methods
- Understanding internal and third-party audits and requirements

A collection of security process data

Security control implementation should be based on the outcome of risk assessment, and it is part of risk mitigation strategy. A strategy is based on the security policies, and the implementation and maintenance of a strategy is based on security procedures. One of the key requirements for security control is to demonstrate that the implemented control satisfies the requirements of the risk mitigation strategy, and in turn demonstrate adherence to established security policies and procedures.

Hence, a security control, whether technical, administrative, or physical, should provide sufficient data to establish that *security policies and procedures are continuously and uniformly applied.*

The data pertaining to a security control can be of two forms. One is data that is provided as an input to the control. The other is data that is generated or used during the process of an event and the output of control action. The input data can be a sample data or a live data. The output data of a process is called a *control or audit log*, which also contains the *control action.*

A control log contains triggers and a trace of activities. A control action contains the decision taken based on the activity and the trigger. For example, an e-mail sent out by an employee with confidential information maybe allowed or disallowed based on the security policy. A control log will contain these triggers based on policy and subsequent events as activity logs. Hence, confidential information in the e-mail triggers the security policy. The control action may block, warn, or raise an incident, advise encryption, and so on.

Before implementing a security control, sample test data may be used to verify the accuracy of the control. For example, databases containing information may be used as test data. Similarly, a collection of security process data is critical in establishing the audit trail, along with demonstrating that the application of security policies and procedures are continuous and uniform.

Hence, it is essential that both the input and output data that are used in security process has to be controlled. The following sections describe best practices for the control of security process data.

The control of security process data

Security process data establishes the audit trail including the action taken on a specific security event. Hence, the logs are important for any further investigation and/or to demonstrate adherence to security policies as well as any legal, regulatory, or contractual requirements. Any tampering of the security process data, data corruption, or non-availability will lead to non-compliance. Hence, it is important that this security process data is preserved and controlled as per the established data storage and retention norms as per business policies.

The protection and control of system test data

System test data may contain sensitive information. The selection of test data, protection, and control is a mandatory requirement in many regulatory frameworks. Some such requirements include the following:

- Avoiding operational databases that contain personal or sensitive information
- In case of using personal or sensitive information for testing purposes, then controlled removal of the data from test environment
- Establishing suitable access-control procedures to test systems
- Enforcing the segregation of duties
- Authorization policies for test systems
- Erasing operational information from test systems after the completion of tests
- Logging off all test activities to provide an audit trail

Audit logging

The activities of users, exceptions, and information security events are recorded in audit logs. These logs need to be retained for longer period of time based on data or log retention policies.

Audit logs include the following:

- User IDs and their access events, such as logon and logoff
- Terminal or location from which the user accessed the system
- The result of control action pertaining to the access attempt, for example, allowed or rejected
- Any changes to system configuration
- Accessed information including files and data

- Any bypasses such as deactivation of a security control or using malicious application

Audit logs are essential for future investigations and access control monitoring.

System logs

Monitoring system logs for security events involve segregating the security-related log information from the overall logs. It is also best practice to separately copy or save security event information from system logs to a different file or location.

Administrator and operator logs

System administration or super user accounts have complete control over the system in most of the operating systems. These accounts are also single point of failure in many systems. Monitoring system administration and operator activities are critical to security and hence usage of such accounts must be logged.

Similar to audit logging, system administrator access and the actions performed by the administrator must also be logged. Such a log should be reviewed on a regular basis to demonstrate compliance to system administration monitoring.

Fault logging

Faults in systems may be reported by users or the application fault or error messages should be appropriately logged to an error or a fault-log file. Fault logs should be reviewed periodically to implement corrective measures as well as devise appropriate preventive controls.

Key performance and risk indicators

The data from security processes can indicate several important parameters. One is related to the performance of the security tools and the other is related to risk. For example, a tool monitoring a storage device may provide information, such as the data retrieval time in terms of performance, and provide a capacity utilization to highlight the risk of exceeding the disk quota.

Such data is useful in determining the disaster-recovery and business-continuity needs, and it will help in establishing appropriate plans for business continuity.

Disaster recovery and business continuity

In the context of process data, disaster-recovery and business-continuity plans include backup procedures and recovery mechanisms.

In the event of a system overload, a catastrophic system failure, or the loss of facility, such data is essential for audit trails and for devising suitable BC and DR plans.

Analyzing security process data

Data analysis is one of the core activities used to establish a security violation as well as control effectiveness. Two parameters are used in this industry to indicate the effectiveness of control from the perspective of identified security violations. One parameter is called the false positive rate and the other is the false negative rate. False positive flags an event as a security violation when it is not. On the other hand, false negative fails to flag a security violation.

False positives

A security process or tool may flag an event as a security violation while the event is not. For example, a fingerprint scanner used in identity and access management may reject a legitimate entity after scanning. This may be due to incorrect or insufficient samples of the entity's finger prints. Such a control action is called false positive action.

False negatives

When a security process or a tool allows an illegitimate event to pass through without raising a security violation, then it is called false negative. For example, an unauthorized entity is allowed to access a resource that requires authorization.

The effectiveness of a security control or a process can also be determined by false positive and false negative rates. Generally, such data will provide inputs to adjust the sensitivity settings of a security control.

The effectiveness of a security control

A security control is considered to be effective when the false positive and false negative rates are minimum. This implies that the security control is performing as per the requirement of the security policy.

The effectiveness of a security control can be ascertained from audits. Periodical internal or third-party audits provide the verification and validation of the control implementation and performance.

Internal and third-party security audits

Audits provide a method to validate adherence to security policies and procedures by the business. Audits consist of verification and validation actions to identify compliance and non-compliance. The verification process in an audit checks the availability of suitable processes to support policies and procedures. The validation process in an audit to check adequacy, the correctness of a process, and the adequacy of controls.

Internal audits

When a business audits its processes through its internal audit department, then such an exercise is called an internal audit. An internal audit is generally performed by the business using its own resources. The purpose of an internal audit is to regularly validate various business systems for policy and procedural compliance.

Third-party audits

In third-party audits, an independent agency or entity that is not associated with the business performs the audit. The auditors are external to the organization. The purpose of third-party audits is twofold. One is the independent verification of security posture. The other one is for certification purposes, such as compliance or standards-related certification.

Information system audit controls

In both internal and third-party audits, when the audits are performed on information systems, it is important to consider that such audits have a minimum disruption to business processes.

Some of the best practices in information system audit controls include the following:

- The management, agreement, and acceptance for audit requirements
- Agreement on the scope prior to audit
- Confidentiality and **Non-Disclosure Agreements** (**NDA**) with auditors
- Unless required for audit process, allowing only read-only access of data to the auditors
- Monitoring all auditor access
- Agreed responsibilities of auditors
- Ensuring that the persons carrying out the audit are independent of the activity being audited

Reporting test and audit outputs

The test and audit data has to be presented in a format suitable for making management and administrative decisions. Such a process is called audit reporting, and the outcome is an audit report. A test report can identify specific areas of administrative controls, and it provides the test results of a security-testing activity. An audit report will be a consolidated view of adherence to security policies, procedures, as well as compliance to specific legal or regulatory requirements or information security standards.

Test and audit reports need to be backed up and archived for future investigations or compliance requirements. The time period for such archival varies between standards and regulatory requirements.

Summary

This chapter has covered foundational concepts in controlling, analyzing, auditing, and reporting the security process and test data. The preservation of security test data is essential in the event of audits and establishing audit trail. It is also used in demonstrating the effectiveness of implemented security control. Methods such as analyzing the security data and internal and third-party audits are conducted to provide evidence that the application of security policies and procedures are continuous and uniform.

Next is a review chapter that includes the content from chapters 11 to 14 in an exam cram format. References and further study for the four chapters are provided. A mock test consisting of about 10 questions is also provided.

Sample questions

Q1. Which one of the following is not a security testing control?

1. Vulnerability assessment
2. Penetration testing
3. Departmental tests
4. Denial of Service Tests

Q2. Access is controlled through a retina scanner for the identification, authentication, and authorization of operators to a data center. A legitimate user was erroneously denied access during a scan. Such errors can be categorized under which one of the following?

1. False negative
2. False positive
3. False rating
4. True negative

Q3. The effectiveness of a security control is a measure for which one of the following?

1. Expected outcome of a control action
2. Efficient process
3. Security policy
4. Security procedure

Q4. The collection of security process, test data, and reporting is used to verify what?

1. Security controls are documented
2. Employee awareness about security controls
3. Avoid social engineering attacks
4. Security policies and procedures are continuously and uniformly applied

Q5. Third-party audits are conducted for what?

1. Independent review of security
2. Internal review of security
3. Management review of security
4. Administrative control validation

Q6. Audit logs may include all of these *except:*

1. The terminal or location from which the user accessed the system
2. Passwords provided by the users
3. Any changes to system configuration
4. Accessed information including files and the data

Q7. Identify some of the best practices in the information system audit control? (This is a drag-and-drop type of question. Here, and for similar drag-and-drop questions, you can draw a line from the list of answers from the left to the empty box on the right).

Agreement on the scope prior to audit	
Monitoring all auditor access	Drag and drop your answers here
Agreed responsibilities of auditors	
Write access to audit records to the auditors	

Q8. An organization engages an agency to conduct an independent audit on its systems. Such an audit is known as what?

1. Internal audit
2. Second party audit
3. Third party audit
4. Compliance review

15

Day 15 – Exam Cram and Practice Questions

This chapter provides the concepts that are covered in the fifth and sixth domains of CISSP CBK in a snippet format, which will reinforce the topics learned and serve as an exam cram. A mock test consisting of ten questions from these two domains is provided. Finally, further reading and references are provided.

An overview of exam cram and practice questions

This chapter starts with an exam cram that consists of quick revision points from the fifth domain of the CISSP CBK **identity and access management** and from the sixth domain of **security assessment and testing**. This is followed by a mock test from these two domains. The last topic of this chapter provides additional references for further reading:

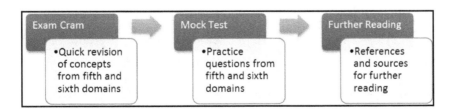

Exam cram

Presented here is a revision of the concepts discussed in the previous four chapters, that is, chapters eleven through fourteen. They are provided in bullet points as snippets that are easy to revise. These snippets are for a quick revision and reinforcement of the knowledge learned:

CISSP CBK Domain #5 – identity and access management

The following bullet points are in an exam cram format for a quick revision. They cover important points from the identity and access management domain. The covered topics include physical and logical access to assets, Identity Management principles and implementation, identity as a service, third-party identity services, access management, authorization mechanisms, identity and provisioning life cycle, and preventing or mitigating access control attacks:

- The overall process of facilitating and managing identities and controlling access to assets while ensuring information security is termed as **identity and access management (IAM)**.
- Identity and access management domain can further be subdivided into two interrelated management activities, such as Identity Management and Access Management.
- Identity and access management consists of four distinctive principles and practices. They are Identification, Authentication, Authorization, and Accountability.
- Authentication, Authorization, and Accountability are together referred to as the Triple A of Access Control.
- Identity management includes some or all of the following:
  - The enrollment of user identifiers.
  - The provisioning of user identities to different systems.
  - Updating all associated accounts whenever there is a change in user information.
  - If the user no longer needs access or is retired, then deprovisioning user accounts that are no longer required.

- When software is delivered as a service through the Internet cloud, then it is generically termed as **Software as a Service (SaaS)**.

- When identity and access management applications and associated services are delivered through subscription-based cloud models, such services are termed as **Identity as a Service (IDaaS)**.

- Access management is facilitated through authentication and authorization processes.

- The access management layer also consists of accountability mechanisms, such as logging and monitoring activities.

- The primary concept in access control is to understand about a *subject* and an *object*.

- A **subject** may be a person, process, or technology component that either seeks access or controls the access.

- An **object** can be a file, data, a physical equipment, or premises that needs controlled access.

- Controlling access to the object by a subject is the core requirement of access control.

- If access to an object is controlled based on certain contextual parameters such as location, time, sequence of responses, access history and more, then it is known as **context-dependent** access control.

- If the access is provided based on the attributes or content of an object, then it is called content-dependent access control.

- Access control models define methods by which a system controls the access to the object by a subject.

- **Discretionary access control** is one in which the subject has some authority to specify the objects that are accessible to them. **Access control list (ACL)** is an example of discretionary access control.

- When access to the object is based on certain rules, then it is called **Rule-Based Access Control (RBAC)**.

- When the access is controlled based on mandatory rules, then it is known as **Mandatory Access Control (MAC).**

- If a centralized authority controls the access based on a specific policy, then the same is referred to as **non-discretionary access control**.

- A **Role-Based Access Control (RBAC)** is a non-discretionary access control based on the subject's role or position in the organization.

- A **task-based access control** is based on a subject's responsibilities in the organization.
- A **lattice-based access control** is one where there is a pair of values that determine the access rights.
- **Decentralized access control** or **Distributed access control** is where the core functions of access are distributed over a network.
- Identity and access management consists of two distinctive activities:
    - One is related to the *identification* of the subject by the system.
    - The other is *authentication* and *authorization,* which is the system's ability to validate the credential supplied by the subject and determine access levels.
- When an entity (subject) is validated against a single credential, then it is called a **one-factor authentication** and generally uses the *what you know* principle.
- When an entity (subject) is validated against two different credentials, then it is called a **two-factor authentication** and generally uses the *what you have* principle.
- When an entity (subject) is validated against two or more different credentials, then it is called a **multifactor authentication** and generally uses the *what you are* principle.
- Authorization is a process of determining the levels of access a subject may have on the object.
- In the identity and provisioning life cycle, there are two distinctive activities. One is user management and the other is system or application access.
- There are many attacks that can be attributed to the compromise of access control systems and processes to gain unauthorized access.
- **Backdoors** are unauthorized open ports created by malicious programs that allow an authorized entity to gain access into the system.
- **Denial-of-Service (DoS)** is a type of attack wherein the legitimate users of the system are prevented from access by disturbing the availability.
- A **Distributed Denial-of-Service (DDoS)** is a type of attack where multiple systems attack a single resource from distributed locations.
- **Hijacking** is an attack in which the session established by the client to the server is taken over by the malicious person or process.
- **Man-in-the-Middle attack** is a type of attack where an attacker hijacks the established session of a client to the server by impersonating a client.
- **TCP hijacking** is a type of attack in which the TCP session of the trusted client to the server is hijacked by an attacker.

- **Malicious codes** executes itself in the client machine and compromises the security.
- The **Trojan horse** is one type of malicious code that comes disguised inside a trusted program.
- When the Trojan horse is activated on a particular event (such as a particular date), then it is called a **logic bomb**.
- **Malicious mobile codes** are the ones that are executed in the client system through the network from a remote server.
- **Password guessing** is one of the attacks that uses various methods to obtain user passwords.
- **Dictionary attacks** are a type of password-guessing attack that checks the encrypted password database with the words found in the dictionary.
- **Brute force attacks** are the means by which the password database is attacked with all the types of letters and possible combinations of characters.
- **Hybrid attacks** combine the dictionary as well as brute force attacks.
- **Replay attacks** are the ones in which the session (such as authentication) is captured and replayed against the system.
- **Scanning** is an attack used to probe the network and system to identify the vulnerabilities for planning a possible attack to compromise.
- **Vulnerability exploitation** is the way of attacking systems by compromising the holes or errors in the operating system or application software to gain access or bypass security controls.
- **Spoofing** is a type of attack used to imitate a trusted entity, thereby making the system trust this imitated entity.
- **Social engineering** is a type of attack used to obtain credential information such as passwords, pin numbers, and so on using social skills, such as impersonation, fake e-mails, and so on.
- In identity and access management, accountability aspects play a major role in establishing preventative, detective, and corrective controls to access control attacks.
- Accountability, in simple terms, can be defined as *monitoring the activities of the authorized user*.

CISSP CBK Domain #6 – security assessment and testing

The following bullet points are presented in an exam cram format for a quick revision. They cover important points from the identity and access management domain. The covered topics include security assessment and testing strategies, security control testing, designing and validating assessment and testing strategies, security testing tools, methods and techniques, and evaluating the effectiveness of controls:

- Risk management involves assessment and testing pertaining to security.
- Security assessment and testing is carried out based on suitably designed assessment and test strategies.
- Security assessment and test strategies are administrative controls that provide processes and procedures to operate and continually assess the effectiveness of controls.
- Security assessment and test strategies are based on risk to assets.
- Information security standards, legal-regulatory frameworks, and best practice recommendations provide a baseline requirements for security assessments and expected test outcomes.
- Vulnerability tests and assessments are performed to ascertain the presence of technical vulnerabilities or some kind of weakness in systems.
- When an identified vulnerability is not published by the application vendor, then it is called a **zero-day vulnerability**.
- When an exploit code is published by security or malicious groups before a patch release by the vendor, then it is called **zero-day exploits**.
- Penetration testing is often performed to ascertain break-in possibilities in systems.
- In **black-box testing**, the network and application details are unknown to the tester.
- In **white-box testing**, the network and application infrastructure is provided to the tester, including configuration details.
- A **grey-box testing** can be considered as a combination of black box and a white box. In this scenario, some information about the infrastructure is known.
- **Log reviews** area a part of monitoring activities.
- Logs reveal a trail of transactions or activities that have taken place and in real-time monitoring scenarios while the activities are going on.

- **Synthetic transactions** are generally used for performance monitoring, and hence, they are directly associated with the availability tenet of the information security triad.
- **Stress tests** are performed to test the robustness of the operational capabilities.
- Denial-of-Service (DoS) is a type of test used to check the availability of a service under different conditions, such as multiple and simultaneous requests.
- **Load tests** are performed to simulate the performance of an application under load.
- **Concurrency tests** are performed to test the application with concurrent user activity.
- **Latency tests** check the round-trip time of a request response.
- **Code review and testing** involves testing the source code of an application for the presence of technical vulnerabilities as well as performance and logical issues.
- A **manual code review** is performed to check for any logical errors based on the application's structure.
- In a **dynamic code review** or testing of a program, the software is executed in a simulated system or a virtual processor.
- In a **static code review**, a software code is analyzed without executing the program code.
- A **misuse case test** is the reverse of a use case test. In other words, doing a malicious act against a system is the misuse case of a normal act.
- An analysis performed to identify metrics for code coverage is called the **test coverage analysis**.
- **Interface testing** is done to ascertain the security during interactions between a user to interfaces and interface to modules.
- An **API test** involves the testing of the functionality, performance, and security of application programming interfaces.
- A **User Interface (UI) testing** can include **Command-Line Interface (CLI)** or **Graphical User Interface (GUI)** testing. The focus of such tests includes operations that can be performed through user interfaces.
- Tests such as pressure, temperature, and environment conditions are used in **physical interface tests**.
- In security effectiveness, the requirements of tools take precedence over efficiency.
- An assurance of effective software and applications is a requirement and is ascertained through security testing.

Mock test

Q1. An interface test is done to ascertain:

1. Pressure, temperature, and environment conditions
2. Metrics for code coverage
3. The round-trip time of a request response
4. Security during interactions between user to interfaces and interface to modules

Q2. Identity management includes:

1. The enrollment of user identifiers
2. The provisioning or deprovisioning of user identities to different systems
3. Whenever there is a change in user information then updating all associated accounts
4. All of the above

Q3. When an identified vulnerability is not published by the application vendor then it is called:

1. Zero-day vulnerability
2. Zero-day exploit
3. Zero-day logic bomb
4. Zero-day threat

Q4. Which one of the following is not a password attack?

1. Dictionary attack
2. Brute force attack
3. Code attack
4. Hybrid attack

Q5. The reverse of a use case test is a:

1. Vulnerability case test
2. Penetration case test
3. Nonuse case test
4. Misuse case test

Q6. A person, process, or technology component that either seeks access or controls the access is called:

    1. Subject
    2. Object
    3. Data
    4. Control

Q7. Synthetic transactions are generally used for:

    1. Performance monitoring and directly associated with the availability tenet
    2. Performance monitoring and directly associated with the confidentiality tenet
    3. Performance monitoring and directly associated with the integrity tenet
    4. Performance monitoring and directly associated with authentication

Q8. Imitating a trusted entity, thereby making the system trust this imitated entity, is known as:

    1. Scanning
    2. Sniffing
    3. Spoofing
    4. Monitoring

Q9. Identify the true statements pertaining to access control from the following (this is a drag-and-drop type of question. Here, and for similar drag-and-drop questions, you can draw a line from the list of answers from the left to the empty box on the right).

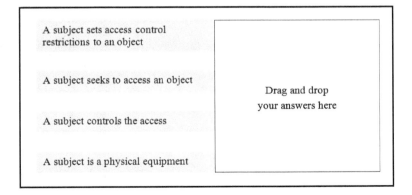

Q10. Which one of the following choices in an audit trail that is unlikely to be contained in the access log file pertaining to physical access?

1. Access attempts
2. Access results such as success or failure
3. Locations accessed
4. Access control list

References and further reading

- **Common Vulnerabilities and Exposure (CVE)**: https://cve.mitre.org/
- **Common Vulnerabilities Scoring System (CVSS)**: https://nvd.nist.gov/cvss.cfm
- **Identity Management white paper from CA Technologies**: https://www.ca.com/us/collateral/ebook/managing-and-governing-identities-in-the-new-open-enterprise.register.html
- **NIST technical guide to information security testing**: http://csrc.nist.gov/publications/nistpubs/800-115/SP800-115.pdf

Summary

This chapter covered some of the important concepts in the form of an exam cram, from the fifth and sixth domains of CISSP CBK. A mock test with a combination of questions from the two domains are provided to test the knowledge learned. Further reading and references are provided to enhance the knowledge in these two domains.

In the next chapter, you will learn security operations with an explanation of core concepts in the operations security, physical and environmental security, equipment security, and monitoring activities.

16

Day 16 – Security Operations - Foundational Concepts

This chapter covers security in operations including physical and environmental security, equipment security, and monitoring activities. The core concepts in the operations security are covered with suitable illustrations.

A candidate appearing for the CISSP exam is expected to understand the foundational concepts and have the knowledge in the following key areas of the **operations security** domain:

- Implementing and managing physical security
- Physical security principles for sites and facilities
- Environmental security practices for sites and facilities
- Logging and monitoring activities
- Understanding and supporting investigations
- Securing the provision of resources
- Operations security
- Resource protection techniques
- Foundational concepts on incident management
- Preventative measures
- Patch and vulnerability management
- Change management principles
- Disaster recovery and business continuity exercises

An overview of operations security

Assets, such as data, are accessed and processed in operational areas through systems and applications. Similarly, access to facilities, such as data centers and operational areas, are facilitated through access control mechanisms. Hence, physical access to operational areas needs to have appropriate controls for strong authentication and authorization.

Observe the following illustration. Users need access to physical facilities such as operational areas. Such physical areas can be subdivided into perimeter and interior sections. Controlling access to operational areas, and the process of identifying and blocking unauthorized intrusions to the operational areas are primary security requirements in this domain. In the scenario of a physical intrusion, it is essential to identify breaches and implement control actions, including investigations:

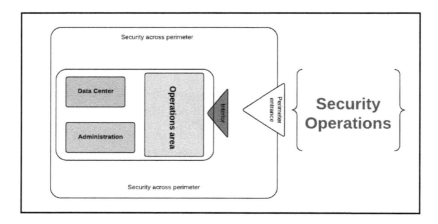

In this module, you will learn about the following:

- Applying secure principles to the site and facility design
- Designing and implementing physical security
- Understanding logging and monitoring activities
- Understanding and supporting investigations
- An overview of investigation types
- An overview of security while the provision of resources
- Understanding operations security
- Employing resource protection techniques

The physical security design

While designing a robust physical security environment, a security professional needs to take into account the following three important parameters:

- The physical facility
- Geographic operating location
- Supporting facilities

National Institute of Standards and Technology (NIST) Special Publication 800-12: An Introduction to Computer Security – The NIST Handbook explains these three parameters next.

Physical facility

The **physical facility** is usually the building, other structure, or vehicle housing the system and network components.

Systems can be characterized, based upon their operating location, as static, mobile, or portable:

- **Static systems** are installed in structures at fixed locations
- **Mobile systems** are installed in vehicles that perform the function of a structure but not at a fixed location
- **Portable systems** are not permanently installed in fixed operating locations

Geographic operating location

Natural threats such as earthquakes and floods; man-made threats such as burglary and civil disorders; communication-related threats such as the interception of transmissions or emanations and electromagnetic interference; and chemical threats such as toxic chemical spills, explosions, fire, and so on; have to be taken into consideration while determining the facility's general **geographic operating location**.

Supporting facilities

Supporting facilities include electric power, heating, and air conditioning, and telecommunications. Disturbances in such facilities or performance degradation would adversely affect the operation of the system or may cause data corruption.

The design should consider the following three primary requirements in terms of security:

- **Unauthorized disclosure** leading to a confidentiality breach
- **Loss of control** over integrity of the information
- **Interruptions** as well as physical damage that could affect availability

Also, one of the most important threats that needs to be considered for physical security is **theft** that could affect all the three.

Physical and operations security controls

Security controls that pertain to physical and operations are predominantly in the authentication and authorization processes. Unauthorized intrusions are a common threat in this domain. The following sections provide some of the common security threats, vulnerabilities, and countermeasures in this domain.

Threats, vulnerabilities, and countermeasures for physical and operations security

We have seen the concept of threats and vulnerabilities in various security domains in the earlier chapters. Though the threats are predominantly common across most of the security domains, the vulnerabilities they could exploit will vary, and the countermeasures are generally unique. Some of the threats and vulnerabilities that could exploit the infrastructure (infrastructure includes IT infrastructure as well) and its associated components are listed here.

Common threats

Some of the common threats to physical environment are as follows:

- Theft
- Heat and temperature

- Humidity
- Organic materials and chemicals that are in gaseous or liquid form
- Organisms such as microbes
- Missiles or bombs that are used as projectiles
- Natural calamities such as earthquake, flood, and so on
- Electrical power disruptions that includes electro-magnetic interference

Common vulnerabilities

Vulnerabilities that the preceding threats could exploit but are not limited to include the following:

- Lack of physical entry controls and accountability
- Lack of fire extinguishers or improper maintenance
- Improper or poor cabling
- Inappropriate chemicals used in the fire extinguishers for the protection of a particular type of asset
- Inappropriate storage of magnetic media
- Weak access controls and intrusion detection systems
- No backup or business continuity plans
- Lack of power control systems

A deeper understanding of these threats and vulnerabilities are essential to do a thorough risk assessment. It is also important to understand relevant specifications pertaining to equipment's as well as physical security standards while designing countermeasures.

Designing physical and operations security controls

Security controls and monitoring processes for physical and operations areas can be subdivided into two main sections. One is related to a perimeter that is external to boundaries, and the other pertains to an interior or operational area. In both these sections, the following core controls need to be considered:

- **Preventative controls**: These are designed to prevent a security event. For example, having a high-raise wall will be a control to prevent intrusion.

- A **security event** is an undesirable activity that could affect he Confidentiality, Integrity, or Availability of an information asset.

The following are some of the examples that are preventive physical controls:

- A high-rise wall
- Fences
- Locks

- Detective controls: These controls are designed to detect an event before it could damage the facilities. The following are some of the examples that are detective physical controls:
  - Fire alarm
  - Intrusion detection systems such a motion and heat sensors
  - Surveillance monitors such as CCTV

- **Reactive controls**: These controls are designed to react in a timely manner to a security event, for example, armed response to an intrusion. The following are some of the examples that are reactive physical controls:
  - Armed responses
  - Mantrap systems

- **Deterrent controls**: These controls are designed to act as a deterrent against an attempt to breach the security; for example, guards and dogs. The following are some of the examples that are deterrent physical controls:
  - Guards
  - Dogs
  - Lighting

Perimeter security

Perimeter security relates to the security considerations pertaining to the boundaries. In other words, securing the entry and exit points of the facility, networks, and so on, will fall under perimeter security.

In physical and operations security domain, the following controls are applicable to perimeter security:

- **Guards** are a form of security control used to prevent, detect, deter, and react to an intrusion event. They also act as a physical access control to the facility. Their ability to adapt to situations is a major plus to this type of security. The disadvantages are related to their availability in hostile environments that do not support human intervention, reliability, and cost.
- **Dogs** are a type of security control used to prevent, detect, deter, and react to an intrusion event. Their ability where a judgment is necessary is, however, limited.
- **Fencing** is an access control for perimeter security. High-rise walls, gates, mantraps, and turnstiles are some of the examples for the same. The following are some of the height requirements pertaining to fencing:
    - 3' to 4' high deters casual trespassers
    - 6' to 7' high is too hard to climb easily
    - 8' high with 3 strands of barbed wire deters most of the intruders

A **turnstile** is a type of fencing that will allow only one person to pass through it at a time and is also called a **baffle gate**. Similarly, a type of vertical post called a bollard is used as a control to protect the facility from vehicle intrusions.

- **Locks** are preventative access control to perimeter security. **Preset locks** have preset internal mechanisms, whereas **programmable locks** have dials that can be programmed to contain digits, letters, or a combination of both.
- **Lighting** is a deterrent control. The purpose of lighting is to discourage intruders as well as detect suspicious movements. NIST standards specify an illumination of 2 feet wide and 8 feet high for critical areas.
- **Closed circuit televisions (CCTV)** are used to monitor live movements as well as provide an audit trail during incident review. **Heat sensors** are also used to monitor the facilities for detecting live movements.
- Access control devices such as **access cards** control physical access to the facility.

Access cards can be categorized as photo cards, digitally encoded cards, as well as wireless cards. When an access card combines with the physical and logical access control as well as contains embedded integrated circuits that can process information, then it is called a **smart card**.

- **Biometric devices** use physical characteristics of a person to identify and provide access to the facility. Some examples of it are fingerprint scanners, retina scanning, and more.

Interior security

Interior security refers to the security considerations pertaining to the facilities that are inside the perimeter. This will include equipment inside the data center and personnel working in such facilities.

One of the most important aspects of interior security is the threats posed by unauthorized intrusions, fire, electrical power, and **Heating, Ventilation, and Air-conditioning** (HVAC).

Unauthorized intrusions

Intrusions to the interior are controlled by motion detectors, mantraps, and more. Motion detectors are used in interior security to detect suspicious movements. They raise an alarm based on the type of motion detection technique used.

Mantrap systems are designed to stop and trap an intruder in between two entrances. Based on the physical access control mechanisms, a mantrap gets activated on detection of suspicious movement either automatically or manually.

Motion detectors

The **wave pattern** is a type of motion detector that would generate an alarm when the wave pattern is disturbed. There are three types of sensors used in wave pattern motion detectors. They are passive infrared, ultrasonic, and microwave sensors.

When an electric field is used around an object being monitored and the field gets charged to raise an alarm, then it is called a capacitance-based motion detector.

Audio detectors are a type of motion detector that passively listen to abnormal sounds to detect motion.

Fire

Fire is a threat that could damage the physical assets, such as computers, networks, as well as the data center.

Fire spreads through **combustible materials**. While fire extinguishers or suppression agents are used to contain the rapid spread of fire, a professional has to be cautious about the type of extinguishing material used.

Fire classes

For fire to catch and spread, a combustible material is required. Based on the type of combustible material, fire is classified into four classes.

National Fire Protection Association (NFPA) provides the following specifications pertaining to the fire classes based on the type of the combustible material; it also classifies them based on suppression mediums:

- **Class A** combustible materials are wood, paper, cloth, rubber. Most of the plastics also fall into this class.
- **Class B** combustible materials are oils, greases, oil-based paints, lacquers, and flammable liquids and gases.
- **Class C** is predominantly electrical equipment that is energized.
- **Class D** refers to flammable chemicals, such as magnesium and sodium.

Fire detectors

Fire detectors are controls for detecting and responding to heat, flames, or smoke. Depending upon the type of detection, they can be classified as heat, flame, or smoke sensors.

Fire suppression mediums

Fire suppression is critical to protect lives, operational systems, and the data center. Using a suitable or applicable fire suppression medium is important if you want to have effective protection:

- **Water, soda acid, CO^2**, and **Halon** are some of the fire suppression mediums
- **Portable fire extinguishers** predominantly use Carbon Dioxide (CO^2) or soda acid
- **Halon** is a suppressing medium that is no longer allowed to be used, as it is designated as an ozone depleting substance

Water sprinklers

Fire extinguishers use either water sprinkler or gas dischargers to suppress fire.

Water sprinklers are of four types. They are Wet pipe, Dry pipe, Deluge, and Preaction:

- **Wet pipe** sprinkling systems always contain water and the valve opens when the heat rises above 165°F
- In **Dry pipe** sprinkling systems, water flows from the outer valve when the heat rises above the threshold level
- **Deluge** sprinkler systems are used to discharge large volumes of water
- **Preaction** combines wet as well as dry pipe systems such that the water flow is controlled

Gas dischargers

Gas discharge systems use CO_2 or Halon instead of water and are usually used under the raised floor of the data centers. However, CO_2 can be used only in an unattended data center as it will have a harmful effect on humans.

Electrical power

Clean **electrical power** is a requirement for proper equipment functioning. If the power is not clean, then it will result in spoiling or damaging the equipment. This may lead to the malfunctioning of devices, leading to unavailability and the corruption of data.

The following are some of the most important terms that are related to electrical power that could affect equipment:

- When the power fluctuates due to interference, the effect is called **noise.**
- When there is a charge difference between neutral, hot, and ground electrical wires, it results in **Electromagnetic Interference (EMI).** This interference is caused by electromagnetic waves.
- **Radio Frequency Interference (RFI)** is caused by radio waves generated by the electrical system components such as cables, florescent lights, and so on.

The following definitions are related to electrical power that a candidate should be thorough with:

- When there is a momentary power loss, it is called a **Fault**
- If the power loss is complete, then it is called a **Blackout**
- When there is a momentary low voltage, it is called a **Sag**
- When the voltage is low for a prolonged period of time, it is called a **Brownout**
- When the voltage is temporarily high, then it is called a **Spike**
- If the voltage is high for a prolonged period of time, then it is called a **Surge**
- When the incoming power at the beginning is high, then it is called a **Inrush**
- When there is a steady interference, it is called a **Noise**
- When the interference is of short duration, it is called a **Transient**
- When the power is non-fluctuating, then it is called a **Clean**

Humidity is the percentage of water vapor present in the air. For proper functioning of the computer systems, the humidity levels should be between 40 and 60 percent. If the humidity is low, then due to dryness, static electricity would set in. If the humidity is high, then due to wetness, some of the components would rust.

Operations/facility security

Facility security concerns the management of facility controls. Some of the important controls that need attention are auditing and emergency procedures.

Auditing

Auditing is a process to check and validate the effectiveness of controls. The primary tool that assists in the audit is an audit trial. In physical and operational security domains, auditing is primarily done from the scope of physical access controls and operational procedures. The focus of the audit is to ascertain that the threats and vulnerabilities to physical access are identified, suitable mitigation to the risks is being implemented, and the effectiveness of physical access controls is ascertained.

While doing audits with the scope of physical security of information systems, the following points need to be considered:

- The physical location of the information systems is a primary factor. Environmental factors, such as proximity to toxic chemical installations and locations that are in the seismic zone and close to seashore, should be avoided at best.

Seismic zones are regions where earthquakes are known to occur.

- Adherence to HVAC specifications for server and network equipment, their proper functioning, and maintenance. It is better not to have windows in the data center, and the doors are designed to maintain positive air pressure.

 Positive air pressure implies that the air flows out of the room when the door is opened.

- The usage of raised floors in data centers and all the cables and ducts are run under the raised floors.

 Based on various specifications, a raised data center floor can be anywhere between 300 mm to 800 mm, depending upon the floor area

- It is important to check the adequacy of access control mechanisms. The usage of smart cards, proximity cards, biometric sensors, and mantrap systems for data center access control should be encouraged. An audit trail has to be established for auditing the use of credentials.
- A periodic vetting of personnel working in critical installations such as data centers.
- Access controls to support infrastructure such as telecommunication rooms, power control rooms housing UPS, and batteries.
- Fire detection and suppression controls based on the recommended specifications.
- An adequacy of lighting and emergency lighting.
- An adequacy of water, temperature, and humidity sensors along with their alarm functions.
- Avoiding obvious sign boards and directions to critical installations.
- Insurance coverage.

Audit trail

An **audit trail** contains all the recorded events. The events may be security related or general activities. One of the most important audit trails in physical and operational security domains is the access details to the data center and other control rooms. The access details should contain the access attempts, the result such as success or failure, as well as the location accessed.

The record of access events is stored in a file called logs. An **access log** contains the events that are related to access attempts, and **error logs** contain the exceptions.

Generally, access logs contain event-related details, such as the date and time of the access attempt, the result of the access attempt in terms of success or failure, the location where the access was granted, the person who was authorized, and the modifications to the access privileges.

Emergency procedures

Physical security also deals with procedures that need to be followed during emergencies. An emergency is an undesired event that may disturb operations for a prolonged period of time. The impact of an emergency event could be devastating in terms of human loss, facility loss, connectivity disturbances, and equipment and data loss. Proper procedures need to be developed; personnel are trained on such procedures and are periodically tested for effectiveness and continued usability.

The upcoming sections deal with emergency procedures that an information security professional should be aware of.

Startup and shutdown procedures

During an emergency, the IT systems may be shutdown intentionally or automatically and may be required to be relocated to a different site. Similarly, data maybe moved to a different system at a remote site. System **startup and shutdown procedures** lay down guidelines and activities that need to be performed in a way that security could not be compromised during system/data migration or relocation. These procedures should include emergency procedures to address the requirements when a disaster strikes. Some of the startup and shutdown procedures include the following:

* Checking all the cables before startup to ensure that they are not loose
* Checking that the power strip is turned on and the power plug is tightly placed

- Checking that the peripheral devices are properly connected and powered on as per procedures
- Booting the systems to a single user or a multi-user mode as per security requirements
- Activating network connections in either manual or automatic mode based on security requirements
- Ensuring that the system shuts down completely during system halt
- Avoiding the physical reset of the operating system
- Ensuring that all the programs are closed before shutdown
- In case of unplanned or unexpected shutdown, ensuring that the system is restarted in diagnostic mode, so that any data corruption is checked before loading the operating system

Evacuation procedures

Evacuation procedures address the priorities in terms of evacuating assets from the disaster site and properly handling such assets. The following points should be considered while developing and testing evacuation procedures.

Personnel are the first to be secured during an emergency or disaster. It is important that evacuation procedures should address a secure evacuation of personnel first:

- Emergency exits are clearly marked and should lead to an open space
- A floor plan with a clear marking of emergency locations and indicating the current location should be available in all the strategic locations
- Emergency lights should be installed at strategic locations throughout the facility
- A clearly marked assembly area has to be set up, and the personnel should be advised to assemble and remain in the assembly area during evacuation
- Automatic shutdown of equipment, such as air conditioners during a fire alarm, should be considered
- Equipment such as fire extinguishers should be available at strategic locations
- The maintenance of fire extinguishers must be up to date
- Trained personnel designated as a warden or a supervisor who should direct and control emergency procedures should be available
- The roles and responsibilities of building wardens or supervisors and other sub wardens should be clearly defined, and their action plans including coordination should be documented clearly

- Identification mechanisms such as different colored helmets or coats for identifying relevant support personnel should be used

Training and awareness

Training and awareness plays an important role during emergencies. Most importantly, the personnel need to be aware of the emergency procedures. To achieve this, organizations should conduct periodical **mock tests** to ensure that the activities that need to be performed during an emergency or disaster are rehearsed and any kind of deviation is documented. These mock tests allow the security planners to fine-tune the emergency procedures and that percolates into the training activities. Periodical mock tests are also called **evacuation drills**.

The following points should be covered in training, awareness programs, and evacuation drills:

- Evacuation drills should be periodically conducted
- The success and failure of such drills should be properly documented, and the lessons learned from such exercises should be updated in the emergency procedures and training manuals
- An explanation of different alarm types should be given
- An explanation of different identification mechanisms for support personnel should be given
- Actions to be taken by personnel when the alarm signals
- The location of assembly points
- Security procedures to be followed if moving computer equipment

Protecting and securing equipment

Physical security also concerns with the physical protection of equipment as well addressing various security requirements pertaining to the media where the data is stored.

Theft is one of the most important threats that needs to be addressed for personal computer, laptop, and media protection.

Equipment security

Equipment security involves protection from theft and unauthorized access. Some of the controls include the following:

- **Cable locks** are used to physically secure PCs and laptop computers. These locks prevent the computers or laptops from being detached and taken away.
- **Encryption** is used to make folders and files secure such that unauthorized disclosure and modification is prevented.
- **Full disk encryption** is used to encrypt the data in laptops. This is to ensure that even if the laptop is lost, the content is not disclosed. This method is also used to ensure that the system is not compromised using a technique called cold boot attack.

 Cold boot attack is used to retrieve the information such as password or encryption keys from the DRAM memories even after the power is removed. This is due to the data-remanence property of DRAM memories.

Modern technologies include a security token to control access to laptops as well as remote laptop-security mechanisms that enable the owner to remotely access and disable the laptop over the Internet.

Port protection is used to ensure that media devices, such as CD-ROM, floppy drive, **Universal Serial Bus** (**USB**) memory sticks, **Wireless-Fidelity** (**Wi-Fi**) ports, and printers and scanners, are not accessible to unauthorized personnel. The purpose of port protection is to prevent downloading or transferring confidential information and/or intellectual property by unauthorized users to a portable medium. Port protection also assists in preventing the spread of malware.

BIOS checks use password protection during the boot up process so that the access to the operating system is controlled. These checks are called **pre-boot authentication**.

Computer hardware equipment is prone to failure due to various factors such as vibration, electrical fluctuation, electromagnetic interference, and so on. For critical systems such as servers, high availability is a primary requirement.

There are two important parameters used in the IT industry to qualify server grade equipment:

- One is **Mean Time Between Failure (MTBF)**, which is a time measurement that specifies the average time between failures. This time is called the useful life of the device.

- The other parameter is **Mean Time To Repair** (**MTTR**), which indicates the downtime or the average time required to repair the device after a failure.

Media security

Storage media such as hard disks, backup tapes, CDs/DVDs, and diskettes need additional security measures to ensure the security of the data they contain. The controls should ensure to prevent data disclosure and modification by unauthorized entities.

The following controls need to be considered for media security:

- Storage controls are the primary means to protect the data in storage media such as hard disk, magnetic tapes, CDs, and so on. The primary consideration should be controlling access to the data, which is usually achieved by encryption. Additional security considerations are required when backup media is stored off the site.
- Maintenance is a regular process to ensure that the data in the storage media is not corrupted or damaged. Media handling procedures are used to ensure this.
- The users and operators should be provided with the proper usage instructions to handle the media.
- Media usage should be in accordance with the established policies and procedures.
- **Data destruction** is done by way of formatting the media. One-time formatting may not completely delete all the data. **Degaussing** is an effective method of destroying the data in magnetic media.
- **Data remanence** is the residual data that remains when the data is not completely erased or destroyed. When the media is reused, this may result in unauthorized disclosure of sensitive information. It is a good practice to prevent **media reuse** by physically destroying the media. In case of reuse, there should be policies and procedures to ensure that the data is destroyed.

Computer investigations

Computer investigations are also called **computer forensics.** This process deals with collecting, preserving, and producing the evidence that pertains to computer crimes. Evidence must be handled to ensure it is admissible in a court of law.

Evidence in computer investigations is a piece of information that supports a conclusion. From the legal perspective, evidence maybe oral or written statements, physical objects, computer files, computer data, or other documentary material that is admissible in a court of law.

Most of the evidence pertaining to computer crimes is intangible in nature. It maybe stored in a magnetic medium, such as tape, disk drive, or in memory. Information such as location, time, discovery, securing, controlling, and the maintenance of the evidence needs to be followed. This activity is called **chain of evidence**.

The cycle of activities from discovery of evidence to preservation, transportation, admission in the court, and to return to the owner is called the **evidence life cycle**.

Summary

This chapter covered physical security design and some of the common threats, vulnerabilities, and the related countermeasures pertaining to the physical and operational security domains. The focus of coverage was to understand different controls, such as preventive, detective, reactive, and deterrent, that are applicable to the physical and operational security domains, along with a few examples associated with each of them.

This chapter also covered concepts related to perimeter security as well as interior security while focusing on some of the standard specifications, such the height of the walls, recommended illumination levels, the types of fire extinguishers, the type of material used, as well as concepts related electrical and magnetic disturbances.

Auditing, investigations, and their role as detective and monitoring controls were addressed at the end of the chapter.

In the next chapter, we will cover incident management, disaster recovery, and business continuity-related concepts that pertain security operations.

Sample questions

Q1. Operations procedures are generally considered as:

1. Draft documents
2. Draft policies
3. Formal documents
4. Formal records

Q2. Operations security is used to ensure:

1. Correct and secure operation of information processing facilities
2. Correct and insecure operation of information processing facilities
3. Incorrect and secure operation of information processing facilities
4. Incorrect and insecure operation of information processing facilities

Q3. Preventive controls are all *except:*

1. Preventing a security event
2. Setting up a rule in firewall so that malicious traffic is filtered
3. Identifying intrusion detection
4. Identifying a virus

Q4. Compensating controls are called:

1. Preventive controls
2. Detective controls
3. Recovery controls
4. Alternative controls

Q5. Which of the following statements are true pertaining to the parameter that indicates the Mean Time Between Failure (MTBF) of devices?

MTBF is a time measurement that specifies an average time between failures	
MTBF is known as the useful life of the device	Drag and drop your answers here
MTBF is the average time required to repair the device	
Higher MTBF means more reliable device	

Q6. Reliability of a device is more if its:

1. MTBF is more and MTTR is more
2. MTBF is more and MTTR is less
3. MTBF is less and MTTR is more
4. MTBF is less and MTTR is less

Q7. A momentary low voltage is called:

1. Sag
2. Spike
3. Fault
4. Blackout

Q8. A periodical mock tests rehearsing the steps of actions to be taken during an emergency is also known as:

1. Table top review
2. Evacuation drills
3. Fire fighting
4. Shutdown of systems

17
Day 17 – Security Operations - Incident Management and Disaster Recovery

This chapter covers incident management and disaster recovery concepts from the perspective of physical and operational security domains. Concepts related to incident management controls, business continuity planning process, and disaster recovery planning are covered with relevant examples and illustrations:

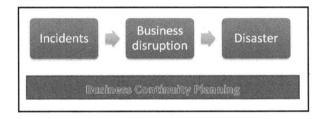

Observe the preceding diagram. Incidents may cause disruption to business processes and activities. In turn, an unattended incident may also lead to disaster. A suitable business continuity planning process with disaster recovery planning will ensure continuity in business operations.

In this chapter, we will cover the following topics:

- Foundational concepts on incident management
- Preventative measures
- Patch and vulnerability management

- Change management principles
- Disaster recovery and business continuity exercises

Incident management and reporting

An incident is an event that could possibly violate information security. The violation may breach confidentiality, integrity, and the availability requirements of information assets. Primarily, incidents happen due to weaknesses in the systems and operational processes and procedures.

When a systematic and procedural way of managing incidents is established in an organization, then it is called **incident management**.

Incident management consists of incident reporting and response to such reports.

Incident reporting refers to the mechanism of reporting suspected weaknesses and incidents to the management by employees, contractors, and third-party users.

The examples of incidents

The following are some of the examples of incidents:

- **Access violation** is a type of incident where an unauthorized entity either tries to gain access to the system and/or successfully gains access.
- The **malfunction of hardware and software** could possibly affect the availability of the systems. It is also possible that data could be corrupted, compromising integrity.
- **Human errors** such as wrong inputs to the system, improper configuration, and the violation of established procedures could compromise security.
- **Uncontrolled system changes** could affect system security in a manner that prevents the system from being restored to its previous secure state, and/or the other users of the system are unaware of the changes.
- **Noncompliance with policies and procedures** is an incident that could compromise the established secure practices.
- A **physical security breach** is an incident that could compromise information security controls.

Incident management objective and goals

The objective of information security incident management is to manage incidents in an effective manner to mitigate the risks by timely actions.

The goals of incident management are as follows:

- Establishing, implementing, and maintaining suitable procedures for reporting information security-related incidents and weaknesses by employees, third-party contractors, and outsourced entities
- Establishing, implementing, and maintaining escalation procedures related to information security incidents
- Establishing the designated points of contact for reporting information security incidents and weaknesses
- Periodically conducting awareness programs for employees, third-party contractors, and outsourced service providers about information security incidents, weaknesses, and reporting procedures
- Ensuring that the reported incidents are properly dealt with and corrective actions are taken
- Establishing procedures to percolate the lessons learned from incidents into the awareness programs and management procedures

Incident management controls

Incident management involves actions that are predominantly corrective in nature. For example, fire fighting is a corrective exercise. However, certain preventive actions are taken to control the onset of an incident. The following are some of the security controls, systems, and actions that can help in managing incidents.

Intrusion detection systems

As this name implies, **Intrusion Detection Systems** (**IDS**) are detective controls that detect unauthorized intrusions to the premises, such as data centers or computer networks.

Vulnerability assessment and penetration testing

In physical, operational, and network security, vulnerability assessment and penetration testing are periodically conducted to identify the weaknesses in the access control mechanisms and test the possibility of unauthorized intrusion.

Patch management

Computer applications contain vulnerabilities, in other words, errors. These applications are generally executable files and are produced by different software vendors. The vulnerabilities that are identified after the final release of such applications are periodically fixed by these vendors by releasing software code containing the patches. Patch management refers to applying patches to the existing applications or the patching of computers in a systematic way. Applying the patches to the test system before applying them to production systems, and creating rollback mechanisms if the applied patch affects the existing applications are considered to be patch management controls. Patch management has to be validated as a part of the compliance-monitoring activity.

Configuration management

An improper configuration of IT systems may lead to systems compromise, affecting the confidentiality and integrity of the systems. Configuration errors will also affect the availability. Configuration management refers to maintaining the right configuration of systems and documenting and managing the changes to the systems.

Business Continuity Planning (BCP)

From the operations security perspective, BCP is to ensure that the continuity of IT operations is maintained from the primary or alternate locations during an incident or disastrous events based on the business continuity requirements. An important consideration is that the security levels are maintained during such operations.

Before we plunge deeper into the myriad concepts of the BCP domain, let's recap some of important concepts in the risk assessment and risk management areas:

- Risk is the probability that a threat agent could exploit vulnerability and the resulting impact. The impact may be related to the loss of money, resources, customer confidence, reputation, or legal and regulatory noncompliance and related issues.
- Threat is an event that could affect business operations.
- Vulnerability is a weakness in the system that a threat could exploit.

In the BCP domain, our focus will be on specific threat events that could cause devastating impacts on the functioning of the organization as a whole, and the IT infrastructure in particular. The examples of such events are fire, flood, earthquake, tornado, or terrorist attacks. Generally, an organization may not have controls to prevent such events. Such events are termed as disruptive events. In other words, an event that could impact regular operations for a prolonged period of time can be termed as a disruptive event.

Business Continuity Planning (BCP) is a process that proactively addresses the continuation of business operations during and in the aftermath of such disruptive events. The aim is to prevent interruptions to operations.

BCP goals and objectives

BCP requires coordinated efforts by a team of personnel drawn from different business functions of an organization. Let's quickly review the goal and objectives pertaining to the BCP process.

The **goal** of BCP is to ensure the continuity of business operations without affecting the organization as a whole.

While designing the BCP, **availability** should be considered as the most important factor.

People are the most important assets in business operations. Hence, life safety or preventing human loss is one of the primary objectives of BCP. Another important objective of BCP is to avoid any serious damage to the business.

BCP process

BCP involves the following steps. These simplified steps form a life cycle model for the BCP process:

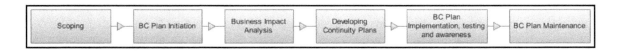

1. Scoping should be thought of in terms of assets, operations, and business processes.

   Scoping is a very important activity in a BCP process. The scope of a BCP primarily focuses on a business process. For example, if the scope of BCP is **Customer Relationship Management (CRM)** processes, then we're looking at the CRM-related information systems: data, people associated with customer management, and facilities such as the servers, data center, backup media, and so on. By focusing on a business process and defining the scope, we will be able to see an end-to-end link of all the associated assets, operations, and processes. Therefore, the primary criterion of BCP scoping is to ensure that it is **appropriate**, which means ensuring that the scoping process covers all the essential resources.

2. Initiating the planning process.

   The Business Continuity Planning process is initiated by establishing the **roles and responsibilities** of personnel involved. Generally, a BCP committee is formed with personnel drawn from critical business units. The function of a BCP committee is to create, test, and implement the plans. The critical component in planning this process is the support and involvement of senior management throughout the process, life cycle.

3. Performing **Business Impact Analysis (BIA)**.

   BIA is a type of risk assessment exercise that tries to assess qualitative and quantitative impacts on the business due to a disruptive event. Qualitative impacts are generally operational impacts such as inability to deliver, whereas quantitative impacts are related to financial losses. In general, BIA uses *What-If* scenarios to assess the risks. For example, take a look at the following:

   - **What** will be the financial loss **if** CRM server is down for 4 hours?
   - **What** will be the operational issues **if** the system administrator is not available during an emergency update of the system?
   - **What** will be the legal ramifications **if** the customer data is corrupted or stolen? A matrix of *What-If* is created and analyzed to develop suitable mitigation strategies for the risks. In BCP terminology, such a risk mitigation strategy is called a *continuity plan*.

4. Developing the BCP.

> Business Continuity Plans are proactive measures that identify critical business processes required for the continuity and sustainability of the business based on BIA. For example, let's assume if the organization has a **Service Level Agreement (SLA)** with its customers and a maximum of 2 hours of continuous downtime of its CRM services, then continuity plans need to address the systems that are needed to ensure an adherence to the SLA proactively. The organization needs a strategy or plan, and the same should be consistent across all business units. Defining the continuity strategy and documenting the same are two important functions that constitute the development of BC plans.

5. BC plan implementation, testing the plans, and creating awareness to the personnel.

> The senior management must approve the properly documented business continuity plans and, upon approval, the plans are implemented. Personnel associated with business continuity strategy and operations must be made aware of the continuity processes; the plans have to be periodically tested and updated based on the lessons learned from such tests.

6. The BC plan maintenance.

> The BCP life cycle also includes the maintenance of the plans. The primary driver for plan update is based on incidents, periodic risk assessments, and changes to the business environment. The plans need to be periodically reviewed and updated based on business changes, technology changes, and/or policy changes.

BCP best practices

The following best practices are gleaned from many BCP-related standards and guidelines. They form the base for a successful BC Planning process.

BCP should be as follows:

- **Appropriate**: The scoping process should be covering the essential resources
- **Adequate**: Based on Business Impact Analysis, the adequacy of available resources pertaining to continuity and recovery should be established

- **Complete**: The plan should include all the resources required based on the analysis

BCP resources should include the following:

- An availability of processes
- An availability of people to implement the processes

BCP processes should include the following:

- Testing the plans
- Day-to-day functions/activities to be performed to make the plan effective and ready at all times

BCP measures should include the following:

- Preventative measures to control known issues
- Facilitating measures to act in a timely manner on issues that are reasonably not under the control of the organization

BCP should identify the following:

- Mission-critical systems
- Business impact due to nonavailability of critical systems (loss of revenue, loss of profits, inability to comply with laws, damage to reputation, and so on)
- Preventive controls
- Recovery controls

BCP objectives include the following:

- **Recovery Time Objective** (**RTO**): This is a timeframe within which the systems should be recovered (indicated in terms of hours or days)
- **Recovery Point Objective** (**RPO**): This is the maximum period of time (or amount of transaction data) that the business can afford to lose during a successful recovery

BCP procedures include the following:

- Procedure for testing the plans
- Procedure for updating the plans

BCP plans should contain the following:

- **Notification**: To whom and, in case the concerned personnel is not available, who holds the secondary responsibility.
- **Call trees**: The list of personnel associated with continuity operations and their contact details.
- **Response teams**: Who should respond during a disruptive event? For example, an event such as fire requires trained teams to handle evacuation and other specific procedures.
- Updating mechanism for contacts.
- A step-by-step procedure for recovery.
- Appropriate testing.
- Restoring a primary site to normalcy or a stable state.
- Required records and the format of the same.
- The awareness of people.

Disaster Recovery Planning (DRP)

Disaster recovery is a process that enables the business to recover from an event that affects the normal business operations for a prolonged period of time.

At this point, I would like to highlight the similarities and differences between BCP and DRP processes:

- Both BCP and DRP are targeted at continuity or the resumption of business processes, as the case may be.
- Both the processes address the actions to be taken when an incident happens or a disruptive event strikes.
- BCP focuses on the continuity of business processes. For example, power failure is an incident. It is not a disastrous event. BCP will address this using continuity processes such as an Uninterrupted Power Supply (UPS) system or a power generator. However, BCP focuses on the continuity of the business processes from the holistic perspective of the business itself.
- DRP focuses on recovery procedures due to disastrous events. For example, earthquake strikes the location. This is not the same situation as a power failure. Even having a UPS or a generator is not going to be helpful. DRP will address this by resuming the critical business processes from an alternative site.

Disaster Recovery Planning (**DRP**) is a process for the following:

1. Developing procedures that define the actions to be taken during and after disastrous event.
2. Testing the procedure for effectiveness.
3. Updating the procedures to reflect the lessons learned from the testing process.

Goals and objectives

The **goal of disaster recovery planning** is to effectively manage the operations during disaster and ensure a proper coordination of different teams.

The **objective of disaster recovery planning** is to continue the business/IT operations in a secondary site during disaster and restore back to the primary site in a timely manner.

Components of disaster recovery planning

Some of the components of disaster recovery include these:

- The identification of suitable teams to coordinate the recovery process
- The resumption of business from alternate sites or recovering data from a backup
- Communications with employees, external groups, and media
- Financial management including insurance

Recovery teams

In disaster recovery, various teams play important roles. The most important teams are as follows:

- **The recovery team**: On the declaration of a disaster, this team is entrusted with implementing the recovery procedures
- **The salvage team**: This team will be responsible for returning business operations to the primary site

Recovery sites

A **primary site** is the one where normal business operations, including IT operations, take place.

A **secondary site** is referred to as a backup to the primary site. Generally, secondary sites are geographically located in a different region.

Business resumption from alternative sites

The following are some of the disaster-recovery activities that are related to continuing business from an alternative site.

A reciprocal agreement

A **reciprocal agreement** is an arrangement with another company having additional computing facilities that can be utilized during contingency. The term reciprocal implies that it is a mutual agreement that both the companies may utilize the computing facilities of the other in the event of a disaster. However, such agreements are not legally binding, as it is a simple arrangement.

Subscription services

This means paying or subscribing to facility management services that use third-party backups and processing facilities. This type of arrangement is called a **subscription service**:

A type of subscription that services a company may be contracted based on the **Business Impact Analysis (BIA)**, **Recovery Time Objectives (RTO)**, and **Recovery Point Objectives (RPO)**.

BIA, RTO and RPO are explained in the previous chapter.

- A **hot site** is an alternate backup site that is fully configured with computer systems, **Heating, Ventilation, and Air Conditioning (HVAC)**, and power supply. This site also contains all the applications as well as the data to commence the operations immediately. Hot sites are highly expensive. Typically, a business operation that needs to be resumed within 24 hours would consider a hot site.

- A **cold site** contains no computer or other computing equipment. Only HVAC and power are available here. The computers, the computing equipment, applications, and data need to be installed before commencing the operations. Cold sites are the least expensive. Typically, a business operation that can be resumed in a span of a week to 10 days would consider this option.
- A **warm site** is in between hot and cold sites. In this type of arrangement, the computing facilities such as computers, other communication elements, HVAC, and power are available. However, applications and data need to be installed before commencing the operations. This type of site is less expensive than a hot site. Typically, a business operation that needs to be restored within a span of 24 hours to 96 hours would consider this option.
- **Dual sites** refer to mirroring the exact operations and data in alternative sites. From the recovery perspective, this type of sit is instantaneous in business resumption. However, they are very expensive to maintain. Typically, business operations that cannot afford any downtime at all would consider this option.

Backup terminologies

The following concepts are applicable to hot sites and dual sites in terms of backup and restorations:

- **Electronic vaulting** is a batch process used to dump the data at periodical intervals to a remote backup system.
- **Remote journaling** is a parallel processing system that writes the data in a remote system at the alternate site. This type of backup is used where the RTO is less and a high degree of fault tolerance is required.
- **Database shadowing** is used to duplicate the data into multiple sites from the remote journaling process. This type of system is used where the fault-tolerance requirement is of the highest degree.

Testing procedures

Disaster recovery plans should include various testing procedures so that the plans can be tested for adequacy and correctness. The lessons learned from such tests can be incorporated into the plans for better preparedness during a disaster.

The following are some of the industry standard tests pertaining to disaster recovery planning processes:

- A **checklist review** is a review process for checking the disaster recovery plan by managers of various business units. The following table shows a general checklist. This list is at the macro level. Further lists should be generated at micro level to drill down to finer details:

	Disaster Recovery Planning - General Checklist	
1	Is updated diagram of network connections and devices are available?	☐
2	Is updated diagram of network connections and devices for DR site are available?	☐
3	Is DR network tested and the results are documented?	☐
4	Are patches are applied to DR site systems?	☐
5	Does the DR Plan document specify the information systems to be available in the DR site? (for example. Accounting system, CRM etc.,)	☐
6	Does the DR Plan specify the applications and the Data to be available in the DR site?	☐
7	Is backup data available at the DR site?	☐
8	Is backup is based on recovery requirements as per the DR Plan?	☐
9	Is backup data tested frequently for integrity? (sanity checks to see the data is not corrupted)	☐
10	Is service contacts list is available?	☐
11	Does the DR Plan identify resource allocation such as equipments and communication?	☐
12	Does the DR Plan identify the staff allocation at remote sites?	☐

- A **structured walk-through** is a **tabletop exercise** in which a management team of various business units meets and reviews each and every step in a sequential manner. Any deficiencies or missing steps are discussed and updated in the plan. While a checklist review is used to check the availability of the resources such as documents, systems, people, communication facilities, backup, and more, the structured walk-through checks the recovery processes step by step over a tabletop review.
- A **simulation test** is a testing process used to simulate the event in a testing environment. This test is expected to provide vital inputs from the actions of various response teams, and any deficiency can be corrected, including the training requirements. This type of test is also called a **walk-through test** or **drill**. A simulation test is more comprehensive than a tabletop exercise.

- A **parallel test** is a testing process used to test the coordination of other essential groups such as medical, fire services including internal teams, and the adherence to communication procedures. This type of test is used for testing the functionality of the plans. Hence, it is referred to as a **functional drill**.

- A **full test** is a type of test that tries to simulate a real emergency or a disaster event. This test involves the participation of all the associated teams and groups as well as a real shutdown of the primary site, and the commencement of operations from the remote site.

Summary

This chapter covered incident management and disaster recovery related concepts, as they relate to physical and operational security. Business continuity planning processes, implementation, and testing procedures are further covered, with emphasis on some of the best practices.

In the next two chapters, we will cover security requirements in software and application development processes and activities.

Sample questions

Q1. An access violation is called:

1. Data Encryption Standard
2. Procedure
3. Incident management
4. Incident

Q2. A systematic and procedural way of managing incidents is known as:

1. Configuration management
2. Incident management
3. Change management
4. System management

Q3. If an event could possibly violate information security, then such an event is known as:

1. Problem
2. Confidentiality breach
3. Incident
4. Integrity breach

Q4. A full test in a disaster recovery testing is called:

1. A functional drill
2. Simulation test
3. Emulates real emergency or disaster scenario
4. All of the above

Q5. Providing wrong inputs to the system can be classified as:

1. Problem
2. Vulnerability
3. Incident
4. Threat

Q6. A periodical mock test rehearsing the steps of actions to be taken during an emergency is also known as:

1. Table top review
2. Evacuation drills
3. Fire fighting
4. Shutdown of systems

Q7. Which of the following can be classified as an incident?

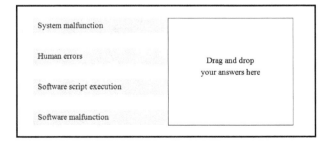

Q8. Which one of the following disaster-recovery tests is also called a functional drill?

1. Checklist review
2. Table top exercise
3. Simulation test
4. Parallel test

18

Day 18 – Software Development Security - Security in Software Development Life Cycle

This chapter covers foundational concepts in various software development life cycle models, and it discusses security requirements in software development processes and assurance requirements in the software.

A candidate appearing for the CISSP exam is expected to have foundational concepts and knowledge in the following key areas of the **software development security** domain:

- Software development life cycle models
- Security in the software development life cycle
- Security controls in development environments
- Assurance requirements in software
- Software security testing
- Security impact analysis on acquired software

An overview of software development security

Software is a core building block in an IT infrastructure. Applications are the outcome of software development, and they are most important from the perspective of security, as they deal with data.

Applications provide a way to achieve tasks that are related to the input, processing, and the output of data. Besides this, applications are used to store, retrieve, process, transmit, or destroy data. Therefore, it is of paramount importance to ensure the security of applications:

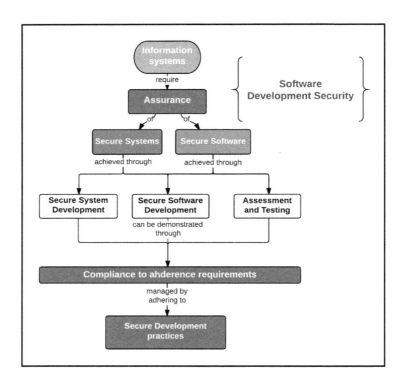

Observe the preceding diagram. The primary area that a security professional should focus on is the addressing of security requirements at the design stage of the application itself. An application contains software code, and it is important that secure coding practices are used throughout the **Software Development Life Cycle** (**SDLC**) processes.

In this module, you will learn about the following:

- Systems engineering concepts
- Security in the software development life cycle
- Software development life cycle models
- An overview of enforcing security controls in development environments

Systems engineering

Systems engineering is a term that connotes the application of engineering concepts while designing application systems that are complex and large.

A system may be defined as the combination of elements or parts that work together to produce an output. In other words, systems are used to achieve an objective. In a system, parts or elements are interrelated.

Many organizations in the world publish standards, models, principles, and practices pertaining to systems engineering. One of them is the **International Council on Systems Engineering** (**INCOSE**), which is a not-for-profit membership organization, founded to develop and disseminate the interdisciplinary principles and practices that enable the realization of successful systems. **Software Engineering Institute** (**SEI**) at Carnegie Mellon University develops and maintains a **Capability Maturity Model** (**CMM**) pertaining to software development process maturity.

According to INCOSE, *Systems Engineering is an interdisciplinary approach and means to enable the realization of successful systems. It focuses on defining customer needs and the required functionality early in the development cycle, documenting requirements, then proceeding with design synthesis and system validation while considering the complete problem.*

When a system is developed using the system engineering processes, then development activities go through a life cycle model and are called System Development Life Cycle (SDLC). Software development is an activity in system development life cycle models.

A system development life cycle model consists of many processes. It starts from establishing the needs (initiation) and runs to archiving or destruction (disposal).

The National Institute of Standards and Technology (NIST) special publication 800-14 titled *Generally Accepted Principles and Practices for Securing Information Technology (IT) Systems* defines five phases in terms of the system development life cycle.

The following diagram illustrates the five phases of the System Development Life Cycle as defined in the NIST 800-14:

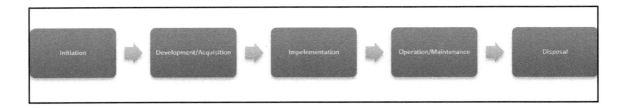

System Development Life Cycle

Initiation phase

The **initiation phase** establishes the need for the system and creation of the associated documentation. It is necessary to conduct a sensitive assessment at this phase, and the scope of the assessment is to look at the sensitivity of the information to be processed as well as the sensitivity of the system itself. Sensitive assessment establishes the data protection needs in the developed or acquired system.

Development/acquisition phase

The second phase is the **development/acquisition phase.** During this phase, a system is designed, purchased, programmed, developed, or otherwise constructed. This phase requires three activities to be performed:

- Determining security requirements
- Incorporating security requirements into specifications
- Obtaining the system and related security activities

Implementation phase

The third phase is the **implementation phase**. This phase emphasizes the testing and installation of the systems. There are very few primary requirements in this phase pertaining to security:

- Installing and/or turning-on controls, such that security features are enabled and configured
- Performing security testing on some particular parts of the system that are developed or acquired
- Security testing the entire system
- Obtaining system security accreditation

Operation/maintenance phase

The fourth phase is the **operation/maintenance phase**. In this phase the system is operational and performs its work. In this phase, the system may be modified or upgraded based on the requirements.

Some of the important security considerations in this phase are as follows:

- Security operations
- Security administration
- Operational assurance
- Monitoring
- Auditing

Disposal phase

The final phase in the system development life cycle is the **disposal phase**. This phase involves the disposition of information, hardware, and software.

Some of the security considerations in this phase areas follows:

- Archiving and retrieval
- Media sanitization

Software development life cycle

Software development is a part of the systems development life cycle. Within the development phase, there are many stages and processes. The activity or cycle starts from a specification development based on which the overall system is designed and implemented.

The software programs are written based on the system design, the system is documented and the operating procedures are written too.

During the entire process of the software development life cycle, other activities are involved to ensure the functionality of the developed application. Verification and validation are the two important activities during development and implementation.

Verification is used to establish the adherence to software specifications, whereas **validation** is used to establish the fitness of the system as outlined in the design and requirements.

Software development models

Life cycle models are used for software development purposes. The objectives of such models are to develop quality software applications or products that meet specifications, customer requirements, and financial viability in terms of budgets and timelines.

Simplistic model

A **simplistic model** is the one that takes an approach of sequential stages in software development. In this model, the concept of rework does not arise, and it assumes that each and every stage of development is finalized before moving to the next stage. One of the popular models in simplistic software development is the waterfall model.

Waterfall model

The **waterfall model** is a type of simplistic model where the development flows like water falling from top to bottom through a series of steps. In this model, activities such as requirements analysis, design, implementation, testing, integration, and maintenance are completed in a sequence. This model's top-down only approach will have difficulty when a rework has to be done on the system design or the software application:

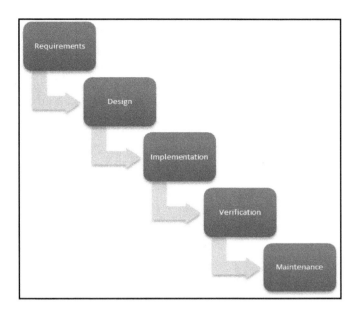

Waterfall model

Complex models

Software development models are considered to be complex when the scope or requirements are uncertain during the initiation of the project. A complex model expects that the scope, requirements, or specifications may change during the development phase. Hence, such models have to be accommodating to include the changes, and development processes should have robust change management processes and strong integration methods. One of the popular methods that is considered to be following a complex model is an agile framework.

When a software development life cycle model uses iterative methods and processes, then such models are called iterative models. In such models, reworking is allowed to improve the systems. Some of the examples of this model include an incremental model and a spiral model.

Incremental model

This model allows the segregation of software development processes into multiple builds or modules. An incremental model can, in a way, be visualized as similar to a multiple waterfall model with each build following its own set of processes. Some of the advantages of such models include flexibility, smaller iterations, and parallel development. Disadvantages include a higher cost than simplistic models, and complete scope and design should be ready before the development:

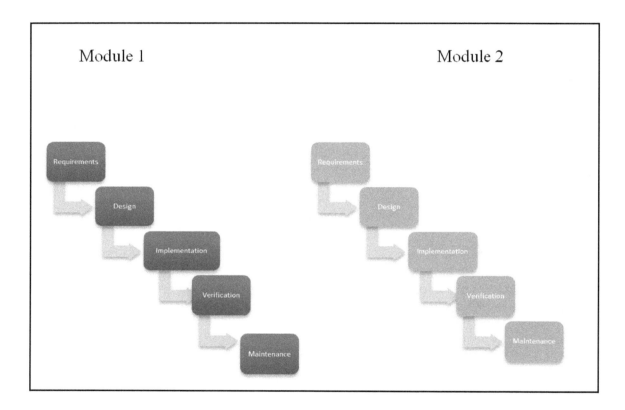

The incremental model

Spiral model

The **spiral model** is a type of iterative model. This model specifies design as well as prototyping stages. This model proposes top-down as well as bottom-up approaches so that rework is possible:

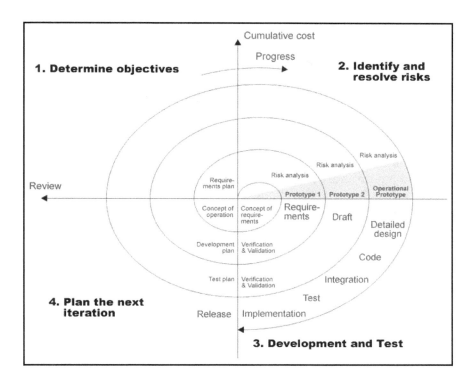

Agile framework

This framework emphasizes the concept of iterations throughout the software development life cycle. An Agile method can use incremental models. However, the development model is considered to be *Agile* when it adheres to the *Agile manifesto* that was published in the year 2001 by a consortium of software developers.

The agile manifesto envisages individuals such as software programmers and their interactions, working software (for example beta versions) instead of only documentation, customer or stakeholder involvement throughout the development, and continuous development that includes quick response to changes.

One of the popular agile programming methods is called **Extreme Programming** (**XP**). There are two core objectives of such programming. One is producing high-quality software, and the other is productivity enhancements. Extreme programming generally has multiple short development cycles. Agile development methods are considered to be more suitable from the perspective of security.

Security in software development

In software development, secure processes are required during development to produce a secure software. Therefore, security during development stages and the security of the developed software are interrelated and necessary for overall security.

Security controls in software development

The software development process follows the cycle of design, development, testing, and integration. Security controls are necessary in all these stages. The following sections describe some of the best practices pertaining to the security controls in software development.

Separation of development, test, and operational facilities

In order to prevent inappropriate developer access to production systems, controlled access to operational systems for developers and testers should be implemented. Hence, to prevent unintended operational system changes, the separation of development, test, and operational facilities should be implemented.

Change control processes and procedures

Formal change control processes and procedures are necessary to ensure that the changes in development processes and implementation are done in a controlled manner. This is to prevent the corruption of data or programming. Change control processes should take into account and follow documentation, specification, testing, quality control, and controlled implementations.

Whenever there is a change in the system or application, performing risk assessment on the impact of the proposed change is necessary. Establishing suitable security controls based on the assessment is important for security.

Similarly, a version of the operating system may change after the application is deployed. The porting of the application to other operating systems may also be planned after the initial deployment in one operating system. In both scenarios, a technical review on the security of the application software has to be done due to the operating system changes. Primarily, integrity procedures should be reviewed.

Any change control processes and procedures should take into account business continuity requirements and include tests for the BCP.

Vendor-supplied software packages

Any changes to the vendor-supplied software by internal development personnel should be avoided. If a change is necessary, it may either be done by the vendor, or it should be done internally after obtaining consent from the vendor. This is to ensure the validity of the warranty. Similarly, any changes provided by the vendor to the software by way of patches should be tested thoroughly in a test environment before updating to operational systems. The tests should also contain rollback mechanisms in case of failure.

Avoiding covert channels

In a software application, covert channels may be introduced by developers with malicious intent. A covert channel can provide a path for information leakage, circumventing security controls. They may also have functions for evading monitoring controls. Hence, covert channel analysis is necessary to ensure data confidentiality.

Summary

This chapter covered systems engineering concepts and various phases in the process. Software development is in the development phase of a systems engineering process. Software development follows life cycle models. When a development model follows simple and sequential methods, then it is called a simplistic model, and where iterations are allowed throughout the cycle, then such a model is called a complex model. Security in the development, test, and operational implementations is critical to overall software security. Some of the important security controls in development include change control procedures and technical review for security.

In the next chapter, we will cover assurance requirements in the software and related security testing procedures.

Sample questions

Q1. Which one of the following activities is performed during the development/implementation phase of the system development life cycle?

1. Performing security testing on particular parts of the system that are developed or acquired
2. Auditing
3. Sensitive assessment
4. Monitoring

Q2. Information leakage-related issues can be addressed through:

1. Circumvent analysis
2. Information channel assessment
3. Covert channel analysis
4. Channel security process

Q3. Which of the following software development models is an iterative model? (This is a drag-and-drop type of question. Here, you can draw a line from the list of answers on the left to the empty box on the right).

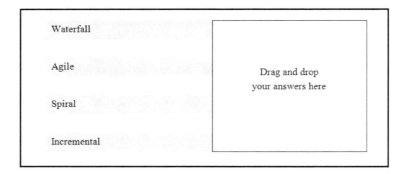

Q4. Validation is used to:

1. Establish the adherence to software specifications
2. Fitness to the system as per the design and requirements
3. Monitor code review timelines
4. Design user interfaces

Q5. The following list provides various phases of system security life cycle *except:*

1. Integration phase
2. Initiation phase
3. Implementation phase
4. Disposal phase

Q6. At what phase of system development life cycle should the sensitive assessment be conducted?

1. Acquisition phase
2. Initiation phase
3. Disposal phase
4. Operation phase

Q7. Patch management is a systematic way of applying the patches to the applications. Identify appropriate action while applying patches from the following:

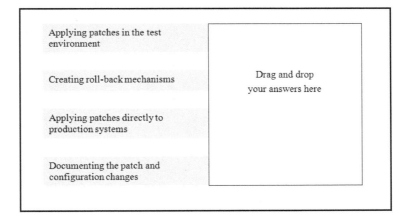

Q8. Which one of the following software development life cycle frameworks emphasize the iteration throughout the development life cycle?

1. The Agile framework
2. The Spiral model
3. The Incremental model
4. The Waterfall model

19

Day 19 – Software Development Security - Assessing effectiveness of Software Security

This chapter covers methods to assess the effectiveness of security in software. Effectiveness is used to ensure that the software has sufficient security controls, and these controls are performing as expected. Software quality and effectiveness is based on assurance requirements, and such requirements are based on performance and security. Hence, parameters such as performance and security must be demonstrable. Monitoring activities such as logging plays an important role in determining the performance and the security control effectiveness of the software.

Overview

Assurance in software means that software performance is as per the design and has effective security controls available. Observe the following diagram:

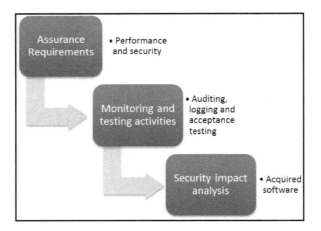

In this module, you will understand the following:

- Assurance requirements in software
- Auditing and logging, risk analysis and mitigation, and acceptance testing
- Security impact analysis on the acquired software

Security in information technology systems

Information technology systems can be broadly classified as follows:

- Object-oriented systems
- Artificial intelligence systems
- Database systems

The preceding systems may be centralized or decentralized in the way that they are distributed.

Object-oriented systems

Object-oriented systems use the concept of *objects* that work together with other objects in a system to achieve certain objectives. Related and common tasks are grouped together as an object. Such systems are considered more reliable and less prone to security issues due to changes in the software code.

The following are some of the concepts of object-oriented systems.

Object-oriented programming (OOP)

An object-oriented programming method uses the collection of objects that communicate and coordinate with other objects to achieve a desired objective. Sending or receiving messages and processing instructions are some of the functions of these objects.

Some of the fundamental concepts that are used in object-oriented programming are as follows:

- **Class**: This defines the characteristics and behaviors of an object
- **Object**: This is a pattern, example, or model of a class
- **Instance**: When a class creates a specific object during runtime, then it is called an instance of that class
- **Method**: This signifies the abilities of an object
- **Message passing**: This is the communication process to invoke a method by one object to another
- **Inheritance**: Classes have subclasses; these subclasses inherit characteristics from the main class
- **Encapsulation**: This is a wrapper and can conceal the functional details of an object to the class
- **Abstraction**: This is used to simplify a complex structure by modeling
- **Polymorphism**: This is when treating derived class members are treated just like their parent class members
- **Object-Oriented Analysis (OOA)**: This is an analysis process for producing conceptual model, and **Object-Oriented Design (OOD)** is used to design the ways (how) in which to implement the conceptual model produced in the analysis process

The security in object-oriented software

Software developed through object-oriented methods are generally considered to be secure. Only the data that is required for the process is accessible to the class, and the other system data is not accessible. This data-hiding method makes object-oriented software more secure, and so, they are prone to less data corruption.

Artificial Intelligence (AI) systems

AI is science and engineering of making intelligent systems. AI systems perceive their environment and take action, which maximizes the chance of success. Due to the adaptability of AI systems based on the environment and the circumstances, a *success* in an AI system is determined on the successful decisions that the system makes.

AI systems are used in information technology in an attempt to mimic human brains in perception and decision-making. From a security perspective, an artificial intelligence system can be a protector from attacks as well as a perpetrator of attacks.

An **expert system** is an artificial intelligence based system that tries to reproduce the performance of one or more human experts.

Neural network is a type of artificial intelligence system that tries to mimic the neural processing of the human brain. They are used in applications such as speech recognition, image analysis, software agents, and so on.

Database systems

A database system defines the storage and manipulation of data, while a **Database Management System (DBMS)** is a set of software programs that are used to perform and control the operations of a database system.

DBMS consists of a modeling language, data structures, database query language, and transaction mechanisms.

Threats and vulnerabilities to application systems

As a security professional, one must s on the following while considering security for applications:

- **Asset**: An asset is basically a resource. It may be a computer, operating system, database management system and so on.
- **Threat**: This is an event that could compromise an asset by exploiting the weaknesses or vulnerabilities in the asset.
- **Threat agent**: A threat cannot manifest on its own. It needs an agent to exploit vulnerabilities. For example, hacking is a threat. Not having suitable patch management control or monitoring control is a vulnerability. Hacking is done by a hacker. Hence, a malicious hacker is a threat agent for unethical hacking.
- **Vulnerability**: This is a weakness in the system that a threat agent could exploit. Inappropriate change controls or insufficient security testing in a software development process is an example of weak development processes. Such weaknesses could introduce vulnerabilities in the software.
- **Attack**: This is a technique used by a threat agent to exploit vulnerabilities. For example, a malicious hacker would inject a malformed data to a web application to exploit a weakness for gaining access.
- **Countermeasures**: These are preventative, corrective, or reactive steps to address vulnerability or an attack.

Web application security

Web applications are becoming popular and used more and more by the government, universities, and business organizations. The convenience of delivering services such as banking, e-commerce, e-governance, and education from a centralized location to the users around the world is taking this technology to dizzying heights. However, the **World Wide Web (WWW)** or the Internet is an open network that can be accessed by anyone using a connected computer. Due to its open nature, web applications are prone to innumerable security threats and vulnerabilities.

Common web application vulnerabilities

Open Web Application Security Project (OWASP) is a volunteer-based project that lists the following vulnerabilities that are common to web applications.

OWASP groups and classifies viruses, worms, Trojan horses, and logic bombs as non-target specific threat agents:

- **Access control vulnerability**: Vulnerabilities in access control mechanisms or code include authentication and authorization related errors. Some of the common issues include the following:
  - Password management errors including empty passwords, hard coded passwords, or password aging
  - Authentication bypasses
  - Unsafe mobile codes
- **Code permission vulnerability**: This type of vulnerability is due to improper permission setup for the code to run. The exploitation of such a vulnerability would give higher privilege access to programs.
- **Code quality vulnerability**: The quality of code is based on various parameters. Vulnerabilities such as leftover debug code, memory leak, undefined behavior, undefined initialization, and so on will affect the quality of code from a security perspective.
- **Cryptographic vulnerability**: Vulnerabilities that arise due to algorithm issues are categorized under this category. Some of the vulnerabilities pertaining to cryptography include insecure or incorrect algorithms, inappropriate use of algorithms, implementation errors, and key management problems.
- **Environmental vulnerability**: Vulnerabilities related to environment configuration such as improper setup or insecure default settings will fall under this category.
- **Error-handling vulnerability**: Information leakage, improper handling of error conditions, null pointer exceptions, and so on will fall under error-handling vulnerability.
- **General logic error vulnerability**: This includes logical errors due to branching or process priority.
- **Input validation vulnerability**: Here, the sanitization of data provided during the input is insufficient. For example, a form element expecting an input of a number may be provided with a code as input. If such a code is not validated at the input stage, then it may be executed internally in the application, thereby creating a security violation.

- **Logging and auditing vulnerability**: This includes weak monitoring mechanisms.
- **Password management vulnerability**: This includes insufficient password rules and password strength.
- **Path vulnerability**: This includes multiple paths to the target resource with some of them being insecure.
- **Protocol error**: This signifies weaknesses related to communication protocols.
- **Range and type error vulnerability**: This vulnerability is related to upper and lower bound memory errors.
- **Sensitive data protection vulnerability**: This vulnerability is related to weak encryption and/or sensitive data in publicly accessible locations.
- **Session management vulnerability**: This vulnerability is related to weaknesses in preserving session data.
- **Synchronization and timing vulnerability**: This vulnerability is related to race conditions that allow an insecure process to be executed before a security control implementation.
- **Unsafe mobile codes**: These are the codes executed at the client side that have weaknesses which may allow unauthorized access.
- **Use of dangerous API**: This includes weaknesses in Application Programming Interfaces.

Security impact analysis

The preceding vulnerability list can be compromised through various attacks. In-house developed software or acquired software should be thoroughly tested for various attack scenarios, and their impact has to be determined. The following list provides some of the common application attacks that need to be tested in applications:

- Abuse of functionality
- Data structure attacks
- Exploitation of authentication
- Injection such as code injection or SQL injection
- Malicious code attack
- Path traversal attack
- Probabilistic techniques
- Protocol manipulation
- Resource depletion

- Resource manipulation
- Sniffing attacks
- Spoofing

 Many of these listed attacks are explained in the previous chapters.

Monitoring and testing activities

Monitoring the application, and testing the security controls is an important step for software security assurance. Application controls are mechanisms used to preserve confidentiality, integrity, and availability of the application systems and the data they process, store, or transmit. Such application controls are important to address vulnerabilities and thwart attacks.

Some of the important application controls that need to be addressed during development processes include the following:

- **Memory and address protection** is a control used to ensure controlled access to the memory and address locations by the application. The core focus is to limit access and prevent overwriting other memory areas.
- **Access control** is a process used to ensure access to authorized entities and block unauthorized entities.
- **File protection** is a mechanism used to ensure that files are accessed and modified by authorized entities in a controlled manner.
- **Authentication** is a process used to identify and authorize legitimate entities.
- **Reliability** is a quality parameter used to assure that the application systems are performing efficiently and effectively.

Summary

This chapter covered performance and assurance requirements in software applications. Information technology application systems such as object-oriented systems, Artificial Intelligence systems, Database management systems, and other application development systems have inherent security and performance controls.

However, software and applications need to be tested for security during development and regularly after implementation. Such tests need to focus on published and known vulnerabilities as well as unknown vulnerabilities based on attack scenarios.

The next chapter is a revision chapter for the chapters 16 to 19. References and further study on the preceding four chapters are provided. An exam cram as well as a mock test consisting of about 10 questions is also provided.

Sample questions

Q1. A class in an object oriented system defines:

1. Characteristics and behaviors of an object
2. Performance requirements
3. Security requirements
4. Monitoring requirements

Q2. The core focus of memory and address protection control is to:

1. Circumvent security controls
2. Authentication security
3. Limit access and prevent overwriting other memory areas
4. Secure information channels

Q3. Which of the following are application controls? (This is a drag-and-drop type of question. Here, you can draw a line from the list of answers from left to the empty box on the right).

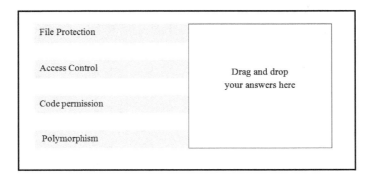

Q4. Preventative, corrective, or reactive steps to address vulnerability or an attack are a:

1. Vulnerability
2. Threat
3. Countermeasure
4. Reliability

Q5. An artificial intelligence system that tries to mimic the processing ability of the human brain is known as:

1. Expert system
2. Brain mapping
3. Neural network
4. Speech recognition

Q6. In object-oriented programming, treating derived class members just like their parent class members is termed as:

1. Encapsulation
2. Abstraction
3. Polymorphism
4. Method

Q7. Artificial intelligence system tries to mimic human brains primarily in:

1. Numerical ability
2. Linguistic ability
3. Perception and decision-making
4. All of the above

Q8. Some of the important application controls that need to be addressed during development processes include all of the following *except*:

1. Memory and address protection
2. Formatting the disk
3. Access Control
4. Reliability

20

Day 20 – Exam Cram and Practice Questions

This chapter summarizes the concepts covered in the seventh and eighth domains of CISSP CBK in a snippet format that will reinforce the topics learned; it will serve as an exam cram as well. A mock test consisting of ten questions from the two domains is provided. Finally, further reading and references are provided.

Overview of exam cram and practice questions

This chapter starts with an exam cram that consists of quick revision points from the seventh domain of the CISSP CBK, **security operations**, and the eighth domain called **software development security**. This is followed by a mock test from these two domains. The last topic of this chapter provides additional references for further reading:

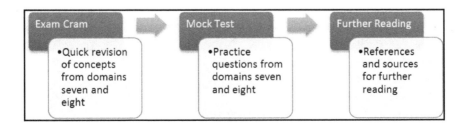

Exam cram

Presented here is the revision of the concepts discussed in the previous four chapters, that is, chapters sixteen through nineteen. They are provided in bullet points as snippets that are easy to revise. These snippets are for a quick revision and reinforcement of the knowledge learned.

CISSP CBK Domain #7 â□□ security operations

The following bullet points presented in an exam cram format are for a quick revision. They cover important points from the security operations domain. The covered topics include implementing and managing physical security, physical security principles for site and facilities, environmental security practices for site and facilities, logging and monitoring activities, understanding and supporting investigations, securing the provision of resources, operations security, resource protection techniques, foundational concepts on incident management, preventative measures, patch and vulnerability management, change management principles, and disaster recovery and business continuity exercises:

- Physical access to operational areas needs to have appropriate controls for strong authentication and authorization.
- Controlling access to operational areas and, in the process, identifying and blocking unauthorized intrusions to the operational areas are primary security requirements.
- Physical security design should include security parameters for the physical facility, the geographic operating location, and supporting facilities.
- The physical facility is usually the building, other structures, a vehicle housing the system, and network components.
- Based on their operating location, systems are characterized as static, mobile, or portable.
- Natural threats, such as earthquake and flooding, and man-made threats, such as burglary, civil disorders, and so on, characterize the security of the geographic operating location.
- **Supporting facilities** are those services (both technical and human) that underpin the operation of the system.
- Unauthorized intrusions are a common threat to physical security.
- Other threats for physical and operations security include theft, heat and temperature, humidity, electrical disruptions, and more.

- Lack of physical entry controls, lack of accountability, insufficient business continuity plans, lack of power controls systems, and more are some of the common vulnerabilities in this domain.
- Security controls including monitoring processes for physical and operations are subdivided into perimeter security and interior security.
- High-rise walls, fences, and locks are preventative controls in this domain.
- Fire alarm, motion detectors, and more, are detective controls in this domain.
- Armed response, mantrap systems, and more are reactive controls in this domain.
- Guards, dogs, and lighting are some of the deterrent controls in this domain.
- Perimeter security relates to the security considerations pertaining to the boundaries. Securing the entry and exit points of the facility, networks, and more will fall under perimeter security.
- **Guards** and dogs are the form of security control to prevent, detect, deter, and react to an intrusion event.
- **Fences**, high-rise walls, gates, mantraps, and turnstiles are some of the access control mechanisms for perimeter security.
- A **turnstile** is also called a baffle gate.
- Locks such as preset or programmable ones are preventative access control mechanisms in physical and operations security domain.
- Lighting is a deterrent control and is used to discourage intruders as well as detect suspicious movements.
- Closed circuit television, heat sensors, and biometric devices are used in physical and operation security as monitoring and access control mechanisms.
- Interior security refers to the security considerations pertaining to the facilities that are inside the perimeter.
- Unauthorized intrusions are detected through motion detectors and controlled through mantrap systems.
- Fire is an important threat to be considered for physical and operations security.
- Based on the type of combustible material, fire is classified as Class A, Class B, Class C, and Class D.
- **Class A** combustible materials are wood, paper, cloth, rubber. Most of the plastics also fall into this class.
- **Class B** combustible materials are oils, greases, oil-based paints, lacquers, and flammable liquids and gases
- **Class C** is predominantly some electrical equipment that is energized.
- **Class D** refers to flammable chemicals such as magnesium and sodium.
- Fire detectors are based on heat, flame, or smoke detection.

- Fire-suppression mediums include water, soda acid, CO^2, and halon.
- **Halon** is a suppressing medium that is no longer allowed to be used, as it is designated as an ozone-depleting substance.
- Fire extinguishers include water sprinklers and gas dischargers.
- Water sprinklers consist of wet pipe, dry pipe, deluge, and preaction.
- Gas dischargers generally use CO^2 as an extinguisher.
- Clean **electrical power** is a requirement for proper equipment functioning.
- Some of the electrical power-related parameters that could affect equipment's include **noise, Electromagnetic Interference (EMI)**, and **Radio Frequency Interference (RFI)**.
- For proper functioning of the computer systems, the humidity levels should be between 40 and 60 percent.
- **Auditing** is a process to check and validate the effectiveness of controls. The primary tool that assists in the audit is an audit trail.
- **Audit trail** contains all the recorded events. One of the most important audit trail in the physical and operational security domains is the access details to the data center and other control rooms.
- The record of access events is stored in a file called a log. The access log contains the events that are related to access attempts, and error logs contain the exceptions.
- Physical security also deals with procedures that need to be followed during emergencies. An emergency is an undesired event that may disturb operations for a prolonged period of time.
- **System startup and shutdown** procedures lay down guidelines and activities that need to be performed in a way so that security can not be compromised during system/data migration or relocation.
- **Evacuation procedures** address the priorities in terms of evacuating assets from the disaster site and properly handling such assets.
- Training and awareness plays an important role during emergencies. The personnel need to be aware of the emergency procedures. **Periodical mock tests are conducted** to ensure that the activities that need to be performed during an emergency or disaster are rehearsed and all deviances are documented. Such tests are also called **evacuation drills**.
- Physical security is also concerned with the physical protection of equipment as well.
- Equipment security controls include cable locks, encryption, port protection, switches, BIOS checks, and more.

- **Mean Time Between Failure** (**MTBF**) is a time measurement that specifies an average time between failures. This time is called the useful life of the device.
- **Mean Time To Repair** (**MTTR**) indicates the downtime or the average time required to repair the device.
- Data destruction is done by way of formatting the media or degaussing it.
- **Degaussing** is an effective method of destroying the data in a magnetic media.
- **Data remanence** is the residual data that remains when the data is not completely erased or destroyed.
- Computer investigations are also called **computer forensics**. This process deals with collecting, preserving, and producing the evidences that pertain to computer crimes.
- Information such as location, time, discovery, securing, controlling, and maintenance of the evidence is called the **chain of evidence**.
- The cycle of activities from the discovery of evidence to preservation, transportation, admission in the court, and returning to the owner is called the **evidence life cycle**.
- An **incident** is an event that could possibly violate information security. The violation may breach the Confidentiality, Integrity, and Availability requirements of information assets.
- When a systematic and procedural way of managing incidents is established in an organization, then it is called **incident management**.
- Incident management consists of incident reporting and response to such reports.
- Incident management involves actions that are predominantly corrective in nature.
- Some of the incident management controls include intrusion detection controls, vulnerability assessment and penetration testing, patch management, and configuration management.
- **Business continuity planning** (**BCP**) is used to ensure that the continuity of IT operations is maintained from a primary or alternate location during an incident or disastrous event based on the business process requirements.
- In the BCP domain, our focus will be on specific threat events that could have a devastating impact on the functioning of the organization as a whole, and the IT infrastructure in specifically.
- BCP is a process that proactively addresses the continuation of business operations during and aftermath of disruptive events. The aim here is to prevent interruptions to operations.
- The **goal of BCP** is used to ensure the continuity of business operations without impacting the organization as a whole.

- While designing the BCP, **availability** should be considered as the most important factor.
- People are the most important asset in business operations. Hence, life safety or preventing human loss is one of the primary objectives of BCP. Another important **objective of BCP** is to avoid any serious damage to business.
- **Business Impact Analysis** (**BIA**) is a type of risk assessment exercise that tries to assess qualitative and quantitative impacts on the business due to a disruptive event.
- BCP should be appropriate, adequate, and complete.
- BCP resources should include the availability of processes and people to implement the processes.
- **Recovery Time Objective** (**RTO**) is the timeframe within which the systems should be recovered (indicated in terms of hours/days).
- **Recovery Point Objective** (**RPO**) is the maximum period of time (or amount) of transaction data that the business can afford to lose during a successful recovery.
- Disaster recovery is a process that enables the business to recover from an event that affects normal business operations for a prolonged period.
- Both BCP and **Disaster Recovery Planning** (**DRP**) are targeted at continuity or the resumption of business processes as the case may be.
- The **goal of disaster recovery planning** is to effectively manage the operations during disaster and to ensure proper coordination of different teams.
- The **objective of disaster recovery planning** is to continue the business/IT operations in a secondary site during disaster and restore them back to the primary site in a timely manner.
- On declaration of disaster **the recovery team** is entrusted with implementing the recovery procedure
- **The salvage team**: This team will be responsible for returning business operations to primary site.
- A **primary site** is the one where normal business operations including IT operations take place.
- A **secondary site** is referred to as a backup to the primary site. Generally, secondary sites are geographically located in a different region.
- A **hot site** is an alternate backup site that is fully configured with computer systems; Heating, Ventilation, and Air Conditioning (HVAC), and power supply.
- A **cold site**, as the name implies, contains no computers or other computing equipment. Only HVAC, power, and the office space are available.

- A **warm site** is between hot and cold sites. In this type of arrangement, the computing facilities, such as computers and other communication elements, as well as HVAC and power are available.
- A **dual site** refers to mirroring the exact operations and data in alternative sites.
- **Electronic vaulting** is a batch process used to dump the data at periodical intervals to a remote backup system.
- **Remote journaling** is a parallel processing system that writes the data in a remote system at the alternate site. This type of backup is used where the RTO is less and a high degree of fault tolerance is required.
- **Database shadowing** is used to duplicate data into multiple sites from the remote journaling process. This type of system is used where a fault-tolerance requirement is of the highest degree.
- **Checklist review** is a review process for checking the disaster recovery plan by the managements of various business units.
- A **structured walk-through** is a tabletop exercise that the management team of various business unit meets to review each and every step in a sequential manner.
- A **imulation tessimulation test** is a testing process used to simulate the event in testing environment.
- A **parallel test** is a testing process used to test the coordination of other essential groups such as medical and fire services, including internal teams and adherence to communication procedures.
- A **null test** is a type of test that tries to simulate a real emergency or disaster event.

CISSP CBK Domain #8 – software development security

The following bullet points presented in an exam cram format for a quick revision. They cover important points from the software development security domain. The covered topics include software development life cycle models, security in the software development life cycle, security controls in development environments, assurance requirements in software, software security testing, and security impact analysis on the acquired software:

- Systems engineering is a term that connotes the application of engineering concepts while designing application systems that are complex and large.

- When a system is developed using the system engineering process, then the development activity goes through a life cycle model and is called a **System Development Life Cycle** (**SDLC**). Software development is an activity in system development life cycle models.

- A system development life cycle model consists of many processes. They start from establishing the needs (initiation) and go through to archiving or destruction (disposal).

- Software development is a part of systems development life cycle. Within the development phase, there are many stages and processes. The activity or cycle starts from specification development based on which the overall system is designed and implemented.

- Software development models include simplistic models, such as the waterfall model, iterative models, such as the incremental model or the spiral model, and complex models, such as the agile framework.

- Some of the important security controls in the software development include the following:
    - The separation of development, test, and operational facilities
    - Change control processes and procedures
    - Security controls and the testing of vendor-supplied software packages
    - Checking and covert channels

- Object-oriented systems use the concept of *objects* that work together with other objects in a system to achieve certain objectives.

- An object-oriented programming method uses a collection of objects that communicate and coordinate with other objects to achieve a desired objective. Sending or receiving messages and processing instructions are some of the functions of these objects.

- **Object-Oriented Analysis (OOA)** is an analysis process for producing conceptual model, and **Object-Oriented Design (OOD)** is used to design the ways (how) in which to implement the conceptual models produced in the analysis process.

- Artificial intelligence systems are used in information technology that tries to mimic human brains in perception and decision making. From a security perspective, an artificial intelligence system can be a protector from attacks as well as a perpetrator of attacks.

- An **expert system** is an artificial intelligence-based system that tries to reproduce the performance of one or more human experts.

- **Neural network** is a type of artificial intelligence system that tries to mimic the neural processing of the human brain. They are used in applications such as speech recognition, image analysis, software agents, and more.
- A database system defines the storage and manipulation of data, while a **Database Management System** (**DBMS**) is a set of software programs that are used to perform and control the operations of a database system.
- Common web application vulnerabilities fall under the categories of access control, code permission, code quality, cryptographic, environmental, error handling, logic errors, validation, and more.

- Common attacks on web applications include attacks on functionality, data structure, authentication, protocol, resource, and more.
- **Memory and address protection** is a control used to ensure controlled access to the memory and address locations by the application. The core focus is to limit access and prevent overwriting other memory areas.
- **Access control** is a process used to ensure access to authorized entities and to block unauthorized entities.
- **File protection** is a mechanism used to ensure that files are accessed and modified by authorized entities in a controlled manner.
- **Authentication** is a process to identify and authorize legitimate entities.

- **Reliability** is a quality parameter used to ensure that the application systems are performing efficiently and effectively.

References and further reading

- **Common Vulnerabilities and Exposure** (**CVE**): https://cve.mitre.org/
- **Common Vulnerabilities Scoring System** (**CVSS**): https://nvd.nist.gov/cvss.cfm
- **OWASP**: https://www.owasp.org/index.php/Main_Page
- NIST Special Publication 800-12: An Introduction to Computer Security – The NIST Handbook: http://fas.org/irp/doddir/other/nist-800-12/

Summary

This chapter covered some of the important concepts in the form of an exam cram from the seventh and eighth domains of CISSP CBK. A mock test with a combination of questions in the two domains is provided to test the knowledge learned. Further reading and references are provided to enhance the knowledge in these two domains.

The next chapter consists of an exam cram from all the domains, and it also covers a mock test consisting of 150 questions.

Sample questions

Q1. Memory and address protection is a control used to ensure:

1. Controlled access to physical facility
2. controlled access to the memory and address locations by the application
3. Controlled access to hardware
4. Vulnerability assessment

Q2. A tabletop exercise is also known as:

1. Simulation test
2. Parallel test
3. Structured walkthrough
4. Full test

Q3. An artificial intelligence-based system that tries to reproduce the performance of one or more human experts is called:

1. Hybrid system
2. Expert system
3. Computer networks
4. Database system

Q4. The timeframe within which systems should be recovered (indicated in terms of hours/days) is known as:

1. Recover Point Objective
2. Recovery Data Objective

3. Recovery Test Objective

4. Recovery Time Objective

Q5. Software development is part of the:

1. Database development life cycle

2. Document model

3. System development life cycle

4. Disaster recovery process

Q6. A batch process to dump the data at periodical intervals to a remote backup system is called:

1. Journaling

2. Data vaulting

3. Database shadowing

4. Tape backup

Q7. A type of Risk Assessment exercise that tries to assess qualitative and quantitative impacts on the business due to a disruptive event is called:

1. Group risk assessment

2. Business Plan Analysis

3. Business Impact Analysis

4. Business process analysis

Q8. Incident management is:

1. Establishing systematic and procedural way of managing incidents

2. Operations security controls

3. Memory protection

4. Documenting Business Continuity Plans

Q9. Which one of the following is not a backup process?

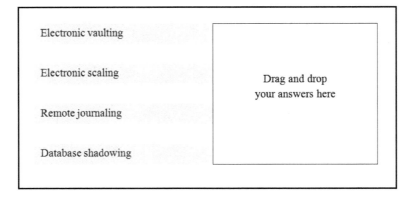

Q10. Which of the following are Class C combustible materials?

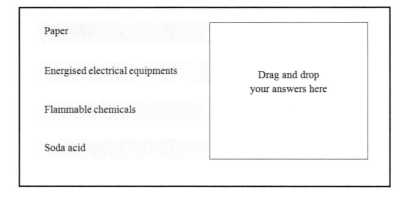

21
Day 21 – Exam Cram and Mock Test

This chapter covers some of the important concepts that are covered in all the eight domains of CISSP CBK in a snippet format that will reinforce the topics learned, and it will serve as an exam cram. A mock test consisting of 180 questions from all the eight domains is provided. Further reading and references are provided towards the end of this chapter.

An overview of the exam cram and mock test

This chapter starts with an exam cram that consists of quick revision points from all the eight domains of the CISSP CBK. This is followed by a mock test consisting of about 180 questions from all the domains. The last topic of this chapter provides additional references for further reading:

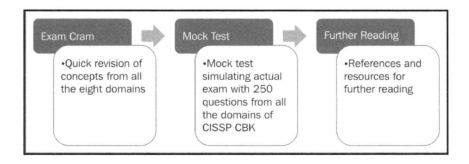

Exam cram

Presented here is a revision of some of the important concepts from all the domains of CISSP CBK. They are provided in bullet points as snippets that are easy to revise. These snippets are for quick revision and reinforcement of the knowledge learned:

- **Risk** is defined as an exposure of the asset to loss, injury, or damage due to threats, vulnerabilities, and attacks.
- **Asset protection** requirements are identified through a structured method of risk analysis, evaluation, and assessment.
- Risk analysis, risk evaluation, risk assessment, and risk mitigation strategies are the components of **risk management**.
- Identifying threats and vulnerabilities, attacks, estimating potential impact, and establishing and implementing suitable controls to treat the risk are functional steps in risk management.
- Risk analysis that provides risk values in numeric terms, such as monetary values, is known as **quantitative**.
- Risk analysis that provides risk values in non-numeric terms, such as high-low-medium, is called **qualitative**.
- Security controls are identified through **risk mitigation strategies**.
- **Risk treatment** includes accepting, transferring, reducing, or avoiding the risk.
- Monitoring, reviewing, communicating the results, and improving the security posture are continual improvement processes in the **risk management cycle**.
- **Security posture** is the overall plan of the organization pertaining to its security. It includes security governance, policies, procedures, and compliance.
- **Information security** is the preservation of the Confidentiality, Integrity, and Availability (CIA) of assets:
    - **Confidentiality**: Unauthorized users should not *view* the information
    - **Integrity**: Unauthorized users should not *modify* the information
    - **Availability**: To ensure authorized users can *access* the information whenever they need to
- **Threat** is an event that could compromise the information security by causing loss or damage to assets. **Vulnerability** is a hole or weakness in the system.
- Threat can exploit vulnerabilities through **threat agents**. A threat event, through its agents, exploiting a vulnerability is called an **attack**. The end result of an attack could be a **security violation**.

- **Security violation** is a compromise of the confidentiality, integrity, and the availability requirement of the asset.
- The **information life cycle** includes handling, processing, transporting, storing, archiving, and destroying the information.
- **Information protection** includes risk management, risk reporting, and accountability.
- Aligning and integrating information security with enterprise governance and IT governance frameworks is called **information security strategy.**
- **Information security policy**states the management intent, support, and direction for security.
- Procedures, guidelines, and standards are called **administrative controls.**
- **Technical controls** are used to support management and administrative controls through information systems.
- **Due diligence** is understanding risk and estimating the risk values, and **Due care** is implementing security governance.
- **Privacy** is the protection of Personally Identifiable Information (PII) or Sensitive Personal Information (SPI) of individuals.
- A **computer crime** is a fraudulent activity that is perpetrated against computers or IT systems.
- In computer crime, the term computer refers to the role it plays in different scenarios: crime committed against a computer, crime committed using the computer, and computer incidental in the crime.
- **Data breach** is a security incident in which sensitive, protected, or confidential data is copied, transmitted, viewed, stolen, or used by an unauthorized entity.
- **Code of ethics** is based on the safety of the commonwealth; duty to principals such as employers, contractors, people whom a professional works for; and duty to each other.
- The (ISC)[2]**code of professional ethics** includes four clauses. They are:
    - Protect society, the commonwealth, and the infrastructure
    - Act honorably, honestly, justly, responsibly, and legally
    - Provide a diligent and competent service to principals
    - Advance and protect the profession
- A **personnel security** policy concerns people associated with the organization such as employees, contractors, and consultants.
- Risk mitigation strategies address risks in terms of availability of the assets are addressed through business continuity management processes.

- An event that could impact regular operations for a prolonged period of time can be termed a **disruptive event**.
- Addressing the risks by way of plans and procedures for the continuation of business operations during and after a disruptive event is called **Business Continuity Planning (BCP)**.
- **Asset security** is based on asset classification and CIA values; and asset classification helps to devise suitable security controls.
- The **need-to-know principle** establishes that one has to demonstrate specific needs to know or access information that is classified as sensitive.
- Core secret, top secret, secret, confidential, public trust, and unclassified are the types of **information classification** in the United States.
- Private and public sector corporate entities classify information under four categories such as confidential, private, sensitive, and public.
- Data that remains even after erasing or formatting from the digital media is called **residual data**, and the property to retain such kind of data is called **data remanence**.
- Privacy laws stipulate data collection limitations pertaining to personal data.
- The **segregation of duties** or the separation of duties is a security control measure used to ensure that mutually exclusive roles are not assigned to a single user concurrently.
- Data can be traditionally grouped under three categories such as Personally Identifiable Information (PII), Intellectual Property (IP), and Non-Public Information (NPI).
- **Data in Motion** refers to the information as it moves around the organization. Information that is stored within the organization is considered to be **Data at rest**. Information that is used by the staff and the data that is available in endpoints is considered as **Data in Use**.
- **Data Loss Prevention** controls are based on who is causing the incident. What actions are carried out by the individual to cause such an incident? Who else is involved and where? And what action is taken?
- **Hashing** is a method in which a cryptographic value is computed and periodically validated based on the contents of the document. Hashing uses mathematical algorithms to compare hashes, and it provides integrity.
- Establishing the identity of the receiver or sender in a digital communication is accomplished through **digital signatures**.
- A secure disposal of media, labeling, access restrictions, formal records of authorized recipients, the storage of media, data distribution, marking, the review of distribution lists, and the control of publicly available information are a few **data handling controls**.

- **Security engineering** is based on design principles, practices, and models to ensure confidentiality, integrity and availability requirements of information assets.
- **Trusted Computer Systems** refer to such systems that have a well-defined security policy, accountability, assurance mechanisms, and proper documentation.
- Encapsulation is a technique to hide information from unauthorized entities.
- **Abstraction** is the process of hiding the details and exposing only the essential features of a particular concept or object that are encapsulated.
- **Logical Security Guard** is a security mechanism used to control the communication between entities that are labeled lower-sensitive and high-sensitive.
- In information security, the term **assurance** means the level of trust or the degree of confidence in the satisfaction of security needs.
- A computer security model **Take-grant protection model** specifies obtaining (taking) rights from one entity to another or transferring (granting) of rights by one entity to another.
- The **Bell LaPadula security model** focus on confidentiality; this model prescribes access controls to classified or confidential information. A simple way to remember this model is-**no read up and no write down**.
- The **Biba model** focuses on data integrity. A simple way to remember this model is-**no read down and no write up**.
- The **Clarke Wilson model** focuses on integrity and aims to address multilevel security requirements in computing systems.
- The primary purpose of vulnerability and penetration tests is to identify, evaluate, and mitigate the risks due to **vulnerability exploitation**.
- Testing from an external network with no prior knowledge of the internal networks and systems is referred to as **black-box testing.**
- Performing the test from an external network or within the network with the knowledge of networks and systems is referred to as **white-box testing.**
- Testing from an external and/or internal network with some knowledge of internal networks and systems is referred to as **gray-box testing**. This is usually a combination of black-box testing and white-box testing.
- An **algorithm** in cryptography is a series of well-defined steps that provide the procedure for encryption/decryption.

- If only one key is used, then it is called **symmetric key encryption**; if two keys are used, then it is called **asymmetric key encryption**; and if no key is used, then it is called .

- When the key stream algorithm operates on a single bit, byte, or computer word such that the information is changed constantly, then it is called **stream cipher**.

- If the algorithm operates on a block of text (as opposed to a single bit or byte), then it is known as **block cipher**.

- **Digital signature** is a type of public key cryptography where the message is digitally signed using the sender's private key.

- **Steganography**refers to the art of concealing information within computer files such as documents, images, or any multimedia content.

- **IEEE 802.11** is set of standards for **Wireless Local Area Networking** (WLAN). **Wired Equivalent Privacy** (WEP) and **Wireless (Wi-Fi) Protected Access** (WPA) are some commonly used protocols for encryption in this communication standard.

- **Public Key Infrastructure** (PKI) is a framework, which enables the integration of various services that are related to cryptography. This uses asymmetric cryptography and digital certificates.

- When a specific key is authorized for use by legitimate entities for a period of time, or the effect of a specific key for given system is for a period of time, then the time span is known as a **Crypto period**.

- **Cryptanalysis** is the science of analyzing and deciphering codes and ciphers.

- The core structure of **FIPS140** recommends four security levels for cryptographic modules that protect sensitive information in federal systems, such as computer and telecommunication systems that include a voice system as well.

- **Open System Interconnect (OSI)** is an International Organization for Standardization (ISO) layered architecture standard that defines a framework for implementing protocols in seven layers.

- The primary four layers of the TCP/IP model are the application layer, the transport layer, the network/internet layer, and the data link layer.

- **TCPSYN attacks** technically establish thousands of half-open connections to consume server resources.

- A **tunnel** in a computer network is a secure path or route for the datagram to pass through an insecure or untrusted network, such as VPN.

- Snooping/eavesdropping, Theft of services, and the Denial-of-Service (DOS) are common attacks on communication systems.

- The overall process of facilitating and managing identities and controlling access to assets while ensuring information security is termed **Identity and Access Management (IAM)**.

- Identity and access management consists of four distinctive principles and practices. They are Identification, Authentication, Authorization, and Accountability.

- Authentication, Authorization, and Accountability are together referred to as **Triple A of Access Control**.

- When identity and access management applications and associated services are delivered through subscription-based cloud models, then such services are termed as **Identity as a Service (IDaaS)**.

- **Access management** is facilitated through authentication and authorization processes.

- If access to an object is controlled based on certain contextual parameters, such as location, time, sequence of responses, and access history, then it is known as **context-dependent** access control.

- If the access is provided based on the attributes or content of an object, then it is called **content-dependent** access control.

- A **Role-Based Access Control (RBAC)** is a non-discretionary access control based on the subject's role or position in the organization.

- When an entity (subject) is validated against a single credential, then it is called a **one-factor authentication** and generally uses the what you know principle.

- When an entity (subject) is validated against two different credentials, then it is called as **two-factor authentication** and generally uses **what you have** principle.

- When an entity (subject) is validated against two or more different credentials, then it is called a **multifactor authentication**and generally uses the **what you are** principle.

- When a Trojan horse is activated on a particular event (such as a particular date), then it is called a **logic bomb**.

- **Spoofing** is a type of attack used to imitate a trusted entity, thereby making the system trust this imitated entity.

- Vulnerability tests and assessments are performed to ascertain the presence of technical vulnerabilities or weakness in systems. When an identified vulnerability is not published by the application vendor, then it is called a **zero-day vulnerability**. When an exploit code is published by a security or malicious group before a patch released by the vendor, then it is called a **zero-day exploits**.

- **Penetration testing** is often performed to ascertain break-in possibilities in systems.

- Synthetic transactions are generally used for performance monitoring, and hence, they are directly associated with the availability tenet of the information security triad.
- Concurrency tests are performed to test the application with a concurrent user activity.
- The misuse case test is the reverse of a use case test. In other words, doing a malicious act against a system is a misuse case of normal act.
- An API test involves the testing of functionality, performance, and the security of application programming interfaces.
- **Perimeter security** relates to the security considerations pertaining to the boundaries. Securing the entry and exit points of the facility, networks, and more will fall under this perimeter security.
- **Interior security** refers to the security considerations pertaining to the facilities that are inside the perimeter.
- Based on the type of combustible material, **fire** is classified as Class A, Class B, Class C, and Class D.
- Clean **electrical power** is a requirement for proper equipment functioning.
- Some of the electrical power-related parameters that could affect equipment include Noise, Electromagnetic Interference (EMI), and Radio Frequency Interference (RFI).
- For the proper functioning of computer systems, the humidity levels should be between 40 and 60 percent.
- **Auditing** is a process to check and validate the effectiveness of controls. The primary tool that assists in the audit is an audit trial.
- **Mean Time Between Failure (MTBF)** is a time measurement that specifies an average time between failures. This time is called the useful life of the device.
- **Mean Time to Repair (MTTR)** indicates the downtime or the average time required to repair the device.
- **Degaussing** is an effective method of destroying the data in magnetic media.
- Information such as the location, time, discovery, securing, controlling, and maintenance of the evidence is called **chain of evidence**. The cycle of activities from the discovery of evidence to its preservation, transportation, admission in the court, and return to the owner is called the **evidence life cycle**.
- An **incident** is an event that could possibly violate information security. The violation may breach the Confidentiality, Integrity, and Availability requirements of information assets.

- When a systematic and procedural way of managing incidents is established in an organization, then it is called **Incident Management**. Incident management consists of incident reporting and responses to such reports.
- **Business Continuity Planning (BCP)** is a process that proactively addresses the continuation of business operations during the aftermath of disruptive events. The aim is to prevent interruptions to operations.
- **Business Impact Analysis (BIA)** is a type of Risk Assessment exercise that tries to assess qualitative and quantitative impacts on the business due to a disruptive event.
- **Recovery Time Objective (RTO)** is time frame within which systems should be recovered (indicated in terms of hours/days).
- **Recovery Point Objective (RPO)** is the maximum the period of time (or amount) of the transaction data that the business can afford to lose during a successful recovery.
- **Disaster recovery** is a process that enables a business to recover from an event that affects normal business operations for a prolonged period of time.
- **Systems engineering** is a term that connotes the application of engineering concepts while designing application systems that are complex and large.
- A **system development life cycle** model consists of many processes. They start from establishing needs (initiation) to archival or destruction (disposal).
- **Software development models** include simplistic models such as the waterfall model; iterative models such as incremental model, spiral model; and complex models such as agile framework.
- Some of the important **security controls** in software development include the following:
    - The separation of development, test, and operational facilities
    - Change control processes and procedures
    - Security controls and the testing of vendor-supplied software packages
    - Checking and covert channels
- **Reliability** is a quality parameter used to assure that application systems perform efficiently and effectively.

Summary

This chapter covered some of the important concepts in the form of an exam cram from all the domains of CISSP CBK. A mock test with a combination of questions from all the domains is provided below to test the knowledge learned.

Mock test

Q1. An attack that compromises the information stored in the client machine by web browsers for faster retrieval during subsequent visits is called what?

1. Path traversal
2. Data structure attacks
3. Eavesdropping
4. Cache poisoning

Q2. Which of the following are risk management processes? (This is a drag-and-drop type of question. Here, and for similar drag-and-drop questions, you can draw a line from the list of answers from the left to the empty box on the right.)

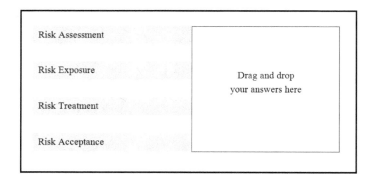

Q3. Primary criterion of a Business continuity planning is to ensure that the scoping is _____.

1. Adequate
2. Large
3. Appropriate
4. Wide coverage

Q4. What is the algorithm used by the Wi-Fi Protected Access 2 (WPA2) protocol for encryption?

    1. RC4
    2. Data Encryption Algorithm (DES)
    3. Advanced Encryption Algorithm (AES)
    4. Triple-DES

Q5. Measurements help in reducing the frequency and severity of security-related issues. Which one of the following is not a right choice for measurements?

    1. Expectations from data privacy requirements
    2. Reduction in number of incidents
    3. More non-conformities during internal or external audits
    4. Expectations from confidentiality requirements of information

Q6. If an attack uses a combination of brute force and dictionary entries to crack a password, then such an attack is called what?

    1. Replay attack
    2. Password attack
    3. Session hijack
    4. Hybrid attack

Q7. Identify from the following list an activity that best describes a management control:

    1. Review of security controls
    2. System Documentation
    3. Network protection
    4. Personnel security

Q8. Brute-forcing of passwords is a

    1. Probabilistic technique
    2. Path traversal attack
    3. Protocol manipulation
    4. Boundary error

Q9. Which of the following are steps in computer system start up and shut down procedures?

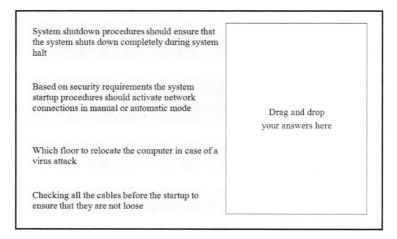

Q10. Which property of a TCP implementation is vulnerable to Denial of Service attacks?

1. Session establishment
2. Three-way handshake mechanism
3. ICMP access
4. Multicasting

Q11. While identifying security awareness training needs, which of the following are appropriate choices to consider?

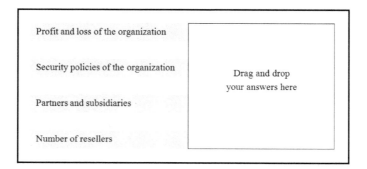

Q12. Which one the following types of hacker is most likely to compromise organizations, computer systems to perpetrate a computer crime for financial gain?

1. Black hat hackers
2. White hat hackers
3. Ethical hackers
4. Vulnerability assessors

Q13. Which one of the following pertaining to lighting is false?

1. Lighting is a reactive control
2. Lighting is a deterrent control
3. For critical areas, the suggested illumination is two feet wide and eight feet tall
4. Lighting discourages intruders

Q14. Which one of the choices is a popular algorithm used in asymmetric key encryption, which is a product of two large prime numbers that derives the key pairs?

1. Rivest, Shamir, and Adleman (RSA)
2. Blowfish
3. Twofish
4. Diffie-Hellman

Q15. An organization monitors the logon sessions of its employees. As per the legal requirements and the system monitoring policy of the organization, it is mandatory that the employee is informed and reminded from time to time about session monitoring. Select the most appropriate method for implementing such a requirement

1. Policy document on the intranet
2. Employee handbook
3. Wall posters
4. Logon Banners

Q16. Ping of death is an example of which one of the following?

1. Denial-of-Service attack
2. A Protocol manipulation attack
3. A Man-In-The-Middle attack
4. A Spoofing attack

Q17. In information security, the level of trust or a degree of confidence on computer systems is known as what?

1. Auditing
2. Assessment
3. Assurance
4. Accreditation

Q18. Common Vulnerabilities and Exposures (CVE) contain the details of published vulnerabilities. These details are called what?

1. A dictionary of vulnerabilities
2. A database of vulnerabilities
3. A list of vulnerabilities
4. Vulnerability exposures

Q19. A time condition in web applications where the state of a resource changes between the time the resource is checked to when it is accessed is called what?

1. Resource management errors
2. SQL injection
3. Race conditions
4. Covert channel

Q20. In public key cryptography, a message is encrypted using the recipient's public key, and the recipient's private key is used to decrypt the message. This process ensures which tenet of information security?

1. Confidentiality
2. Integrity
3. Availability
4. Authenticity

Q21. An attack that redirects a user accessing a legitimate website to an attacker-constructed malicious site without the acceptance or knowledge of the user is known as _____.

1. Phishing
2. SmiShing
3. Fishing
4. Pharming

Q22. The process of packaging the data packets received from applications is known as encapsulation. What is the term that denotes the output of such a process?

1. Database
2. Decapsuatlion
3. Frame
4. Datagram

Q23. Which one of the following statements are true?

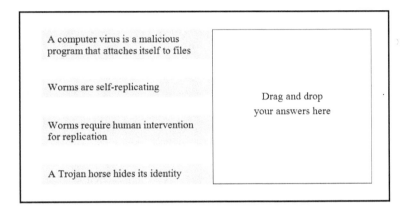

Q24. In an organization, a surveillance monitor, such as Closed Circuit Television (CCTV), is used in critical areas to monitor the movement of personnel. Which of the following controls is least effective for such a monitoring activity?

1. Motion Sensor
2. Heat Sensor
3. Intrusion detection system
4. Fire Wall

Q25. An organization is planning to set up a data center that houses critical business application servers. Which one of the following will be the least important factor to consider for such a facility?

1. The location is not in close proximity to toxic chemical installations
2. The location is not in a seismic zone
3. The location is not very close to a seashore
4. The location is not very close to a metropolis

Q26. In cryptography encrypting, a decrypted message results in what?

    1. A scrambled message
    2. A decrypted message
    3. A plain text
    4. An algorithm

Q27. Which of the following statements pertaining to the Bell-LaPadula model are appropriate?

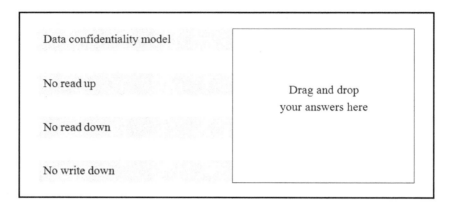

Q28. A prominent application of a Fiber Channel Protocol includes which one of the following?

    1. IPSec
    2. Storage Area Network
    3. Hyper Text Transfer Protocol
    4. File Transfer

Q29. Which one of the following disaster recovery tests is also called a functional drill?

    1. The checklist review
    2. The table-top exercise
    3. A simulation test
    4. A parallel test

Q30. A steady interference to electrical power is called Noise. What is the term used for an electrical power interference of a short duration?

1. Sag
2. Spike
3. Transient
4. Inrush

Q31. A malicious code that tracks user actions is called_____.

1. Botware
2. Worm
3. Spyware
4. Virus

Q32. Which one of the following water sprinkler systems is most appropriate when large volumes of water should be discharged to contain the fire?

1. Dry pipe
2. Wet pipe
3. Deluge
4. Preaction

Q34. Which of the following are true statements pertaining to information security controls?

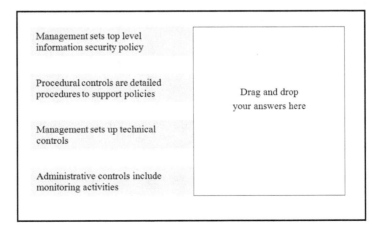

Q35. The charge difference between neutral, hot, and ground electrical wires is called what?

1. Electromatic Interference
2. Electromechanical interference
3. Radio Frequency Interference
4. Electromagnetic Interference

Q36. Residual risk is risk that remains after _____.

1. The implementation of control
2. Before control implementation
3. Risk assessment
4. An incident

Q37. In web applications, the lack of a verification mechanism to ensure that the sender of a web request actually intended to do so is exploited by which one of the following attacks?

1. Cross-site scripting
2. Cross-site request forgery
3. Buffer overflow
4. Path traversal

Q38. An asset is valued at $5,000,000, and it is estimated that a certain threat has an annualized rate of occurrence (ARO) once every three years. The asset has an exposure factor (EF) of 15%. What is the highest amount that a company should spend annually on countermeasures?

1. $250,000
2. $350,000
3. $960,000
4. $450,000

Q39. The activities of a logged in user are monitored and updated to an access log file. This process is known as what?

1. Authentication
2. Audit trail
3. Accountability
4. Access control

Q40. Providing invalid or out-of-bounds inputs to the database system to obtain either database access or the database content using the native language of the database system constitutes a type of attack known as what?

1. Database manipulation
2. Denial-of-Service
3. SQL injection
4. Arbitrary code injection

Q41. Which of the following are threats to physical security?

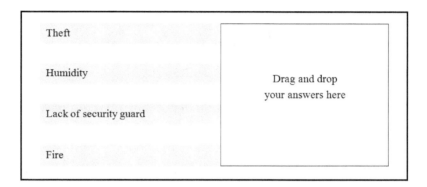

Q42. A high-rise wall in the physical perimeter is a physical security control. Which one of the following is a false statement for such a control?

1. It is preventative physical control
2. It is a deterrent physical control
3. It is corrective physical control
4. It is a control to prevent physical intrusion

Q43. If a periodic port scanning is not performed on the information systems, then there is risk of _____ created by malicious programs.

1. Port forwarding
2. Port mapping
3. Turnstile doors
4. Backdoors

Q44 Business Continuity Planning life cycle includes the maintenance of plans. Which one of the following choices may not provide necessary inputs for updating the plans pertaining to information security?

1. Incidents
2. Results of periodic risk assessments
3. Changes to business environment
4. Changes in tax structure

Q45. The malicious activity of changing data during the input or processing stage of a software program to obtain a financial gain is known as _____.

1. Data diddling
2. Salami slicing
3. Penny shaving
4. Hacking

Q46. Hiding or showing menus in an application depending on the access permissions of a user is known as what?

1. Context-dependent access control
2. Content-dependent access control
3. Mandatory access control
4. Role-based access control

Q47. Identify the false statements from the following options pertaining to information security procedures:

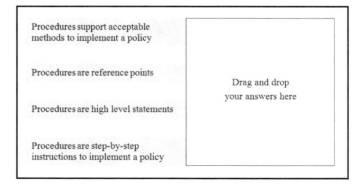

Q48. Which one of the following is not an assurance aim of Public Key Infrastructure (PKI)?

1. Confidentiality
2. Integrity
3. Non-repudiation
4. Availability

Q49. The process of checking and validating the effectiveness of physical security controls is called what?

1. Administration
2. Assessment
3. Auditing
4. Analysis

Q50. Federal Information Processing Standard (FIPS) 140 Security Level 3 does not emphasize which one of the following?

1. A high probability of detection of physical attacks
2. Response mechanisms for physical attacks
3. Identity-based authentication
4. Control of environmental conditions such as temperature, heat, and voltage

Q51. A law that was developed on the basis of the decisions of courts and tribunals is called _____.

1. Civil law
2. Common law
3. Religious law
4. Statute law

Q52. Which one of the following is a false statement pertaining to the Take-Grant model?

1. Take rule: a subject takes rights from another subject
2. Grant rule: a subject grants rights to another subject
3. Create rule: a subject creates new nodes
4. Restore rule: a subject restores its rights over an object

Q53. Providing wrong inputs to the system can be classified as which one of the following?

1. Problem
2. Vulnerability
3. Incident
4. Threat

Q54. The purpose of using Secure Shell (SSH) over TelNet is what?

1. SSH provides shell access to the target system
2. SSH is faster than Telnet
3. SSH encrypts the session and Telnet does not encrypt the session
4. SSH is less expensive than Telnet

Q55. In Cryptography, if a corresponding ciphertext to the block of plaintext selected by the analyst is available, then which type of attack is possible?

1. Ciphertext only attack
2. Adaptive-chosen-plaintext attack
3. Chosen-plaintext attack
4. Known-plaintext attack

Q56. When a sender wants to ensure that the message is not altered during transmission, the sender uses a hash function. The hash value is known as what?

1. Hash digest
2. Checksum
3. Message digest
4. Message code

Q57. A cryptovariable is a:

1. Cryptographic key
2. Cryptographic method
3. Cryptographic text
4. Cryptography type

Q58. Which one of the following is not a type of sensor used in wave pattern motion detectors?

1. Infrared
2. Shortwave
3. Microwave
4. Ultrasonic

Q59. An organization has identified risks to its web servers from hacking attacks through the Internet. Which one of the following may not be a correct strategy to mitigate the risks?

1. Establishing controls to filter the traffic to the server
2. Establishing countermeasures in case of an unauthorized breach to the server
3. Establishing safeguards to protect the information in the server
4. Relocating the server to a different data center

Q60. Which of the following is false for Gas discharge fire extinguishing systems?

1. They use carbon dioxide
2. They are used under the floor in data centers
3. They use water
4. They use halon

Q61. While doing risk assessment for physical and environmental security requirements, which of the following security professionals will be taken into consideration?

1. Physical facility
2. Geographic operating location
3. Supporting facilities
4. Communications systems

Q62. Which of the following statement is false pertaining to the RC4 algorithm?

1. It uses 40 to 256 bits
2. Key sizes are different
3. It is used in less complex hardware
4. It cannot be used for faster processing environments

Q63. Which of the following are risk mitigation strategies?

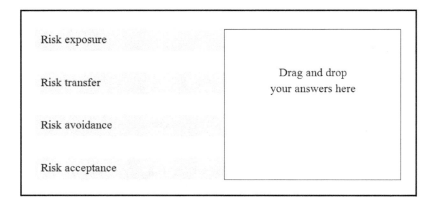

Risk exposure

Risk transfer

Risk avoidance

Risk acceptance

Drag and drop
your answers here

Q64. In digital signature, the process of signing is accomplished by what?

1. Applying the sender's private key to the document
2. Applying the sender's public key to the document
3. Applying the hash function
4. Applying the sender's private key to the message digest

Q65. At what temperature is the valve of wet pipe sprinkling systems designed to open?

1. 164° Fahrenheit
2. 164° Celsius
3. 165° Celsius
4. 165° Fahrenheit

Q66. Which one of the following is not a primary objective of the Orange book?

1. Accountability
2. Assurance
3. Policy
4. Authentication

Q67. IEEE 802.11 is set of standards for which type of the following networking technologies?

1. Wireless Local Area Networking (WLAN)

2. Local Area Networking (LAN)
3. Wide Area Networking (WAN)
4. Metropolitan Area Networking (MAN)

Q68. Identify the least appropriate method from the following to determine the strength or security of a cryptographic key:

1. The length of the key
2. Entropy
3. The quality of the encryption algorithm
4. Initialization vectors

Q69. Which one of the following choices is correct for Annualized Loss Expectancy (ALE)?

1. Single Loss Expectancy divided by the Annual Rate of Occurrence
2. Asset Value multiplied by Exposure Factor
3. Asset Value multiplied by the Annual Rate of Occurrence
4. Single Loss Expectancy multiplied by the Annual Rate of Occurrence

Q70. Which one of the following is false pertaining to the Gray-box penetration testing?

1. The scope of testing can be from external or internal networks
2. While testing from external networks, the details of internal network are is not known to the tester
3. While testing from external networks, the details of internal network are known to the tester
4. While testing from internal network, the details of the network are not known to the tester

Q71. The address pace of Ipv6 is what?

1. 216 IP addresses
2. 2,128 IP addresses
3. 264 IP addresses
4. 232 IP addresses

Q72. Identify the correct statements pertaining to the primary purpose of cryptography:

Conceal the confidential information from unauthorized users	
Ensuring immediate detection of any alteration made to the concealed information	Drag and drop your answers here
Ensuring availability of confidential information all the time	
Converting a plain text to a cipher text	

Q73. A cold boot attack is used to retrieve information such as password or encryption keys from DRAM memories even after the power is removed. Which property of the DRAM memories is this attack trying to compromise?

1. Data Retention
2. Data Emanation
3. Data Remanence
4. Data Encryption

Q74. An exposure factor can be best described as:

1. The rate of occurrence of a threat event
2. Measure of an impact
3. Measure of a vulnerability
4. Measure of risk

Q75. While developing business continuity plans, which one of the following should be considered as the most important requirement?

1. Confidentiality
2. Integrity
3. Availability
4. Business plans

Q76. Replay attacks are due to improper handling of:

1. Authentication process
2. Session data
3. Application inputs
4. Boundary values

Q77. Sending Unsolicited Commercial Email (UCE) is popularly known as:

1. Phishing
2. Pharming
3. SMiShing
4. Spamming

Q78. Identify the correct asset classification criteria from the following:

1. Age
2. Useful degree
3. Useful life
4. Value

Q79. The turnstile type of fencing should be considered in which of the following situations?

1. When a group of people can be allowed at a time through the gate
2. When a mantrap system is required
3. When a single person should be allowed to pass through the gate at a time
4. When intrusion detection systems are installed

Q80. For the proper operation of computer parts, the ideal humidity range should be 40 to 60%. What type of problem will occur if the humidity is above 60%?

1. Electric plating
2. Electro plating
3. Condensation
4. Static electricity

Q81. Threats exploit vulnerabilities through:

1. Associates
2. Adversaries

3. Agents
4. Angles

Q82. Identify the intellectual property-related terms from the following:

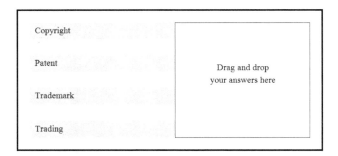

Q83. A strong session management prevents what type of attack?

1. Sniffing
2. Spoofing
3. Hijacking
4. SYN

Q84. Identify the incorrect statements pertaining to security policy:

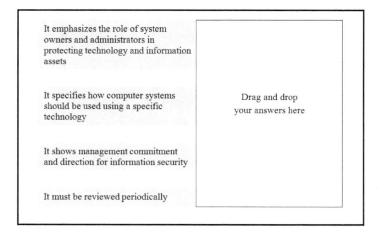

Q85. Which of the following is not a true choice for the Kerberos implementation?

1. It can be used to authenticate network services
2. It can be used to provide third-party verification services
3. It maintains a centralized server
4. The Kerberos server is a single point of compromise

Q86. Basic Input Output System (BIOS) checks can be used to control access to the system using password protection. This control is called what?

1. Pre-boot authorization
2. Pre-boot authentication
3. Boot sector authentication
4. Pre-boot identification

Q87. Which of the following information security models proposes a directed graph?

1. The Biba model
2. The Clark-Wilson model
3. The Take-Grant model
4. The Integrity model

Q88. When a malicious code that came disguised inside a trusted program gets activated on a particular event or date, then such malicious code is called what?

1. A Trojan horse
2. Malware
3. A logic bomb
4. Virus

Q89. An access card that contains integrated circuits and can process information for physical and logical access control is called what?

1. An ATM card
2. A credit card
3. A supplementary card
4. A smart card

Q90. Which one of the following is a correct description of a preventative control?

1. Preventative control is used to predict the occurrence of an undesirable event
2. Preventative control is used to reduce the effect of an attack
3. Preventative controls trigger a corrective control
4. Preventative controls are to prevent security violations

Q91. Which of the following are right considerations while designing a data center?

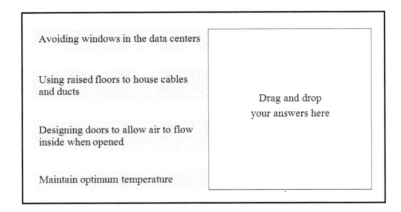

Q92. An access control model that uses a pair of values that are related to the least upper bound and the greatest lower bound in a model is called what?

1. Discretionary access control
2. Non-discretionary access control
3. Matrix-based access control
4. Lattice-based access control

Q93. Secret and hidden channels that transmit information to unauthorized entities based on the response time of the system are known as what?

1. Covert storage channel
2. Covert channel
3. Covert timing channel
4. Covert information channel

Q94. Secure Sockets Layer (SSL) is a popular protocol that uses cryptographic encryption to protect the communication data. Which type of cipher does this protocol use for such a protection?

1. Block cipher
2. Stream cipher
3. Triple-DES
4. Rijndael algorithm

Q95. Which one of the following statements pertaining to combustible materials is false?

1. Cloth and rubber are Class A materials
2. Magnesium and sodium are Class D materials
3. Oils and Greases are Class B materials
4. Water is a Class C material

Q96. The focus of the red book in rainbow series published by the US Department of Defense (DoD) is _____.

1. Integrity
2. Confidentiality
3. Authenticity
4. Confidentiality and Integrity

Q97. Which one of the following pertaining to fire-suppression mediums is false?

1. Halon is a fire suppression medium
2. Halon is a very widely used fire suppression medium
3. Halon is an ozone-depleting substance
4. Halon is no longer allowed to be used as a fire suppression medium

Q98. Which one of the following methods is most suitable for protecting copyrighted information?

1. Steganography
2. Digital watermarking
3. SecureID
4. Digital signature

Q99. Which of the following information security models is also known as a State machine model?

1. The Take-Grant model
2. The Bell_LaPadula model
3. The Biba Model
4. The Clark-Wilson model

Q100. The systematic use of information to identify sources and estimate risk is known as what?

1. Risk evaluation
2. Risk treatment
3. Risk acceptance
4. Risk analysis

Q101. When you want to ensure that the message you sent can be opened only by the receiver, then you will do what?

1. Encrypt the document using your public key
2. Encrypt the document using receiver's private key
3. Encrypt the document using your private key
4. Encrypt the document using receiver's public key

Q102. Portable fire extinguishers predominantly use which fire-suppression medium?

1. Halon
2. Carbon dioxide (CO2)
3. Water
4. Magnesium

Q103. Which of the following choices can be appropriate when an organization needs to resume its critical IT operations in 24 to 48 hours?

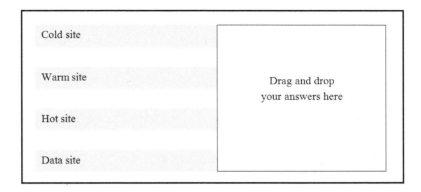

Q104. The amount of time or effort required to accomplish an attack is known as what?

1. Work load
2. Attack vector
3. Work factor
4. Attack factor

Q105. The layer that manages the communication between two computers in the OSI model is called what?

1. The Network layer
2. The Session layer
3. The Data link layer
4. The Application layer

Q106. Fooling an information system to make it trust an entity that has imitated the trusted entity is known as what?

1. Sniffing
2. Social engineering
3. Smurf
4. Spoofing

Q107. Which one of the following controls will be most effective to prevent data theft due to data remanence in the storage media?

1. Degaussing
2. Formatting seven times

3. Physically destroying the media
4. Erasing the data before reuse

Q108. Hash value in cryptography is a computed value based on the contents of the message. What is this computed value called?

1. Primesum
2. Key strength
3. Checksum
4. One-way function

Q109. If an access to an asset is determined by its owner, then such an access control is termed as what?

1. Mandatory
2. Rule based
3. Discretionary
4. Lattice-based

Q110. Which one of the following is a service asset?

1. Computer
2. Air-conditioner
3. Printer
4. Computing

Q111. Which one of the following is false pertaining to the information owners?

1. Owners are entrusted with the day-to-day maintenance of information
2. Owners delegate the maintenance of information to the custodian
3. Owners determine the classification level of the information
4. Owners are responsible for the protection of the information

Q112. An organization is doing risk assessment for the Information Technology department. Which one of the following choices would not yield much input for the assessment?

1. Classification of assets
2. List of threats

3. Vulnerability assessment reports
4. Number of audits

Q113. Which one of the following protocols is most likely to reduce the manual configuration of IP addresses to host computers?

1. Transmission Control Protocol
2. Internet Protocol
3. Dynamic Host Control Protocol
4. Address Resolution Protocol

Q114. IPsec is a set of protocols used to secure Internet communications. Which of the following is not a key function of the protocol?

1. Authentication
2. Encryption
3. Key exchange
4. Key modification

Q115. Randomization vulnerabilities are predominantly concerned with which one of the following?

1. Access control
2. Encryption
3. Authentication
4. Boundary condition

Q116. Providing personnel identification number (PIN) along with a smart card and swiping a finger constitutes what type of authentication?

1. Multi-tier
2. Two-factor
3. Three-factor
4. Factoring

Q117. In Cryptography, when a key is authorized for use by legitimate entries for a period of time, then such a period is called what?

1. Cryptovariable
2. Cryptotime

3. Cryptoperiod
4. Cryptanalysis

Q118. Which one of the following is not true pertaining to Virtual Private Networking (VPN)?

1. VPN is a virtual network within a public network, such as the Internet
2. VPN uses the concept of tunneling
3. A tunnel in VPN is an unencrypted path
4. VPN uses IPsec protocols

Q119. In the Bell-LaPadula model, which one of the following statements is false?

1. The security properties are related to the Mandatory Access Control and Discretionary Access Control
2. The model prescribes access controls to classified or confidential information
3. The security properties are related to the Mandatory Access Control and Non-Discretionary Access Control
4. The focus of the model is confidentiality

Q120. Which one of the following is false pertaining to the TCP/IP protocols?

1. TCP is a connection-oriented protocol, whereas UDP is a connectionless protocol
2. TCP is a connectionless protocol, whereas IP is a connection-oriented protocol
3. Internet protocol works in the Internet layer of the TCP/IP model
4. TCP works in the transport layer of the TCP/IP model

Q121. The concept of least privilege is applicable to what?

1. System administrators
2. Security administrators
3. Users
4. Operators

Q122. Border Gateway Protocols work in which layer of the TCP/IP model?

1. The Application layer
2. The Physical layer
3. The Data link layer
4. The Transport layer

Q123. In Public Key Infrastructure, which of the following is not a key management procedure?

1. Secure storage of keys
2. Secure distribution of keys
3. Secure destruction of keys
4. Secure modification of keys

Q124. Asymmetric key encryption is also known as what?

1. Private key cryptography
2. Private key encryption
3. Public key cryptography
4. Public key infrastructure

Q125. An armed response to an intrusion is called what?

1. Preventive-administrative control
2. Preventive-technical control
3. Reactive-physical control
4. Reactive-administrative control

Q126. An organization is planning to conduct information security awareness training programs for its employees. Which one of the following topics should they consider the most important?

1. Briefing the security requirements of the organization
2. Legal responsibilities of the organization
3. Business controls
4. Usage instructions that relate to information-processing facilities

Q127. At what stage of penetration testing are vulnerability scanners used?

1. Scoping
2. Penetrating testing
3. Information analysis planning
4. Vulnerability detection

Q128. The practice of discovering the full content of a DNS zone via successive queries is called what?

1. Zone transfer
2. Zone Update
3. Zone security
4. Zone enumeration

Q129. The separation of users and data is an example of which type of assurance?

1. Operational assurance
2. Life Cycle assurance
3. System assurance
4. Network assurance

Q130. In computer crime, the role of computers could be which one of the following?

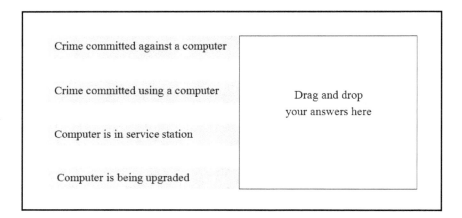

Q131. Which one of the following is not true for Recovery Time Objectives (RTO) pertaining to Business Continuity Planning?

1. It is a timeframe within which the systems should be recovered
2. It is indicated in terms of hours/days
3. The maximum period of time of that transaction data that a business can afford to lose during successful recovery
4. It is based on Service Level Agreements

Q132. The goal of the code of ethics by (ISC) includes which one of the following?

1. Protect society, the commonwealth, and the infrastructure
2. Act honorably, honestly, justly, responsibly, and legally
3. Provide diligent and competent service to principals
4. All of the above

Q133. Which one of the following is a crime committed by way of identity theft?

1. Online purchases through stolen credit cards
2. Selling skimmed credit cards
3. Sending spam mails by spoofing mail addresses
4. Breaking into a bank and stealing money

Q134. Which one of the following attacks does not represent a form of social engineering?

1. Phishing
2. 419 Nigerian spam
3. Denial-of-Service
4. A Trojan horse

Q135. Key loggers capture the keystrokes of the unsuspicious user. Which one of the following attacks represents a behavior that may be capturing the activity information in the network?

1. Spamming
2. Sniffing
3. Replay attacks
4. Pinging

Q136. Which one of the following pertaining to criminal law is not a right choice?

1. It deals with violations of government laws
2. Criminal laws are files by government agencies against an individual or organization
3. It deals with lawsuit files by private parties, such as individuals and corporations
4. The punishment under criminal law includes imprisonment

Q137. _____ is a set of exclusive rights granted to the inventor of new, useful, inventive, and industry-applications:

1. Copyright
2. Patent
3. Trademark
4. Trade secret

Q138. Sarbanes-Oxley mandates a number of reforms to which one of the following?

1. Enhancing corporate responsibility
2. Financial disclosures
3. Combating corporate and accounting fraud
4. All of the above

Q139. Which one of the following statements pertaining to communication protocols is false?

1. A protocol is a communication standard
2. A protocol is network traffic routing device
3. A protocol defines rules pertaining to syntax and semantics
4. A protocol defines rules pertaining to synchronization for communications

Q140. The four upper layers in the OSI model are sometimes referred to as_____.

1. Network layers.
2. Media layer
3. Host layers.
4. Communication layers.

Q141. Spoofing can also be referred to as:

1. Masquerading
2. Disguising
3. Impersonating
4. All of the above

Q142. Which of the following is not a service provided by Domain name System Security Extensions (DNSSEC)?

1. Authentication
2. Accounting
3. Data integrity
4. Authenticated denial of existence

Q143. Which one of the following statements pertaining to Dynamic Host Control Protocol (DHCP) is false?

1. DHCP uses Point-to-Point Protocol (PPP)
2. DHCP uses Network Address Translation (NAT) for assigning IP addresses
3. DHCP is the preferred method of IP allocation to routers and firewalls
4. The address allocation method is termed as Request, Offer, Send, and Accept (ROSA)

Q144. Path traversal is a type of attack that tries to:

1. Compromise the availability of a server
2. Spoof the network traffic
3. Gain unauthorized access to web server directory structures
4. Corrupt the database

Q145. Which of the following cryptographic standards uses three 56-bit keys?

1. Data Encryption Standard
2. Triple-DES
3. Advanced Encryption Standard
4. Blowfish

Q146. Secure Electronic Transaction (SET) is a:

1. Set of standard protocols for file transfer
2. Set of standard protocols for web browsing
3. Set of standard protocols for securing credit card transactions over insecure networks
4. None of the above

Q147. What is the normal range of a raised floor in a data center?

1. 2 to 3 feet
2. 2 meters to 4 meters
3. 300 mm to 800 mm
4. 50 cm to 90 cm

Q148. A periodical mock test rehearsing the steps of actions to be taken during an emergency is also known what?

1. A Table-top review
2. Evacuation drills
3. Fire fighting
4. A shutdown of systems

Q149. Full disk encryption is used to encrypt the data in laptops. This is done to prevent which type of attack?

1. A warm boot attack
2. A hot boot attack
3. A cold boot attack
4. A boot sector attack

Q150. Average time required to repair a device is termed as what?

1. Mean Time Between Failure
2. Useful life of a device
3. Mean Time To Repair
4. Mean Time to Install

Q151. A technique to hide information from unauthorized entities is known as what?

1. Reference monitor
2. Salami slicing
3. Encapsulation
4. Emanation

Q152. Property states that a subject a given security level may not write to any object at a lower security level. Which security model states this property?

1. The Bell-LaPadula Model
2. The Take-Grant model
3. The Biba model
4. The Clark-Wilson model

Q153. In Biometrics, identification provided by a person is verified by a process called one-to-one search. This process can be described as what?

1. Authorization
2. Identification
3. Authentication
4. Access control

Q154. An authority who manages the certificates in a Public Key Infrastructure is known as what?

1. The Root authority
2. The System authority
3. The Certification authority
4. The Digital authority

Q155. Which of the following algorithms are not useful for hashing?

1. MD4
2. MD5
3. MD2
4. RC4

Q156. Kerberos is suitable for preventing what?

1. Spoofing attacks
2. Replay attacks
3. Phishing attacks
4. Decryption attacks

Q157. The disposal phase in system development life cycle is concerned with which one of the following?

1. Disposition of information
2. Disposition of hardware and software
3. Disposition of media
4. All of the above

Q158. In software development, life cycle verification during development and implementation is a process used to check what?

1. Adherence to timelines
2. Adherence to budgets
3. Adherence to software specifications.
4. Adherence to hardware specifications

Q159. What is the biggest concern in using a waterfall model for software development?

1. It is a top-to-bottom approach
2. It is a simplistic approach
3. The activities have to be completed in sequence
4. The approach does not support reworks

Q160. Which of the following are core security considerations for secure software development processes?

1. User authentication
2. Password management
3. Access controls
4. All of the above

Q161. From the security perspective, which of the following procedures is most important during software development processes?

1. Hardware configuration procedure
2. Network setup procedure
3. Change control procedure
4. Documentation procedure

Q162. Failure to properly create, store, transmit, or protect passwords is an example of: what?

    1. Improper network management
    2. Insufficient access controls
    3. Improper credential management
    4. Insufficient authentication mechanisms

Q163. Failure of a web application to validate, filter, or encode user input before returning it to another user's web client is known as what?

    1. Path traversal
    2. Cross Site Scripting
    3. Cross Site Request Forgery
    4. Input validation

Q164. Mobile codes are executed in which one of the following?

    1. Server
    2. Target machine
    3. Network
    4. Routers

Q165. Which of the following are common data structure attacks?

    1. Altering the data in primary memory
    2. Rearranging the order of execution in the memory
    3. Malicious code execution through a data buffer
    4. All of the above

Q166. The encryption of data between the client and the server in an Internet web browsing session can be accomplished using what?

    1. SSL
    2. HTTP
    3. FTP
    4. DHCP

Q167. Which one of the following is not a technical control?

1. Firewall
2. Security policy
3. Intrusion detection systems
4. Anti-virus software

Q168. An organization's security initiatives based on policies, procedures, and guidelines; security awareness training; and risk management together define what?

1. Security setup
2. Security posture
3. Security management
4. Security initiative

Q169. Which of the following parameters are considered for assets during asset classification and help in devising suitable controls for security protection?

1. Value
2. Sensitivity
3. The degree of assurance required
4. All of the above

Q170. Which one of the following classifications of information, if compromised could cause certain damage to national security as per governmental classification types?

1. Top secret
2. Secret
3. Confidential
4. Sensitive but unclassified

Q171. While initiating a business continuity planning process, which of the following is first established?

1. Roles and responsibilities
2. Alternative sites
3. Testing the plans
4. Performing an impact analysis

Q172. Business continuity plans should identify which one of the following?

1. Mission-critical systems
2. Business impact due to no-availability of critical systems
3. Preventive and recovery controls
4. All of the above

Q173. A call tree in Business Continuity Planning represents which one of the following?

1. A list of personnel associated with the continuity processes
2. A list of technical department personnel
3. A list of external auditors
4. A list of administrative staff

Q174. Which of the following are important for Business Continuity Processes?

1. A step-by-step procedure for recovery
2. The appropriate testing of BC plans
3. Awareness of people
4. All of the above

Q175. Half-open connections are a vulnerability in what?

1. SPX protocol
2. HTTP
3. TCP
4. IP

Q176. SYN cookies are:

1. Attacks on TCP protocol implementation
2. Used in Spoofing
3. Security control for SYN attacks
4. A Denial-Of-Service attack

Q177. In client server networking, cookies are:

1. Text files sent by the server to the client
2. A type of attack

3. Viruses
4. Malicious code

Q178. The process of sending ECHO_REQUEST using Internet Control Messaging Protocol is popularly known as what?

1. Digging
2. Pinging
3. Tunneling
4. Echoing

References and further reading

- **CISSP Candidate Information Bulletin (CISSP CIB):** https://www.isc2.org/
- **ISO/IEC 27001 and ISO/IEC 27002:** http://www.iso.org/iso/home/standards/management-standards/iso27001.htm
- **NIST Guide to Protecting Confidentiality of Personally Identifiable Information (PII) – Special Publication 800-122:** http://csrc.nist.gov/publications/PubsSPs.html
- **US Security and Exchange Commission (SEC) laws:** http://www.sec.gov/about/laws.shtml#sox2002
- **HIPAA:** http://www.hhs.gov/hipaa/index.html
- **Federal Trade Commission – GLBA:** https://www.ftc.gov/tips-advice/business-center/privacy-and-security/gramm-leach-bliley-act
- **PCI DSS:** https://www.pcisecuritystandards.org/pci_security/
- **EU Data Protection Act:** https://www.gov.uk/data-protection/the-data-protection-act

Index

I

L

latency tests 237
lattice-based access control 198, 234
legal and regulatory issues
  about 18
  computer crimes 18
  data breaches 22
  import and export restrictions 22
  transborder data flow 22
legislative statute 16
link layer protocols
  Address Resolution Protocol (ARP) 159
  Neighbor Discovery Protocol (NDP) 159
  Reverse Address Resolution Protocol (RARP)
  159
load tests 237
Local Area Network (LAN) 161
log reviews 236
logic bomb 202, 235, 319
logical access
  to assets 185
logical security guard 93
Logical Security Guard 169, 317

M

malicious codes 201, 235
malicious mobile codes 202, 235
malware 77
  about 19
  computer virus 20
  key loggers 20
  spyware 20
  Trojan horse 20
  worms 20
Man-in-the-Middle attack (MIIM) 201, 234
management controls
  about 14
  Information security policy 14
management framework 24
Mandatory Access Control (MAC) 197, 233
manual code review 237
Manufacturing Execution Systems (MES) 197
Mean Time Between (MTBF) 320
Mean Time Between Failure (MTBF) 305

Mean Time Between Failures (MTBF) 256
Mean Time to Repair (MTTR) 320
Mean Time To Repair (MTTR) 257, 305
Media Access Control (MAC) 159, 160
media layers 140
media reuse 56, 257
media security controls
  data destruction 257
  data remanence 257
  maintenance 257
  media usage 257
  storage controls 257
memory and address protection 309
message digest 123, 172
misuse case test 237
misuse case testing 216
mock tests 255
Multi Protocol Label Switching (MPLS) 160
multi-factor authentication 199
multifactor authentication 234, 319

N

National Fire Protection Associations (NFPA) 249
National Information Assurance Certification and
  Accreditation Process (NIACAP) 95, 170
National Institute of Standards and Technology
  (NIST)
  about 17, 24, 243
  evaluation phase 45
  identification phase 45
National Security Agency (NSA) 171
need-to-know principle 80, 316
Network Address Translation (NAT) 143
Network Interface Cards (NIC) 160
network layer protocols
  about 156
  functions, carrying out 157
  Internet Protocol (IP) 157
  IPsec protocols 158
network security
  about 137, 138
  architecture 139
  layered architecture 139
  protocol 139
  technologies, using 139